U.S. Department of Defense

History of the German Campaign in Russia (1940-1942)

Sharp Ink 2024

U.S. Department of Defense

History of the German Campaign in Russia (1940-1942)

Strategy & Operational Execution

Sharp Ink, 2024
Contact: info@sharpinkbooks.com

ISBN: 978-80-283-7070-1

Contents

FOREWORD

Clausewitz observed of Russia that "it was a country which could be subdued only by its own weakness and by the effects of internal dissension. In order to strike these vulnerable spots of its body politic, Russia would have to be agitated at the very center." In reading this study, the military student will realize how dearly the Germans had to pay for ignoring Clausewitz's advice.

The purpose of this study is to describe German planning and operations in the first part of the campaign against Russia. The narrative starts with Hitler's initial plans for an invasion of Russia and ends at the time of Germany's maximum territorial gains during the battle for Stalingrad. A subsequent volume will depict the course of events from the Russian counteroffensive in November 1942 to the capture of Berlin in April 1945.

The material for this study was obtained from German military records now in the custody of The Adjutant General, Department of the Army. Monographs by former German general officers who had an active part in the planning and operations provided additional information. The authors of these monographs, prepared for the Historical Division, United States Army, Europe, include Generaloberst (Gen.) Franz Halder, Chief of Staff of the German Army from 1938-42; Generaloberst Gotthard Heinrici, a former corps, army, and army group commander on the Russian front: and several others.

The study was written by Mr. George E. Blau of the Special Studies Division, Office of the Chief of Military History. In his presentation, the author made every effort to give an objective account of Germany's initial efforts to conquer Soviet Russia in World War II.

PART ONE PLANNING

Chapter 1 Strategic Planning

Initial Discussions (July 1940)

After the conclusion of the French campaign in June 1940 Hitler devoted his attention to initiating plans for the seaborne invasion of England-Operation SEELOEWE. On 16 July he issued the directive for the operation. Three days later, in a speech before the Reichstag, Hitler made peace overtures to Great Britain. When they did not produce the expected reaction in Britain, he could only conclude that his last remaining enemy was continuing the war hoping for a change in the U.S. attitude and for future assistance from the Soviet Union.

On 21 July, after discussing the invasion of England with his military advisers, Hitler asked Field Marshal Walter von Brauchitsch, the Commander in Chief of the Army, to study the Russian problem and submit plans for a campaign against the Soviet Union. In regard to the latter the following was mentioned:

1. The concentration of attack forces would take 4 to 6 weeks.
2. The military objective would be to defeat the Russian Army or at least to seize so much Russian territory that the armaments plants in eastern Germany, particularly those in Berlin and Upper Silesia, and the Romanian oil fields would be beyond the range of Russian air attacks. At the same time the German ground forces would have to advance far enough to bring important production centers of European Russia within striking distance of the Luftwaffe.
3. The political aims would include the creation of an independent Ukraine and a confederation of Baltic States under German domination.
4. The Army would need approximately 80-100 combat divisions; the Soviet Union had some 50-75 good Russian divisions in Europe. If the campaign against Russia was launched that autumn, some of the German air power committed against Britain would have to be transferred to the East.

Chart 1. German Chain of Command (1 July 1940)

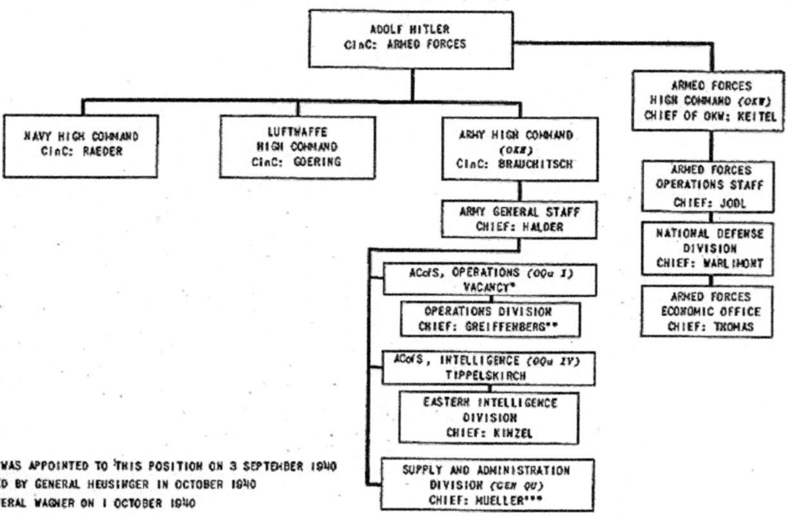

*GENERAL PAULUS WAS APPOINTED TO THIS POSITION ON 3 SEPTEMBER 1940
**AILING; REPLACED BY GENERAL HEUSINGER IN OCTOBER 1940
***REPLACED BY GENERAL WAGNER ON 1 OCTOBER 1940

Map 1. General reference map of Eastern Europe.

The following day, Brauchitsch informed Generaloberst (Gen.) Franz Halder, Chief, Army General Staff, of the discussions that had taken place at the previous day's conference and asked him to study the various problems involved in an operation against Russia. Halder thereupon requested Lt. Col. Eberhardt Kinzel, Chief, Eastern Intelligence Division, to brief him on Russian troop dispositions and asked Col. Hans von Greiffenberg, Chief, Operations Division, to assign a special assistant to the preparation of a tentative plan for a campaign against the Soviet Union. [See *chart 1.*]

On the basis of data provided by Kinzel on 26 July, Halder concluded that an attack launched from assembly areas in East Prussia and northern Poland toward Moscow would offer the best chances for success. After the seizure of Moscow the Russian forces defending the Ukraine and the Black Sea coast would be compelled to fight a series of battles with reversed front. [See *map 1.*]

The first draft of the Operations Division plan placed the main effort south of the Pripyat Marshes. The plan also called for 100 divisions. Halder, however, preferred to place the main effort north of the Pripyat.

Two days later, 29 July, Generalmajor (Brig. Gen.) Erich Marcks was temporarily assigned to Army High Command headquarters to draw up a campaign plan against the Soviet Union. General Marcks was chief of staff of the Eighteenth Army, which had recently been assigned to the Russian border and was preparing plans for defense against a possible Russian attack.

The same day General der Artillerie (Lt. Gen.) Alfred Jodl, Chief, Armed Forces Operations Staff, informed Col. Walter Warlimont, Chief, National Defense Division, and a group of officers working on his staff that Hitler had made up his mind to start a preventive war against Russia. The Army and Luftwaffe were to employ all available forces to eliminate forever the Bolshevist danger in the East. Since an eventual conflict between the National Socialist and Communist ideologies was inevitable, the Fuehrer preferred to extend the war into eastern Europe right then to being forced to resume hostilities after a few years of intermittent peace. Originally, Hitler had intended to invade Russia in the autumn of 1940, but Field Marshal Wilhelm Keitel had pointed out the difficulties of a winter campaign in Russia and had presented convincing evidence that the existing road and rail net in the newly acquired Polish territories would not be capable of supporting the assembly of strong German forces. Hitler had thereupon postponed the campaign, setting the tentative invasion date for mid-May 1941.

The first task confronting the officers present at the conference was to draft a directive-later issued under the code designation AUFBAU OST (BUILD-UP EAST)-stipulating the requirements for a prompt concentration of forces in western Poland. Strict secrecy concerning the plan was to be observed by everybody. The conferees queried Jodl whether it was assumed that Great Britain would be completely subjugated by spring 1941 or whether Germany was to become involved in a two-front war by its own volition. Jodl replied that the campaign against Russia would be conducted independently of developments in the West. He added: "In the autumn of 1941, after the consummation of the Russian defeat, our Luftwaffe will appear in the skies of western Europe in greater strength than ever before."

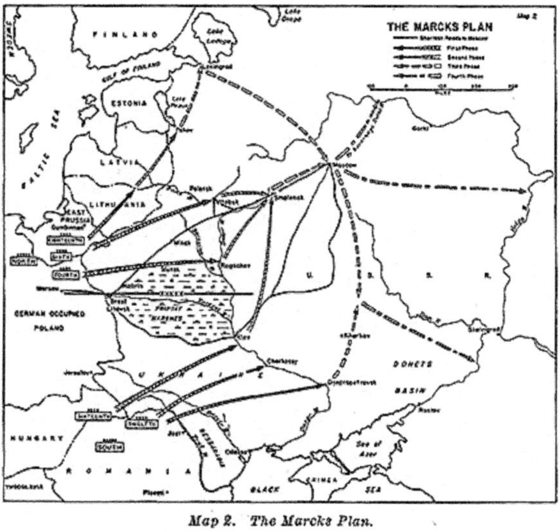

Map 2. The Marcks Plan.

On 29 July, also, data provided by the Navy made it obvious that the seaborne invasion of England could not be undertaken before the middle of September 1940 because of the Navy's inability to carry out and secure landings on a sufficiently wide front. The invasion was to be indefinitely postponed on 17 September.

On 31 July, toward the end of a conference at Berchtesgaden that was mainly concerned with Operation SEELOEWE, Hitler declared that a showdown with Russia would have to take place the following spring. The quicker the USSR was defeated, the better. The entire campaign made sense only if the Soviet Union was smashed in one fell swoop: territorial gains alone would prove unsatisfactory, and stopping the offensive during the winter months might be dangerous. Therefore, it was best to wait until May 1941 and then bring the campaign to a successful conclusion within five months. It would have been preferable to conduct the operation during the current year, but that solution did not seem practicable. Two converging thrusts were envisaged-a southern drive toward Kiev and into the Dnepr bend, with the Luftwaffe neutralizing the Odessa area; and a northern one across the Baltic States in the direction of Moscow. A secondary operation, by which the Baku oil fields were to be seized, was to take place later. To realize this plan Hitler directed that the strength of the Army, instead of being cut as recently ordered, was to be increased by the activation of 40 divisions.

It remained to be seen to what extent Finland and Turkey might be interested in such an operation. After the successful conclusion of the campaign the Ukraine, White Russia, and the Baltic States would come under German domination, whereas Finland could expand its territory toward the White Sea.

On 1 August Marcks and Halder discussed the campaign: the objective, rail and road communications, and the possible course of operations as well as the missions of the Navy and Luftwaffe. Two large forces were to be formed, one for the drive on Kiev, the other for that on Moscow. Halder pointed out that the Kiev force would operate from insecure bases if it jumped off from Romania. Also, the seizure of the Baltic States would have to be a secondary operation that would not interfere with the drive on Moscow. Halder then asked Marcks to put his plan in writing, including details pertaining to organization, logistical support etc.

The Marcks Plan (5 August 1940)

On 5 August Marcks submitted his plan which read essentially as follows:

a. Objective. The objective of the campaign was to defeat the Russian armed forces so that the Soviet Union could not threaten Germany in the future. German troops would have to seize all territory west of the line Rostov-Gorki-Archangel to eliminate the danger of Russian bombing attacks on Germany.

From the military-economic viewpoint Russia's most valuable regions were the food and raw-material producing areas of the Ukraine and the Donets Basin as well as the armament-production centers around Moscow and Leningrad. The industrial areas of Asiatic Russia were not greatly developed. The principal objective was Moscow, the nerve center of Soviet military, political, and economic power; its capture would lead to the disintegration of Soviet resistance.

b. Terrain. To the north and west Moscow was screened by huge forests and swamps which extended from the White Sea past Leningrad through Vitebsk to a line Kobrin-Slutsk-Kiev. [See *map 2.*] The Pripyat Marshes, forming the southern part of this forest and swamp area, divided the western border region of Russia into two separate theaters of operation. The most extensive forests were between Leningrad and Moscow and in the Pripyat Marshes. The intermediate area was crossed by the main highways extending from Warsaw and East Prussia via Slutsk, Minsk, and Vitebsk to Moscow.

South of the Pripyat Marshes were the lightly wooded regions of eastern Poland and the Ukraine. The terrain was favorable, but mobility was limited by the scarcity of good roads — only one main west-east highway via Kiev — and by the Dnepr River which constituted a major obstacle.

Because of its better road net the area north of the Pripyat permitted greater mobility, whereas the Ukraine offered better terrain conditions. In the north fighting would, of necessity, be largely restricted to roads.

c. Russian Tactics. The Red Army would adopt defensive tactics except along the Romanian border, where it might attack in an attempt to seize the Romanian oil production centers. In any event heavy air attacks on the oil fields would have to be expected.

On the other hand, the Russians could not repeat the maneuver of 1812, by which they had avoided giving battle. A modern force of 100 divisions could not simply abandon its sources of supply. It was therefore to be assumed that the Red Army would take up defensive positions which would protect most of European Russia, including the eastern Ukraine. The general line Dvina River-Polotsk-Berezina River-eastern edge of the Pripyat Marshes — Prut or Dnestr Rivers would serve this purpose, especially since it was partly fortified from earlier days. A withdrawal to the Dnepr also seemed feasible. West of their prepared positions the Russians would probably fight a delaying action.

d. Strength Estimates.

Russian Military Strength, August 1940

Distribution of forces	Infantry divisions	Cavalry divisions	Mechanized brigades
Total	151	32	38
Border defense	55	9	10
Forces total:			
Facing Japan	34	8	8
Facing Turkey	6	1	----------
Facing Finland	15	--------	2
Available for use against Germany	96	23	28

By spring 1941 the German Army would have 24 panzer, 1 cavalry, 12 motorized infantry, and 110 infantry divisions, or a total of 147 divisions, available for a campaign against Russia. This figure did not include the occupation forces to be left in western and northern Europe.

e. Disposition of Russian Forces. As of August 1940 the main concentrations were in the Baltic States in the north and in the Ukraine in the south. In general, the Russian troops in the west were about equally divided between the areas north and south of the Pripyat Marshes with a reserve force around Moscow. It could be assumed that the same disposition would hold in any war with Germany. Whether a point of main effort would be formed in the north or south would depend upon political developments. In all probability the troop strength in the north would exceed that in the south. Once the Russian lines had been pierced, the Red Army, being spread over a wide front, would no longer be able to coordinate its maneuvers and would be destroyed piecemeal.

The Russian Air Force was a redoubtable opponent whose attacks against the few major highways might be very effective.

f. Conduct of Operations. In view of the dimensions of the theater and its division into two parts by the Pripyat Marshes, it seemed unlikely that a decisive victory over the Russian Army could **be scored in one single operation. During the initial phase two separate offensives would have to be launched against the main concentrations of Russian forces; later, beyond the extensive forests, the operation could be unified.**

The German Army would have to concentrate its forces in the northern part of the theater, crush all opposition, and capture Moscow. To this end it would build up its main effort between Brest Litovsk and Gumbinnen and advance first toward the line Rogachev — Vitebsk. Weaker German forces assembled between Jasi and Jaroslav, south of the Pripyat, were to attack in the direction of Kiev and the Dnepr southeast of that city. They would thus forestall a Russian offensive on Romania and form the southern arm of a pincers that would be closed east of the upper Dnepr. To the north of the main effort, a secondary attack force would thrust across the Baltic States toward Leningrad and seize the Russian naval bases.

1. The Offensive in the South. An attack against the Russian forces in the Ukraine would have to be launched to protect the Romanian oil fields. If the main effort could have been made from Romania and secondary thrusts from northeastern Hungary and southeastern Poland, this operation might have become the principal attack across the Dnepr toward Moscow. But neither the political situation in the Balkans nor the road and rail nets in Hungary and Romania would permit the assembly of the necessary forces prior to the tentative date set for the launching of the campaign. A thrust from southeastern Poland in the direction of Kiev and the middle Dnepr, though quite feasible, could not possibly be made the principal operation because the maneuvering space was too narrow and the distance to Moscow too great.

This southern thrust, however, would have to be executed with sufficiently strong forces to destroy the Russians in the western Ukraine and gain the east bank of the Dnepr. Any further advance would have to be coordinated with the principal operation in the northern part of the theater and could be conducted either due eastward toward Kharkov or northeastward. In any event, the main effort of the offensive in the south would have to be on the left, with Kiev the principal objective. A secondary attack force, jumping off from Romanian territory, could link up with the main-effort grouping along the middle Dnepr. Three major roads would be available for the advance toward the river line between Dnepropetrovsk and Cherkassy. The Romanian Army could participate in the occupation of Bessarabia, Odessa, and the Crimea.

2. The Main Effort. The main effort was to lead to the destruction of the Russian forces west of Moscow by a direct thrust on the capital. Once in possession of Moscow and northern Russia, elements of the main-attack force would turn south and seize the Ukraine in conjunction with the southern groups.

The principal attack would have to be directed from East Prussia and the northern part of Poland toward Moscow because no decisive operation could be launched from Romania and an initial sweep toward Leningrad would only lengthen the distance to be covered and lead into the dense forests northwest of Moscow.

During the advance on Moscow the left flank would be protected by a special force that was to be committed across the Dvina River toward Pskov and Leningrad. After capturing the latter important industrial city this force might operate in conjunction with the main-attack force.

The road and rail nets west of the Russian border were capable of supporting the advance on Moscow. The terrain that had to be crossed by the forces jumping off from East Prussia was difficult. They would have to traverse a forest and lake belt between the Dvina and Dnepr. There, the battle for the traffic arteries would be decisive. Airborne troops would have to take possession of the eastern exits from large forest areas and thus keep the roads open.

3. Movements. Since surprise and speed were of the essence, armored and motorized infantry forces supported by tactical air power were to break through the enemy lines, with ordinary infantry divisions following closely to encircle and destroy the isolated enemy forces. The strength of the first attack wave was limited by the relatively small number of through roads. At most, two division-size units could advance abreast on any one road. The bulk of the infantry with its horse-drawn vehicles would have to march on such side roads as were available. As a result, all units would have to be deployed in great depth. The enormous width of the funnel-shaped theater necessitated keeping strong motorized forces in reserve and so distributing them that they could easily be shifted within the theater.

g. Distribution of German Forces.

Distribution	Divisions				
	Total	Panzer	Mtz. Inf.	Inf.	Cav.
Totals	147	24	12	110	1
Army Group South					
Total	35	5	6	24	------
Twelfth Army	12	2	4	6	------
Sixteenth Army	17	3	--------	14	------
Army Group Reserves	6	--------	2	4	------
Army Group North					
Total	68	15	2	50	1
Fourth Army	19	6	--------	12	1
Sixth Army	20	6	--------	14	------
Eighteenth Army	15	3	--------	12	------
Army Group Reserves	14	--------	2	12	------
Army High Command Reserves	44	4	4	36	------

h. Primary Missions of the Ground Forces. The primary mission of Army Group South was to destroy the Russians in the western Ukraine and to establish bridgeheads across the Dnepr from which the army group forces could continue eastward or northeastward.

Army Group North was to seize Moscow. To accomplish this, motorized units would have to drive through the forest areas between Rogachev and Vitebsk with airborne troops assisting them at the forest edges. If the Russians chose to make a stand between the jump-off line and the forests or the Dvina, they would have to be pushed northward, away from the direct route to Moscow. While the reduction of these enemy forces was under way, the armored and motorized units were to move on until they reached the Russian capital.

i. The Mission of the Air Force. The Luftwaffe was to neutralize the Soviet Air Force, disrupt rail and road communications, prevent the concentration of Russian ground forces in the forests areas, support the German spearhead units with dive-bomber attacks, prepare airborne operations, and secure the air above traffic bottlenecks.

j. The Mission of the Navy. The Navy was to neutralize the Russian fleet in the Baltic, safeguard the iron ore shipments from Sweden, and transport supplies across the Baltic as soon as the Army had seized the ports.

k. Logistics. A special staff was to be formed to coordinate supply problems and establish bases behind the two army groups. It was anticipated that the Russians would attempt to carry out large-scale demolitions and destroy supply dumps, rail lines, and bridges. This could be partially prevented by keeping them off balance and by preparing appropriate countermeasures. In the Ukraine, Lithuania, and Latvia agents might be able to seize bridges and railroad installations and thus prevent their destruction. All railroad tracks beyond the former Polish border would have to be converted from the Russian wide to normal gauge.

A military administration would have to be set up for the occupied areas. In the Baltic States, White Russia, and the Ukraine the military government agencies would have to work toward turning their authority over to autonomous, non-Communist local governments.

l. Time Phasing. The most favorable season for the campaign was from mid-May to mid-October. After a mild winter, it might be possible to start as early as the beginning of May.

It was anticipated that all units needed for the initial operations would be assembled before the outbreak of hostilities. In the event of an unexpected outbreak of fighting, the forces scheduled to be assembled in the Army Group North area would need approximately 10 days to arrive in their designated areas and those in the south 9 days.

During the initial phase of the German offensive the Russians would probably fight delaying actions over distances of up to 250 miles, until they reached their prepared positions. The German infantry divisions would take three weeks to cover this distance. The panzer divisions would have to advance so rapidly and penetrate so deeply that the Russians would be unable to man a continuous defense line. The issue of the entire campaign would depend on the success of the armored thrusts.

The struggle for the forest areas and river courses would dominate the second phase. Since the depth of this zone was 60-120 miles, it would take 2-4 weeks to cross it. At this stage the German forces would either achieve a decisive breakthrough or destroy the previously shattered Russian forces individually.

During the third phase Moscow and Leningrad would have to be seized and the drive into the eastern Ukraine initiated. The distances to be covered were 250 and 200 miles respectively. Whether this phase could be executed immediately after the second would depend upon the condition of the railroads, the serviceability of the track-laying and wheeled vehicles, and the degree of success hitherto achieved. If the Russians were beaten, a few armored or motorized divisions would suffice to keep them off balance, and to seize Moscow and Leningrad and thrust deep into the eastern Ukraine. This would require one or two weeks if sufficient tanks and motor vehicles were available. If, however, the bulk of the Red Army was still capable of offering organized resistance, the start of the third phase would have to be delayed until sufficient supplies were brought up to support the continuation of the offensive. In this case it might be 3-6 weeks, depending on the time needed for the supply buildup.

The fourth and last phase of the offensive would see the Germans pursuing the Russians to the Don, the Volga, and the Severnaya Dvina. The distances to be covered were 250 miles in the south and up to 500 in the center and north. After the Germans had captured Kharkov, Moscow, and Leningrad, the Soviet command would have lost control over its forces but complete occupation of the territory acquired during this phase would be neither possible nor necessary. Motorized forces and rail-transported infantry would be responsible for this operation. The time needed for this phase was estimated at 2-4 weeks.

The total time required to attain the designated objective would therefore vary between a minimum of 9 and a maximum of 17 weeks.

In the event that the Soviet government did not collapse or make peace, the offensive might have to be continued to the Ural Mountains. After the destruction of their armed forces and the loss of their most valuable European territories, the Soviets would probably no longer be capable of conducting military operations but could still set up a government in Asia and maintain a state of war for an indefinite period.

To this plan General Marcks added recommendations for the preparation of the campaign, including details regarding signal communications; the construction and improvement of roads, bridges, railroad facilities, and billeting areas; the organization, equipment, and training of troops; and the procurement of cartographic material.

General Marcks discussed his plan with General der Kavallerie (Lt. Gen.) Ernst Koestring, the German military attaché in Moscow, during the latter's presence at Army High Command headquarters. Koestring did not agree that the seizure of Moscow would be the key to victory. In his opinion the capture of Moscow would not be decisive because the Soviet Union had vast industrial resources beyond the Urals. Moreover, with their ability to improvise, the Russians would be able to reorganize their transportation net without Moscow.

Staff Work (August-September 1940)

At the beginning of August the National Defense Division of the Armed Forces High Command completed the directive for AUFBAU OST. It stated that greater military use was to be made of those German-occupied territories of Poland which had not been incorporated into the Reich. The increasing threat of air attacks on western Germany made it imperative to utilize the comparatively safe eastern territories for the activation and training of new units. The necessary accommodations and facilities had to be built; supply depots had to be transferred from west to east; and road, rail, and signal communications had to be improved. The directive was signed by Keitel and issued to all interested military and civilian agencies.

The Army General Staff and technical service divisions were particularly interested in implementing the directive, and a number of organizational measures were initiated by General Halder and his assistants. In September, personnel of the Operations Division under the direction of the new Assistant Chief of Staff, Operations, General-leutnant (Maj. Gen.) Friedrich Paulus, began to work on a strategic survey based on the Marcks plan.

General Jodl had meanwhile asked his subordinates in the National Defense Division to prepare a campaign plan for his own information. This study was to be drawn up without recourse to the plans that were being prepared by the Army, because Jodl wanted to check the Army plans before they were submitted to Hitler. The National Defense Division plan, submitted to Jodl on 19 September, stressed the need for concentrating the attack forces north of the Pripyat Marshes so that they could take the shortest route to Moscow via Smolensk. Three army groups were to be employed; after Army Group Center had seized the Smolensk area, the continuation of the offensive was to depend upon the progress made by Army Group North. If the latter proved to be sufficiently strong to sustain the drive on Leningrad, Army Group Center would employ all its forces on the continuation of its thrust on Moscow. In the event, however, that Army Group North should be unable to make satisfactory progress, Army Group Center would have to halt its advance and divert forces to lend assistance.

In the Finnish Theater of Operations the National Defense planners wanted to concentrate all available German and Finnish forces in the south; no attack in the direction of Murmansk was contemplated. The thrust from southern Finland was to be coordinated with the advance of Army Group North and was to be directed across the Karelian Isthmus toward Leningrad or from east of Lake Lodoga toward Tikhvin.

The strategic survey then being prepared by the Operations Division of the Army probably influenced the National Defense Division plan because of the close relationship between the Armed Forces and Army High Command personnel on the operating level.

Admiral Raeder's Suggestions (26 September 1940)

On 26 September the Commander in Chief of the Navy, Adm. Erich Reader, suggested to Hitler that Germany should support the Italian attempt to seize the Suez Canal, whose possession would be vital for a farther advance across Palestine and Syria. Once this had been achieved, Turkey would be at Germany's mercy. The Russian problem would then have an entirely different aspect, since the Soviet Union was basically afraid of Germany. Under such circumstances it would be doubtful whether an invasion of Russia from the north would still be necessary.

In expressing his approval of Raeder's ideas, Hitler stated that Russia would have to be tempted to turn toward Persia and India, where she could gain access to the open sea. That would be far more important to Russia than her position in the Baltic. Hitler, also, was of the opinion that the Soviet Union was apprehensive of Germany's power.

Strategic Survey (October 1940)

During October 1940 the Operations Division completed the preparation of a strategic survey which was submitted to General Halder on 29 October. In this study the Army General Staff formulated its own ideas regarding the most appropriate strategy for a campaign against the Soviet Union. The authors of the study realized that the Red Army's numerical strength, the vast terrain to be covered, the adverse conditions of the Russian theater, and the necessity of defeating the Soviet Union with a minimum of delay raised a series of problems for which in many instances no fully satisfactory solutions could be found. On the other hand, ever since the Red Army had performed so badly during the campaign against Finland in the winter of 1939-40, the average German General Staff officer had a low opinion of the military potential of the Soviet Union. Moreover, it was generally assumed that the people in areas recently occupied by the Soviet Union were anti-Russian and anti-Communist, and that disaffection in the Ukraine, the Crimea, and the Caucasus was equally widespread. The purges of 1937 were considered as evidence of the vulnerability of the Soviet Union.

The major factors considered in the study were as follows:

a. Manpower. The ratio of strength between German and Russian forces was not at all favorable. Against the approximately 170 Soviet divisions plus ample reinforcements estimated to be stationed in western Russia the Germans could at best put only 145 — including 19 armored divisions — into the field. Small contingents of Romanian and Finnish forces could be added to this total, but their equipment, capabilities, and combat efficiency were below the German. In other words, the German offensive forces would not have the advantage of numerical superiority. The only method of compensating for this deficiency was to mass forces at crucial points and take risks at others.

The relative combat efficiency was not as clear cut. To be sure, the German forces had had more combat experience; their leaders were experienced in maneuvering large motorized forces, and the individual soldier was self-confident. The Russian soldier, however, was not to be underestimated, and it remained doubtful whether the Red Army would show immediate signs of internal disintegration. On the other hand, Russian leadership was certainly below the German average, particularly in making quick decisions in a war of movement.

The element of surprise in launching the attack would probably compensate for some of the German numerical inferiority. Extensive deceptive measures were to be taken to achieve surprise, but Hitler's pretext that preparations along the Russian border were merely a deliberate deception to divert British attention from an imminent invasion of England could not be maintained indefinitely. In the final analysis, surprise was limited to the timing and direction of the German attack; to hope for more seemed unrealistic.

b. Space. The tremendous width and depth of European Russia was another problem that deserves serious consideration, especially in view of the disproportion of strength. Everything would depend on the German Army's ability to prevent the Russians from exploiting this space advantage. Whether they would give battle near the border or attempt an organized withdrawal could not be foreseen. In any event, it was essential to engage the enemy as soon as possible, if his quick destruction was to be achieved. The distribution of the German forces and the application of deceptive measures had to conform with this intention. The Russians had to be denied any opportunity to withdraw into the depths of European Russia where they could fight a series of delaying actions. This objective could be attained only by strict application of the principles of mass, economy of force, and movement. Substantial Russian forces were to be cut off from their rear communications and forced to fight on reversed fronts. This was the only method by which the German Army could cope with the factor of space during the offensive operations. Lacking the necessary forces, the German Army could not mount an offensive along the entire front at the same time, but had to attempt to open gaps in the front at crucial points, envelop and isolate Russian forces, and annihilate them before they had a chance to fall back.

c. Time. The problem of selecting the most propitious time assumed far more importance than on any previous occasion. For operations in Russia the May-to-October period only seemed to offer a reasonable guarantee of favorable weather. The muddy season began in late October, followed by the dreaded Russian winter. The campaign had to be successfully concluded while the weather was favorable, and distances varying from five to six hundred miles had to be covered during this period. From the outset the German campaign plan would be under strong pressure of time.

d. Inteligence Information. The intelligence picture revealed two major Russian concentrations — one in the Ukraine of about 70 divisions and the other in White Russia near and west of Minsk of some 60 divisions. There appeared to be only 30 divisions in the Baltic States.

The disposition of the Red Army forces did offer the Soviets the possibility of launching an offensive in the direction of Warsaw. But, if attacked by Germany, it was uncertain whether the Russians would make a stand in the border area or fight a delaying action. It could be assumed, though, that they would not voluntarily withdraw beyond the Dnepr and Dvina Rivers, since their industrial centers would remain unprotected.

e. Analysis of Objective Area. The almost impassable forests and swamps of the Pripyat Marshes divided the Russian territory west of the Dnepr and Dvina Rivers into two separate theaters of operation. In the southern part the road net was poor. The main traffic arteries followed the river courses and therefore ran mostly in a north-south direction. The communication system north of the Pripyat Marshes was more favorable. The best road and rail nets were to be found in the area between Warsaw and Moscow, where the communications ran east and west and thus in the direction of the German advance. The traffic arteries leading to Leningrad were also quite favorable. A rapid advance in the south would be hampered by major river barriers — the Dnestr, the Bug, and the Dnepr — whereas in the north only a single river, the Dvina, would have to be crossed. By thrusting straight across the territory north of the Pripyat one could strike at Moscow. The Red Army would not simply abandon the Russian capital, and in the struggle for its possession the Germans could hope to deliver a telling blow.

By contrast, the area south of the Pripyat region was of minor military importance; there the Soviets could more readily trade space for time and withdraw to a new line, possibly behind the Dnepr River. On the other hand, the south offered tempting economic targets, such as the wheat of the Ukraine, the coal fields of the Donets Basin, and the faraway oil of the Caucasus. The Army's immediate interest, however, was to attain military victory, not economic advantages. The quicker the campaign was over the more decisive the victory, the more certain would be the eventual accrual of economic advantages.

For these reasons the Operations Division arrived at the conclusion that the main effort should be concentrated north of the Pripyat Marshes and that the principal thrust should be directed via Smolensk toward Moscow.

The Preliminary Plan (November-5 December 1940)

During November the Army High Command was primarily concerned with preparations for an attack on Gibraltar and armed intervention on the Balkan Peninsula. At the same time, the training and equipment of the newly activated divisions proceeded according to schedule. Molotov's visit in Berlin on 12-13 November aroused some hope that Hitler's intentions might be modified by a change in Soviet policy. When Admiral Raeder saw the Fuehrer on the day after Molotov's departure, he found that Hitler continued to plan for an attack on Russia. Raeder suggested that such a conflict be delayed until a victory had been won over Britain. His reasons were that a war with the Soviet Union would involve too great an expenditure of German strength and that it was impossible to foretell where it would end. Raeder then explained that the Soviets were dependent on German assistance for building up their navy and would therefore not attack Germany for the next few years.

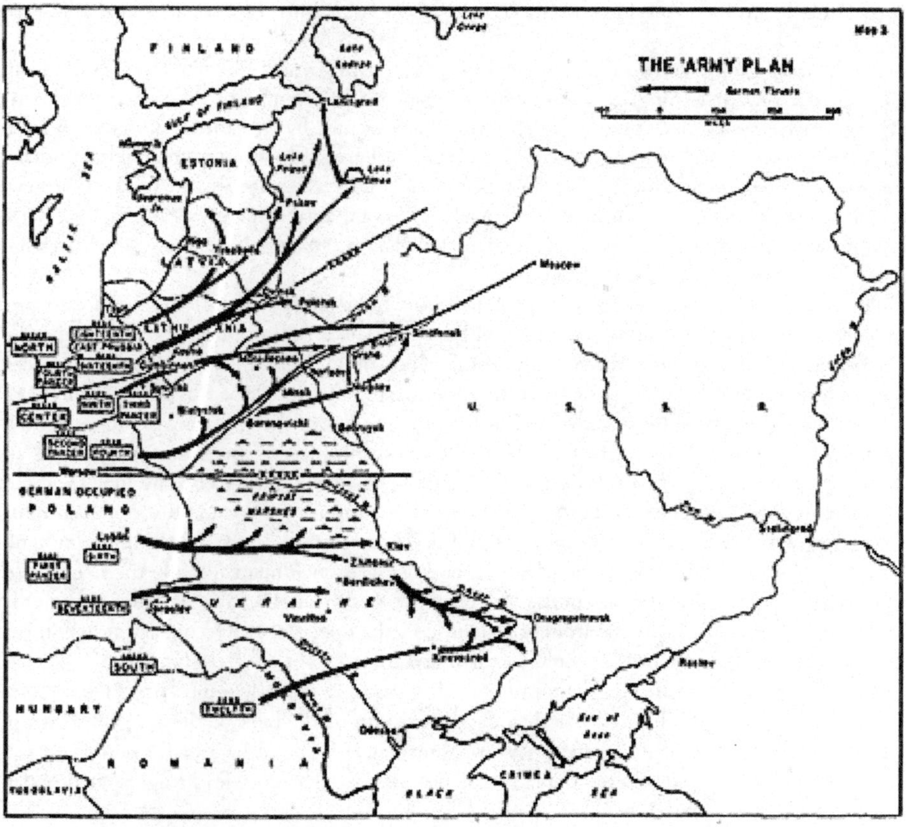

Map 3. The Army Plan.

In November the Soviet Government made the first official inquiry at the German Embassy in Moscow with regard to German troop concentrations in the former Polish provinces adjacent to the Russian border. General Koestring, the German military attaché, was called to Berlin, where he was instructed to reply that the troop movements were incidental to the redeployment after the campaign in the West, the requirements of the occupation, and the better training facilities available in this area.

While these demarches were being carried on, the Army prepared its preliminary plan on the basis of previous staff and concurrent General Staff exercises. On 5 December Brauchitsch and

Halder presented their plan to Hitler at a conference during which the preparations for various future operations were examined. [See DA Pam No. 20-260, *The German Campaigns in the Balkans (Spring 1941),* Map 2.] In his verbal report, Halder first explained the topographical features of the Russian theater and mentioned that the most important industrial centers were in the Ukraine, in Moscow, and around Leningrad. The Pripyat Marshes divided the theater into a northern and a southern part. The roads in the latter were poor; the best rail and road net was to be found in the region between Warsaw and Moscow. The northern part of the theater was therefore more favorable for large-scale maneuvers than the southern. (For this reason the Russians were apparently concentrating more troops in the northern regions than in the south. Another remarkable feature in their distribution of forces was the massing of forces in the vicinity of areas in which Soviet and German spheres of interest overlapped. [See *map 3.*]

The course of the Dnepr and Dvina would be the easternmost limits to which the Russians could withdraw without exposing their industrial centers. German armored wedges would have to drive through the Russian lines and break up the enemy defense system west of these rivers. A particularly strong attack force would have to be assembled for the thrust from the Warsaw area toward Moscow.

Three army groups were to launch the offensive: Army Group North was to thrust from East Prussia toward Leningrad, Army Group Center via Minsk toward Smolensk, and Army Group South toward Kiev. The third drive was to be executed by two armies jumping off from the Lublin and Jaroslav areas respectively, and by a third army thrusting from Moldavia toward the lower course of the Dnepr. The objective of the entire offensive was to reach the course of the Volga and the region around Archangel. The total assault force was to consist of 105 infantry and 32 armored and motorized infantry divisions, strong elements of which were to form the second wave.

Hitler agreed with Halder's plan and added that it was of the utmost importance to prevent the Russians from making a planned withdrawal. The Soviet military potential had to be eliminated and its regeneration made impossible. In planning the initial distribution of forces, every effort would have to be made to destroy the maximum number of Russian units near the border. For this purpose the armored and motorized divisions of the two army groups operating in the northern part of the theater would have to be committed on their adjoining wings. In the north, the enemy forces stationed in the Baltic States would have to be enveloped and cut off. Army Group Center would therefore have to be so strong that it could divert considerable forces northward to assist Army Group North if necessary. Army Group South would jump off later than the other two, with some elements advancing from Romania, while the main force, thrusting southeastward, was to envelop the enemy forces in the Ukraine. Finally, Hitler indicated that Romania and Finland would participate in the operation. A secondary attack in the far north was to be launched by three German divisions.

The Fuehrer did not consider the capture of Moscow as particularly important. He therefore did not want to commit himself whether the destruction of the bulk of the Russian forces in the northern and southern pockets was to be immediately followed by an advance toward and beyond Moscow. He also believed that 130-140 divisions would suffice for bringing the Russian campaign to a successful conclusion.

Upon resuming his report Halder pointed out that according to the most recent data the assembly would take 8 weeks and that the German preparations could not be concealed from the enemy after the beginning or the middle of April at the latest.

General Staff and Command Post Exercises (November-December 1940)

The preliminary plan was tested in a General Staff exercise conducted by the Assistant Chief of Staff, Operations, General Paulus. General Staff officers responsible for the drafting of the plan acted as group leaders. Paulus divided the exercise into three phases: the first began 29 November with the invasion and the initial battles near the border; the second, beginning 3 December, continued the offensive operations to the line Kiev — Minsk — Lake Peipus; and the last, staged 7 December, dealt with reaching the potential objectives beyond this **line.**

After each phase Paulus indicated the premises for the start of the next part of the exercise by explaining the phase line that had been reached, the condition of the troops, the supply situation, intelligence estimate, etc. All participants thus based their ideas on the same data. During the third phase of the game it became evident that the German ground forces would hardly be sufficiently strong to fan out across the funnel-shaped Russian theater if — contrary to the generally prevailing opinion — the Red Army was capable of offering continued resistance. Paulus reported the results and the lessons learned to Halder.

Generalmajor (Brig. Gen.) Eduard Wagner, Chief, Supply and Administration Division, prepared logistical exercises, which were to take place in December and January. Wagner also worked on a logistical plan that was to serve as a counterpart to the strategic survey prepared by the Operations Division. Special emphasis was placed on establishing an efficient supply system in the assembly areas and drawing up a sound base-development plan to guarantee the flow of supplies during the execution of far-reaching operations in the Russian theater.

Concurrent with, but independent of, these exercises the chiefs of staff of the three army groups were asked to work on problems involved in a campaign against Russia. They were briefed by Halder who limited the scope of their investigations to defeating the Russian forces in White Russia and the western Ukraine. Paulus provided them with all the necessary data, and each officer was instructed to arrive at a solution without consulting his fellow workers. The studies submitted at the beginning of December 1940 were carefully scrutinized by both Halder and Paulus. Ideas that were at great variance with those submitted in the preliminary plan were selected as topics of discussion for a conference of all chiefs of staff of army groups and armies which took place at Army High Command Headquarters on 13 and 14 December 1940. The discussions served to clarify a number of problems for which no solution had been found during the various exercises. It was also concluded that the Soviet Union would be defeated in a campaign not exceeding 8-10 weeks' duration.

Economic Survey

In November 1940 Reichs Marshal Hermann Goering ordered General der Infanterie (Lt. Gen.) Georg Thomas, Chief, Armed Forces Economic Office, to study the economic implications of a campaign against the Soviet Union. In the summary of his report Thomas arrived at the following conclusions:

a. During the initial months of an operation which would lead to the occupation of European Russia excluding the Urals, Germany would improve its food and raw material position, if the destruction of Soviet supplies could be prevented, if the Caucasus oil region was seized intact, and if the transportation problem was solved.

b. In the event that hostilities should continue for some time, Germany would benefit only if the transportation problem was solved and the civilian population induced to remain and cooperate. More specifically:

> (1) The destruction of mechanized equipment would have to be prevented and the production of new farm machinery would have to be resumed without delay. Supplies of petroleum, oil, and lubricants (POL) would have to be allocated to agriculture.
>
> (2) The industrial production would depend on the immediate availability of electric power plants and the delivery of raw materials generally unavailable in European Russia.

c. Until the establishment of a link with the Far East, Germany would be short of such strategic materials as rubber, tungsten, copper, platinum, zinc, asbestos, and jute.

d. The area south of the Volga and Don estuaries including the Caucasus would have to be included among the objectives of the operation. The oil produced in the Caucasus region would be essential for the exploitation of any territories occupied in Russia.

e. By occupying European Russia, Germany would seize 75 percent of the total Soviet armament potential and almost 100 percent of the precision-tool and optical industries.

The study was submitted to Hitler who, though recognizing its intrinsic value, failed to make any basic changes in his overall military-political plans.

Directive BARBAROSSA (18 December 1940)

On 6 December General Jodl requested General Warlimont to draw up a directive for the campaign against Russia on the basis of the preliminary plan that had been approved by Hitler. Six days later the draft of Directive No. 21 was submitted to Jodl who made a few insignificant changes and ordered a revised draft prepared. The same day the Navy submitted a report stressing the danger of starting a war on a second front while Germany's naval forces were fully engaged in the struggle against Britain. On 16 December Warlimont submitted the revised draft of the directive to Jodl who was to present it to Hitler the next day. During their conference Jodl and Warlimont discussed the dangers of a two-front war and the serious POL problems it would involve.

On 17 December Jodl presented the draft of Directive No. 21 to Hitler who made some basic changes with regard to the mission of the two army groups that were to be committed north of the Pripyat Marshes. First priority was to be given to the capture of Leningrad and Kronshtadt and to the destruction of the enemy forces in the Baltic States. The advance on Moscow would not be resumed until these objectives had been attained. Only if Russia's military machine collapsed earlier than anticipated would Army Group Center be permitted to drive simultaneously on Leningrad and Moscow.

After the necessary changes had been incorporated in the directive it was signed by Hitler on 18 December and distributed to the services under the new cover name Operation BARBAROSSA. The directive read as follows:

Directive No. 21

Operation BARBAROSSA

18 December 1940

The German Armed Forces must make preparations to crush *Soviet Russia in a lightning campaign,* even before the termination of hostilities with Great Britain (Operation BARBAROSSA).

For this purpose the *Army* will commit all available forces except those needed to safeguard the occupied territories against surprise attacks.

The *Air Force* will earmark sufficient forces in support of the ground operations to guarantee the rapid conclusion of this campaign and to minimize any potential damage eastern Germany might suffer through enemy air attacks. The concentration of air power in the East is, however, subject to certain limitations. First, all German-held military bases and war production centers must be adequately protected against enemy air raids. Second, the air offensive against Great Britain and against its life lines in particular must not be slowed down.

The *Navy* will continue to focus its attention on *Great Britain* while the campaign against Russia takes place.

In due time, i. e., at least eight weeks before the intended start of the operation, I shall issue a directive for the strategic concentration against Soviet Russia.

Any preparations which require more time and are not already under way will be initiated immediately and brought to a conclusion before 15 May 1941.

It is absolutely essential that the preparations for the attack remain unobserved.

The operational planning of the individual services should be based on the following premises:

I. *Overall Plan*

During the initial phase the bulk of the Russian *Army* stationed in western Russia is to be destroyed in a series of daring operations spearheaded by armored thrusts.

The organized withdrawal of intact units into the vastness of interior Russia must be prevented.

During the next phase a fast pursuit will be launched up to a line from which the Russian air force will be incapable of attacking German territory. The ultimate objective of the operation is to screen European against Asiatic Russia along the course of the Volga and thence along a general line extending northward toward Archangel. Thus, if necessary, the German Air Force would be in a position to neutralize the last industrial region remaining in Russian hands, i. e. that situated in the Urals.

As a result of these ground operations the Russian *Baltic Fleet* will rapidly lose its bases and thus cease to be operational.

Any effective interference by the Russian *Air Force* will be eliminated by the delivery of decisive blows at the very beginning of the campaign.

II. *Prospective Allies and their Mission*

Romania's and Finland's active participation in the war against Soviet Russia is to be anticipated; they will provide contingents on either wing of our ground forces.

In due course the Armed Forces High Command will approach these two countries and make arrangements as to the manner in which their military contingents will be placed under German command at the time of their intervention.

Romania will employ elite forces to give at least initial support to the offensive launched by the German southern attack forces. In addition, Romania's mission will call for tying down enemy forces in the south, wherever no German units are committed, and lending assistance in maintaining the lines of communications.

Finland will cover the concentration of the German Force North (elements of Force XXI) which will be transferred from Norway, and the Finnish troops will operate in conjunction with this force. Moreover, Finland will have to neutralize Hanko.

It may be assumed that, by the start of the campaign at the latest, there will be a possibility of using the *Swedish* railroads and highways for the transfer of the German Force North.

III. *The Campaign Plans*

A. *Army* (in conformity with the plans submitted to me by the Army) : For the purpose of the campaign the theater of operations is divided into a southern and northern part by the Pripyat Marshes. The main effort is to be placed *north* of the Pripyat, where two army groups are to be committed.

Of these two army groups the one on the right will be provided with especially powerful motorized infantry and armored forces. Its mission will be to thrust from the area around, but especially north, of Warsaw and to shatter the enemy forces in White Russia. This preliminary operation will set the stage for a pivoting movement performed by strong motorized elements that will drive northward in order to annihilate the enemy forces in the Baltic area in conjunction with the northern army group which will be driving from East Prussia in the general direction of Leningrad. After this most urgent mission has been successfully accomplished, the cities of Leningrad and Kronshtadt must be captured. Only then will the offensive operations leading to the seizure of Moscow, the important communications and armament production center, be continued. Simultaneous drives toward both objectives might be envisaged only in the event of an unexpectedly rapid collapse of the Russian resistance.

During the Russian campaign, Force XXI will continue to consider the protection of Norway as its primary mission. Any excess forces available beyond the scope of this mission will be committed primarily in the north (mountain corps) to secure the Petsamo region and its ore mines as well as the highway connecting Petsamo with

Oulu (Arctic Highway). Together with Finnish contingents these forces will subsequently thrust toward the Murmansk railway in an attempt to prevent supplies from- reaching the. Murmansk area by land.

Whether an operation by a *stronger* German force — consisting of two to three divisions which would jump off from the region around and south of Rovaniemi — can be executed, will depend on Sweden's willingness to make its railroads available for such a concentration of German units.

The bulk of the Finnish Army will coordinate its operations with the advance of the German north wing. Its principal missions will be to tie down the maximum Russian forces by an attack west of or on both sides of Lake Ladoga and to seize Hanko.

The army group committed *south* of the Pripyat Marshes will also attempt a double envelopment. Strong forces concentrated on both wings are to achieve the complete annihilation of the Russian troops in the Ukraine west of the Dnepr. The *main attack* will be directed from the Lublin area toward Kiev, while the forces concentrated in Romania will cross the lower Pruth River and form the other arm of a wide envelopment. The Romanian Army will have the mission of tying down the Russian forces which are to be caught between the two pincers.

Once the battles south and north of the Pripyat Marshes have been brought to a successful conclusion, pursuits will be launched with the following objectives:

In the south the Donets Basin, highly important from a military-economic point of view, must be seized without delay.

In the north Moscow must be reached as soon as possible. economic significance of capturing this city is tremendous. The political and Moreover, German possession of Moscow will deprive the enemy of the most important railway hub.

B. *Air Force:*

Its mission will be to paralyze and eliminate the Russian air force, and to support the Army's operations at the points of main effort, particularly in the Army Group Center area and along the north wing of Army Group South. According to their significance for the course of the campaign, the Russian railways will be severed by air attacks. In some instances most important railroad installations (river crossings!) will be seized by vertical envelopments performed by parachute and airborne troops.

In order to concentrate the entire striking power of the German Air Force on neutralizing the enemy air force and on providing direct support for the Army, the Russian armament industry will not be attacked during the initial phase of the campaign. Once the war of movement has come to a conclusion, such attacks might be considered, particularly against the industrial region in the Urals.

C. *Navy:*

In addition to defending the German coast, the Navy will have the mission of preventing the enemy naval forces from forcing their way out of the Baltic Sea. Once the Leningrad area has been seized, the Russian Baltic Fleet will have been deprived of all its bases. Since its situation will then be altogether hopeless, major naval engagements prior to that time must be avoided.

After the Russian fleet has been eliminated, it will be important to establish full-scale maritime traffic in the Baltic, including the logistical support of ground forces in the northern part of the Russian theater (mine sweeping!).

IV. All orders issued by the commanders in chief of the services on the basis of this directive are to be formulated in such a manner that they leave no doubt on the *precautionary nature of these measures* which are prepared for the event that Russia should change her present attitude toward us. The number of officers to be informed during the preliminary stage must be kept to a minimum. Additional personnel will be initiated as late as feasible, and then only to the extent necessary for the performance of their individual duties. This will minimize the risk of serious political and military consequences that might result from our preparations — for the implementation of which not even a deadline has been set — becoming known.

V. I request the commanders in chief of the services to report to me on their future plans which are to be based on this directive.

All services will submit to me progress reports on their projected preparations through the Armed Forces High Command.

ADOLF HITLER

The generally held opinion that the Russian campaign would be of short duration found its clearest expression in Section III *B* of Directive No. 21, pertaining to the Air Force. By giving the Luftwaffe primarily a ground-support mission and equipping it accordingly, Hitler and Goering expressed their belief that strategic bombing would be unnecessary. The Navy, however, did not anticipate the Russian campaign with so much optimism.

On 27 December Admiral Raeder tried once more to convince Hitler that Germany's most urgent task was to concentrate all its military power against Britain. That country was gaining strength as a result of the Italian reverses in the Mediterranean and the increasing support it received from the United States. On the other hand, Britain could be defeated if Germany turned its entire war potential to strengthening the Navy and Air Force. Any dissipation of strength would prolong the war and jeopardize the final success. In concluding, Raeder raised very strong objections against starting the Russian campaign before Britain was defeated.

In his reply Hitler agreed that greater stress would have to be placed on submarine construction. In general, however, he felt that the Soviet Union's expansionist policy in the Balkans made it mandatory that Germany eliminate its last opponent on the European continent before the final showdown with Britain. For this purpose, the Army would have to be built up first; as soon as the Russian campaign had been won, the needs of the Navy and Luftwaffe would have priority.

Chapter 2 Operational Planning

The Army's Operation Order (3 February 1941)

During January 1941 each army group was informed of its mission as stipulated in Directive No. 21 and ordered to carry out intracommand map maneuvers for the purpose of studying the operation plan in detail and examining the proposed courses of action. A number of command post exercises took place at each army group headquarters, and the ideas formulated on these occasions were discussed in great detail during meetings of Army High Command and army group representatives.

At a conference that took place in Berlin on 31 January, Field Marshal von Brauchitsch told the commanding generals of the army groups that his plans were based on the assumption that the Russians would give battle west of the Dnepr-Dvina line. Later on, when one of the army group commanders asked Halder whether this assumption was supported by facts, the latter replied: "It might easily turn out different."

Some of the ideas expressed during the exercises and meetings were incorporated into the operation order, which was the Army High Command's implementation of Directive No. 21. The order originated from the Operations Division and was eventually signed by Field Marshal von Brauchitsch after Hitler approved it on 3 February. In the introductory part of the order it was stated that preparations for defeating the Soviet Union in a lightning campaign had to be made in the event that the USSR should change its attitude toward Germany. For this purpose armored wedges would have to be driven deep into western Russia and the bulk of the Red Army would have to be destroyed before it had a chance to withdraw.

The Russians would probably try to stem the tide by defending prepared positions along the new and former borders as well as by holding the numerous river lines west of the Dnepr and Dvina Rivers. It was to be expected that the Soviet command would make a special effort to hold the Baltic States and the coastal provinces along the Black Sea as long as possible in order to keep important air and naval bases in its possession. If the battles southeast and northeast of the Pripyat Marshes took an unfavorable turn for the Russians, the next attempt to stop the German offensives would probably be made along the Dnepr and Dvina.

After stating the overall mission of each army group, the order assigned the specific tasks as follows:

a. Army Group South. This army group was to assemble two strong attack forces, one along the Prut River in Romania, the other in the Lublin-Jaroslav area. [See *map 3.*] These two forces were to thrust in the direction of Kirovograd and Kiev respectively, and thus accomplish a double envelopment of Russian forces in the western Ukraine. The significance of Kiev as the capital of the Ukraine, the headquarters of one of the most important military districts of the Soviet Union and the site of vital bridges across the Dnepr, was unquestioned. Here, too, was the point from which, after the initial border engagements, Army Group South was to coordinate any further advance with the movements of Army Group Center.

The southern arm of the pincers was the Twelfth Army, consisting of German and Romanian divisions and including one motorized infantry and two armored divisions. It was to drive northeastward via Kirovograd toward the Dnepr. The connecting link between the two prongs was to be the relatively weak Seventeenth Army, which had no armored units. Since neutral Hungary's territory was not to be used, this army was to assemble southeast of Lublin and advance toward Vinnitsa and Berdichev, in order to pin down the front of the Russian forces that were threatened by a double envelopment.

Forming the northern arm of the pincer, Sixth Army was to assemble in the Lublin area together with First Panzer Group. These two forces were given the most important as well as the most difficult task within the Army Group South mission. They would have to carry the main effort and, in addition to breaking through to Kiev and participating in the encirclement of the Russian forces in the western Ukraine, Sixth Army would have to screen the army group's north flank along the Pripyat Marsh region. In its distribution of attack forces the Army High Command had not allocated any combat elements of this region on the assumption that it was unsuitable for major operations and could therefore simply be kept under observation. In view of the unsatisfactory manpower situation, the Army High Command preferred to save forces for employment in more important attack zones.

After Sixth Army and First Panzer Group had succeeded in breaking through the enemy front, the latter was to speed toward Zhitomir, establish bridgeheads on the east bank of the Dnepr at Kiev and below, wheel southeastward to hit the enemy flank and rear, and link up with Twelfth Army. Covering the left flank of the advancing armor along the Pripyat Marshes, Sixth Army was to follow the First Panzer Group as quickly as possible, first to Zhitomir and then to Kiev. During its direct thrust across the territory west of the Dnepr, Sixth Army was to earmark strong forces for a sudden southeastward diversion.

b. Army Group Center. In the Army Group Center area immediately north of the Pripyat, the Russian salient west of Bialystok offered the possibility for a double envelopment. In this area the principal objective of rapidly destroying major Russian forces seemed more easily attainable than in the area of Army Group South. Exceedingly strong forces were to be massed on both extremities of the army group front while relatively weak ones were to be employed in the center. On the right, Fourth Army, including Second Panzer Group, was to advance along the main highway Baranovichi-Minsk-Orsha, while on the left, Ninth Army, including Third Panzer Group, was to jump off from Suwalki and drive toward Molodechno and Orsha. The objective of these two forces was the encirclement and destruction of all Russian forces between the border and Minsk. Second and Third Panzer Groups were then to move on Smolensk from the southwest and from the northwest respectively, thus preventing a reorganization of enemy forces along the upper Dnepr and Dvina Rivers. Fourth Army was to follow Second Panzer Group, advancing via Bobruysk and Borisov to Mogilev and the area north of that town. At the same time Ninth Army, taking advantage of the Third Panzer Group thrust, was to gain the Dvina at Polotsk and farther upstream.

c. Army Group North. The topography of the Baltic States favored the massing of power on the right of Army Group North. A powerful drive emanating from central East Prussia and directed via Kovno and Dvinsk into the area south of Pskov would cut off the Russian troops stationed in the Baltic States and squeeze them against the Baltic. Moreover, by establishing themselves in the vicinity of Lake Ilmen the German units would be in a favorable position for continuing their advance on Leningrad. The possibility that Army Group Center would support Army Group North was anticipated but was to be made contingent upon Army High Command approval.

At the outset of the operation Fourth Panzer Group, in conjunction with Sixteenth and Eighteenth Armies, was to break through the Russian border defenses in the area bordering on the Gumbinnen-Kovno highway. The armored units were to precede the infantry elements and cross the Dvina at Dvinsk and farther downstream. Their objective was to proceed to the area south of Pskov as quickly as possible, so that they could continue their drive to the north or the northeast in accordance with the overall situation.

After breaking through the Russian border positions, Sixteenth Army was to strengthen its right and follow Fourth Panzer via Dvinsk in the direction of Pskov.

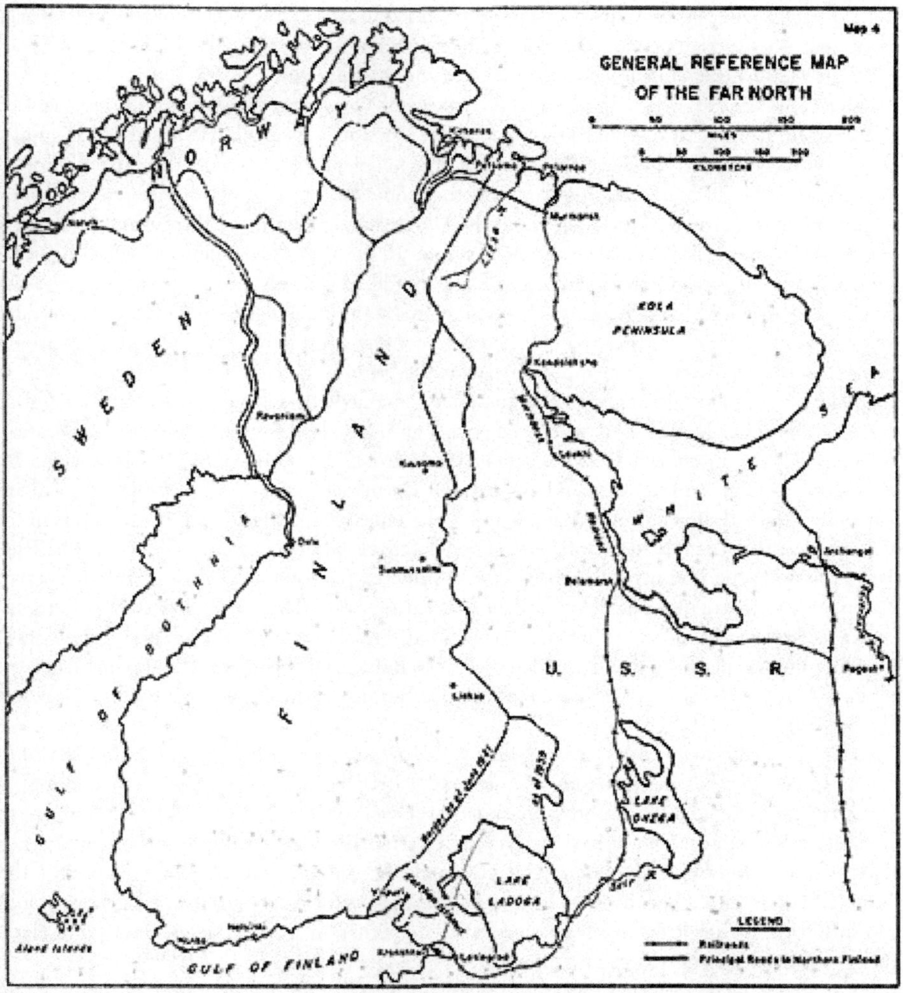

Map 4. General reference map of the Far North.

Eighteenth Army was to mass its forces along and east of the Tilsit-Riga highway, break through the Russian lines, cross the Dvina in the vicinity of Yekabpils, and destroy the encircled Red Army forces southwest of Riga. By quickly driving on to Pskov, the army was to prevent the withdrawal of Russian forces from the area southwest of Lake Peipus and set the stage for a subsequent seizure of Estonia and the islands of Hiiumaa and Saaremaa.

At the beginning of the operation the Army High Command reserves were to be moved up to the areas west of Jaroslav and east of Warsaw, where relatively strong forces were to be assembled, and to the Lublin and East Prussian border areas, where weaker groups were to be stationed.

d. Far North. Finland was to coordinate its offensive across the southeastern border with the Army High Command. The Finnish forces could attack either to the east or to the west of Lake Ladoga, and they were to time their offensive to coincide with Army Group North's crossing of the Dvina River.

The Army of Norway was given a defensive and an offensive mission [See *map 4.*]:

1. To protect Norway against any landing attempt by the British, and, in particular, to strengthen the defense forces in the Kirkenes-Narvik area.

2. To seize the Petsamo area in Finland in order to secure the nickel mines and to bear down upon the Russian port of Murmansk with the intention of seizing it as soon as the overall situation would make sufficient troops available for this mission.

On 2 February Hitler received Field Marshal Fedor von Bock, the commanding general of Army Group Center, with whom he discussed the plans for Operation BARBAROSSA. Bock expressed his belief that the Germans would be able to defeat the Russians, if the latter chose to give battle. He was wondering, however, how they could be forced to make peace. The Fuehrer replied that the German Army's seizure of the Ukraine and capture of Moscow and Leningrad would surely compel the Russians to come to terms. If, however, the Soviets refused to abandon the struggle even then, German motorized forces would have to advance as far as the Urals. He added: "In any event, I am happy that our war production is equal to any demand. We have such an abundance of materiel that we had to reconvert some of our war plants. The armed forces now have more trained manpower than at the beginning of the war, and our economy is in excellent condition." He rejected any possibility of conciliation by exclaiming: "I shall fight!"

At a conference the next day, when the campaign in the Balkans and the Army's operation order were being discussed, General Halder estimated that 100 infantry, 25 cavalry, and 30 mechanized Russian divisions would oppose the German invasion. The average Russian infantry division had direct armored support, but the tanks were of poor quality. In mechanized divisions the Red Army had quantitative superiority, the German Army qualitative. The Russian artillery, though numerically strong, was considered relatively ineffective. Among Russian leaders only Timoshenko was outstanding. But, on the other hand, the Soviet plans were unknown. Near the border were massed strong Red Army forces whose voluntary withdrawal would be limited if the Soviets wanted to keep the Baltic States and the Ukraine in their possession. And the Russians were constructing fortifications, particularly along the northern and southern sectors of the border.

Halder then summarized the instructions issued to the three army groups in the operation order. He added that Army Groups Center and North would jump off with 50 infantry, 9 motorized infantry, and 13 armored divisions, or a total of 72 divisions. Army Group South would have 30 infantry, 3 motorized infantry, and 5 armored divisions, or 38 divisions altogether. Most of the Army High Command reserves would be stationed in the northern part of the theater. Six armored divisions, which were to take part in the campaign in the Balkans, would be transferred to the Russian theater, provided the situation in the Balkans and particularly Turkey's attitude permitted such action.

Hitler interrupted by stating that once the die was cast Turkey would not budge, and that no special protection would be needed in the Balkans. He added that he had no basic objection to the Army's operation plan as presented by Halder: the theater of operations was tremendous; major elements of the Red Army could be trapped only if a tight noose was thrown around them; and he did not expect the Soviets to abandon Leningrad and the Ukraine without a struggle. On the other hand, it was quite possible that, after suffering their initial defeats and having perceived the German objectives, the Russians might stage a large-scale withdrawal to a defense line. In this event the Baltic States and the Leningrad area would have to be seized first because possession of these areas would greatly improve the logistical situation for the continuation of operations. If the center of the line was left in place until the enveloping wings began to apply pressure, the enemy forces would be unable to escape by withdrawing into the depth of the theater.

Halder continued his report by stating that one and one-half divisions of the Army of Norway were to advance toward Petsamo, while a force of approximately equal size was to be moved to northern Finland via Sweden. These two forces were to protect northern Finland and isolate the Russians around Murmansk. The Finns intended to commit 4 corps in southern Finland: 5 divisions were to advance on Leningrad, 3 toward Lake Onega, and 2 on Hanko. They would need strong German support since 15 Russian divisions stood on the other side of the Russo-Finnish border and approximately 1 division was stationed in the Murmansk area.

After Hitler observed that a rapid advance from Romanian territory was essential for safeguarding the oil fields, Halder broached the subject of Hungary. If that nation did not take an active part in the campaign, it should at least permit the use of its territory for detraining and staging purposes. Hitler felt that Hungary would consent to whatever Germany demanded, provided that proper compensation was offered. The necessary agreements would, however, have to be delayed until the last moment in order to maintain secrecy. Finland, Sweden, Hungary, and Slovakia were to be approached with regard to their cooperation only after the German intentions could no longer be concealed. The political leaders of Romania, whose participation in the campaign was certain, were the only ones to whom the German plans could be revealed. In accordance with Hitler's previous instructions, the concentration of forces in the East would be dissimulated as a large-scale deception preparatory to launching the invasion of England.

Halder then discussed matters pertaining to the other services and logistical problems. Flak protection would have to be provided by both the Army and the Luftwaffe. The Navy would have to open supply routes via the Baltic ports as rapidly as possible. The initial transport burden would fall upon truck transportation since the Russian rail lines would have to be converted to normal gauge. It was intended to organize long-distance truck transportation units to haul supplies to distribution points in the field. All transportation matters would have to be coordinated with the Luftwaffe so that no motor vehicle would remain unused. Even then, supply bases were being established in former eastern Poland, and similar installations were to be set up in Romania.

Halder also explained the plans for the strategic concentration of forces. The first echelon was then being moved into the theater. The second echelon was scheduled to begin its movement in mid-March, and these very substantial forces would be concentrated in rear areas away from the border. At the beginning of April Hungary would have to be approached regarding the transit of troops. The third echelon was to begin its movement in mid-April; from then on concealment would become difficult. The transfer of the fourth echelon was foreseen for the period from 25 April to 15 May.

Hitler approved the order as indicated, adding that "the world will hold its breath at the launching of Operation BARBAROSSA."

Initiation of Subordinate Staffs (February-March 1941)

Upon receiving the operation order from the Army High Command, the army group headquarters held map exercises and briefed the army and panzer group headquarters under their commands on their missions. Command post exercises were conducted at army and panzer group level, and special logistical problems were examined. The ideas expressed during these various exercises were incorporated into the drafts of the operation orders drawn up by each army group headquarters. Prior to being issued, these orders were submitted to the Army High Command for final approval.

A little later, corps and division headquarters were briefed on their missions. They then reexamined the tentative operation plans and orders and initiated personnel under their commands, using command post and map exercises for this purpose. The final step in this process of initiation, which actually did not take place until May or June, was to acquaint the lowest-echelon commanders with their future mission and to study the peculiarities of the terrain across which the initial attacks would have to be launched.

On 5 February for instance, General der Infanterie (Lt. Gen.) Georg von Sodenstern, Chief of Staff, Army Group South, conducted a command post exercise in which the operation plan, so far as it pertained to his army group, was put to the test. The participants were the chiefs of staff and operations officers of the armies and corps assigned to Army Group South. The outcome of the exercise revealed the difficulty of effecting an envelopment east of the Dnepr because the Russian forces remaining in the Pripyat area could easily interfere with the progress of the northern arm of the pincers. Another lesson learned was that a number of faulty assembly movements would impede the execution of the initial maneuvers. The necessary changes in the plans were made on the spot. General Halder, who attended the exercise, expressed his satisfaction with the excellent presentation and fruitful discussion.

At this time the question of infantry-armor cooperation during the initial breakthrough was also the subject of particular attention. It was resolved by the decision of the Army High Command to place one infantry corps under the operational control of each panzer group during the initial assault phase. The infantry's mission was to open gaps for the armored forces which would emerge suddenly, thus achieving complete surprise. An additional advantage was that the armored units would thus be able to keep their full striking power for thrusting deep into the Russian theater. As soon as the panzer groups had advanced sufficiently, the infantry corps would revert to the control of their respective armies.

In February General Jodl and his associates in the Armed Forces High Command prepared propaganda material for the invasion, drafted special regulations pertaining to the administration of occupied Russian territories, drew up plans for military cooperation with those nations which had expressed their willingness to join Germany against the Soviet Union, and coordinated functions pertaining to two or more of the armed services. On 20 February Goering formed a small Luftwaffe planning staff and set it up under his own supervision near Berlin.

At the beginning of March logistical exercises took place at Army High Command headquarters, and Army Group South held a supply and administration game based on the lessons learned during Sodenstern's command post exercise of the preceding month. During the following weeks the Armed Forces and Army High Commands issued a series of directives and regulations pertaining mainly to supply and administration.

Changes in Plans (March-April 1941)

Army Group South

On 18 March Hitler decided that Sixth Army was to carry out the main thrust of Army Group South. The plan for a Twelfth Army advance from Moldavia toward the northeast was abandoned. The German and Romanian units assembling along the Pruth were to tie down the opposing forces and pursue them only in the event that they should withdraw. This change in plan had to be made because Hitler contended that the Dnestr was a formidable obstacle that could not be surmounted by a frontal attack without considerable delay. According to the new plan the powerful left of Army Group South was to punch its way to the Kiev area and approach the Dnestr line from the rear. The forces assembled in Moldavia would have to be sufficiently strong to prevent a Russian penetration into Romania, but this danger did not seem acute since Brauchitsch had expressed the opinion that the Russians would not attack Romania unless they were attacked from Romanian territory. According to Hitler, Hungary was to take no part in Operation BARBAROSSA, and Slovakia was to assist only in the concentration and supply of German troops.

The Yugoslav *coup d'etat* on 26 March induced Hitler to expand the operations in the Balkans by attacking Yugoslavia in addition to Greece. The greater scope of the campaign in the Balkans necessitated that an army headquarters assume control of the occupied territories after the end of hostilities. Twelfth Army, which was in charge of the operations against Greece, was selected for this role, and Eleventh Army was designated as substitute headquarters for the forces assembled in Moldavia.

On 30 March 1941 the army group and army commanders reported to Hitler. During this conference the mission of Eleventh Army was discussed, and Hitler ordered the army forces divided into three separate groups, capable of backing up the Romanian divisions in case of need. Since Eleventh Army had thus been given a defensive mission, the motorized forces originally earmarked for that area were transferred to First Panzer Group. The encirclement of the Russian forces in the western Ukraine was to be effected by a single envelopment from the north, during which the armored forces were to thrust to the Dnepr at and south of Kiev, bear southeastward, and follow the bend of the river to its mouth, thus preventing the Russian forces in the western Ukraine from withdrawing across the river.

As a result of the foregoing changes, Directive No. 21 had meanwhile been amended as follows:

> Section II, paragraph 3: In conjunction with the German troops assembled on Romanian territory, Romanian troops will tie down the enemy forces opposite their borders and will also lend assistance in maintaining the lines of communications.
>
> Section III, A., paragraph 6: The army group committed south of the Pripyat Marshes will concentrate its main-effort forces in and to the south of the Lublin area for an attack in the general direction of Kiev. From there strong armored forces will thrust deep into enemy territory and envelop the Russian forces by following the course of the lower Dnepr.
>
> The mixed German-Romanian force in the south will have two missions:
>
> > 1. To secure Romania as a base and thus guarantee the continuity of operations in the southern part of the theater; and
> >
> > 2. To tie down the opposing enemy forces during the advance of the army group's north wing. In accordance with developments in the situation, the mixed force — supported by Air Force contingents — will launch a pursuit to prevent the Soviets from making an organized withdrawal across the Dnepr.

The corresponding changes were also incorporated into the Army's operation order. [See *map 5*.] Army Group South was no longer to concentrate its strength on both its wings; instead, it was to strengthen its left so that mobile forces could pace the drive on Kiev, where they were to bear southeastward and destroy — or at least cut off — all enemy forces still in the western Ukraine.

The missions of the individual armies were changed as follows:

Eleventh Army was to protect Romania against an invasion by Russian troops, tie down the forces opposite the Romanian border by tricking the enemy into believing that major forces were being assembled, and eventually launch a pursuit to prevent the Russians from making an organized withdrawal.

Seventeenth Army was to jab with its powerful left, push back the enemy southeastward, and pursue him via Vinnitsa and Berdichev.

First Panzer Group was to thrust via Berdichev and Zhitomir toward the Dnepr River at Kiev, and then immediately continue its southeastward drive in order to block the Russian routes of withdrawal.

Sixth Army was to screen the north flank of the army group along the Pripyat Marshes and follow First Panzer Group closely up to Zhitomir. Upon receiving specific orders from army group, Sixth Army was to shift strong forces southeastward along the west bank of the Dnepr and join First Panzer Group in the destruction of the Russian forces fighting in the western Ukraine.

The difficulties of such an operation, hinging on a single envelopment, were fully realized by the Army High Command. Its success depended essentially upon whether the Russian leaders would react swiftly to the situation. If they recognized the danger in time, major Russian forces would probably get across the Dnepr River — or at least those opposite the Romanian border. The outcome of the offensive in the south therefore seemed doubtful from the outset.

Map 5. The final plan for Operation BARBAROSSA.

Far North

In the far north Hitler wanted to close in on Murmansk and seize that port, if sufficient attack forces could be made available. The Russians would thus be unable to use Murmansk as a base for attacks against northern Finland and Norway, and British landings along the Kola Peninsula would not materialize. Another drive in the direction of Kandalaksha was planned in order to cut the lines of communications of the Russian troops stationed near Murmansk. Thus, two thrusts were to be staged in northern Finland in addition to the three in the southern part of that country : across the Karelian Isthmus, east of Lake Ladoga, and at Hanko. Initially, it was intended that the two German forces operating in northern Finland would be under the overall command of Field Marshal Carl Gustav Mannerheim, Commander in Chief, Finnish Armed Forces. When the latter refused to assume this additional responsibility, the German Army of Norway was put in charge of the northern and central Finnish theaters of operation. The Finnish Armed Forces Command was to exercise independent command authority over operations in southern Finland.

Delay in the Start

At the beginning of April, immediately after the start of the campaigns in the Balkans, the invasion of Russia was postponed by 4 to 6 weeks. On 30 April Hitler decided that the new D Day was to be 22 June. [See DA Pam 20-260, *The German Campaigns in the Balkans (Spring 1941),* pt. Five.]

The fighting in the Balkans ended with the withdrawal of the British at the end of April. During the second half of that month most of the German divisions engaged in the Balkans were being redeployed for rehabilitation so that they would be available for Operation BARBAROSSA. It was anticipated that, despite the planned invasion of Crete, all ground and air forces earmarked for the strategic concentration preceding the Russian campaign would be ready to jump off, with the possible exception of two panzer divisions that had advanced all the way to southern Greece.

The Draft of Directive No. 32 (11 June 1947)

Throughout this period of intensive planning and preparations Hitler and his military advisers believed in all seriousness that Germany could defeat the Soviet Union within 3 to 4 months. The Russo-Japanese pact of neutrality, concluded on 13 April, did not change any of the German dispositions. On the contrary, so convinced was Hitler of his future success that he made far-reaching adventurous plans even before the start of the Russian campaign. As early as 17 February 1941 he had asked Jodl to draw up a plan for the invasion of India from Afghan territory in order to permit closer German-Japanese cooperation. These and similar ideas met with no objection from the Army. But on 4 June 1941 the latter requested the Armed Forces Operations Staff to state which operations were to be conducted after the defeat of the Russian armed forces. Directive No. 32, "Preparations for the Period after BARBAROSSA" was drafted on 11 June and circulated among the three services for comments. It envisaged the following operations for the future:

a. Seizure of British strongholds in the Mediterranean and the Near East by concentric drives from Libya toward Egypt, from Bulgaria across Turkey, and possibly from the Caucasus across Iran;

b. Seizure of Gibraltar, and the closing of the gate to the western Mediterranean; and

c. Intensification of the siege of Britain and eventually a landing on the British Isles for the *coup de grâce.*

Strategic Concentration (21 June 1941)

The Army High Command had 145 divisions — including 19 armored — available for the invasion of Russia. These divisions were distributed among the individual army groups and armies in conformity with their mission and with a view to rail transport facilities. [See *chart 2.*] The distribution was as follows:

a. Army Group South (Field Marshal Gerd von Rundstedt).

1. Eleventh Army: 7 German and 14 Romanian infantry divisions in northeastern Romania.

2. Seventeenth Army: 7 infantry, 4 mountain and/or light infantry, and 2 security divisions west of Jaroslav.

3. Sixth Army, including First Panzer Group: 11 infantry, 1 security, 3 motorized infantry, and 5 armored divisions southeast of Lublin.

4. Army group reserves: 1 infantry and 2 mountain and/or light infantry divisions.

The total strength of Army Group South was 5 armored, 3 motorized infantry, 26 infantry, 6 mountain and/or light infantry, and 3 security divisions, for a grand total of 43 German plus 14 Romanian divisions. After the start of the invasion Army Group South was reinforced by a gradually increasing number of Italian, Hungarian, and Slovak units.

b. *Army Group Center* (Field Marshal Fedor von Bock).

(1) Fourth Army, including Second Panzer Group: 5 armored, 4 motorized infantry, 18 infantry, 1 cavalry, and 2 security divisions northeast and east of Warsaw.

(2) Ninth Army, including Third Panzer Group: 4 armored, 3 motorized infantry, 1 security, and 12 infantry divisions in and south of the Suwalki area.

(3) Army group reserves: 1 infantry division.

The total strength of Army Group Center was 9 armored, 7 motorized infantry, 31 infantry, 1 cavalry, and 3 security divisions, for a grand total of 51 divisions.

c. Army Group North (Field Marshal Wilhelm von Leeb).

(1) Sixteenth Army: 10 infantry and 2 security divisions east of Insterburg.

(2) Eighteenth Army, including Fourth Panzer Group: 3 armored,. 3 motorized infantry, 1 security, and 10 infantry divisions north, south, and east of Tilsit.

Chart 2. Order of Battle on 21 June 1941

Army groups	Subordinate panzer groups and armies	Assembly areas	Planned direction of attack
North: Field Marshal Wilhelm von Leeb (Attached: First Air Force: General Alfred Keller)	Eighteenth Army: General Georg von Kuechler	North of Tilsit	Estonia
	Fourth Panzer Group: General Erich Hoepner	South and East of Tilsit	Thrust toward Leningrad
	Sixteenth Army: General Ernst Busch	East of Insterburg	Leningrad via Lovat to follow Fourth Panzer Group
Center: Field Marshal Fedor von Bock (Attached: Second Air Force: Field Marshal Albert Kesselring)	Third Panzer Group: General Hermann Hoth	North and East of Suwalki	Northern arm of pincers
	Ninth Army: General Adolf Strauss	Southeast and Southwest of Suwalki	Polotsk, Vitebsk
	Fourth Army: Field Marshal Guenther von Kluge	Northeast and East of Warsaw	Mogilev area, to follow Second Panzer Group
	Second Panzer Group: General Heinz Guderian	Southeast of Warsaw	Southern arm of pincers
South: Field Marshal Gerd von Rundstedt (Attached: Fourth Air Force: General Alexander Loehr)	First Panzer Group: General Ewald von Kleist	Southeast of Lublin	Enveloping maneuver toward Kiev
	Sixth Army: Field Marshal Walter von Reichenau	Southeast of Lublin	North of Kiev, to follow First Panzer Group
	Seventeenth Army: General Karl Heinrich von Stuelpnagel	West of Jaroslav	Vinnitsa
	Eleventh Army: General Eugen von Schobert	East and Southeast of Botosani	Lower Dnepr

(3) Army Group reserves: 1 infantry division.

The total strength of Army Group North was 3 armored, 3 motorized infantry, 21 infantry, and 3 security divisions, for a grand total of 30 divisions.

d. Army High Command Reserves (as of D Day).

(1) In transit and assigned to:
Army Group South — A infantry divisions, Army Group Center — 6 infantry divisions, and Army Group North — 2 infantry divisions.

(2) In transit and unassigned: 2 armored, 1 motorized infantry, 9 infantry divisions.

The total Army High Command reserves were 2 armored, 1 motorized infantry, and 21 infantry divisions, for a grand total of 24 divisions.

e. In Finland.

(1) Finnish Army High Command.

a. Karelian Isthmus forces: 7 divisions west of Viipuri.

b. Karelian Army: 5 divisions, 1 cavalry and 2 light infantry brigades in the area northeast of Lake Ladoga.

c. Other forces: 1 division in the Lieksa area, 1 division blocking Hanko, 1 German division as reserve.

(2) German Army of Norway.

a. Finnish III Corps: 2 Finnish divisions in the Suomussalmi-Kuusamo area.

b. German XXXVI Corps: 1 Finnish and 11/2 German divisions in the area east of Rovaniemi.

c. German Mountain Corps Norway: 2 German mountain divisions in the Kirkenes area.

f. In Norway. 5 infantry and 2 security divisions on occupation duty and guarding coastal areas.

Air Support

Each army group was to be supported by one air force, so that the Fourth, Second, and First Air Forces were to operate in conjunction with Army Group South, Center, and North respectively. Second Air Force was the strongest, whereas First Air Force actually consisted of only one corps. This deficiency was partly compensated for by committing the Fifth Air Force in the far north, where the Luftwaffe contingents were given the threefold mission of guarding the Norwegian coastal waters, striking at the naval base of Murmansk and the convoys heading for that port, and supporting the Army of Norway's operations in northern Finland.

Luftwaffe Strength Figures (20 June 1941)

Unit	Total	Bombers and dive bombers	Fighter planes	Reconnaissance planes
Totals	2,000	1,160	720	120
Fourth Air Force (A Gp South)	600	360	210	30
Second Air Force (A Gp Center)	910	490	390	30
First Air Force (A Gp North)	430	270	110	50
Fifth Air Force (Finland)	60	40	10	10

Other Factors

Perhaps the most striking feature of the distribution of forces for the invasion of Russia was the small number of reserve divisions assigned to the army groups. The Army High Command, however, was in a quandary: the reserve divisions could either be assigned to the Army groups, leaving hardly any strategic reserves, or the Army High Command could retain them under its control. The latter solution was given preference because it offered Hitler a possibility of exercising closer control over the course of operations. In view of the 900-mile width of the attack front, the total reserves were too small to give a safe margin of depth to the strategic concentration and the invasion proper.

The main attack groupings were in the Sixth, Fourth, and Ninth Army areas where, within narrow zones of action, deeply echeloned wedges were to be driven across enemy lines. By contrast, the Carpathian border and the central sector of the Bialystok salient were screened by only weak security units.

The strategic concentration of forces was carried out over a period of several weeks. The rate of troop transfers, moderate in order to maintain secrecy, was not stepped up until the final phase. Most of the divisions of Eleventh Army moved up from Greece, covering up to 500 miles on foot and arriving just before D Day. The initial concentration of forces took place away from the border. From the assembly areas most of the troops reached their jump off positions in a few night marches.

German Army Personnel and Equipment Assembled for the Invasion of Russia (20 June 1941)

Officer and Enlisted Personnel	3,050,000
Horses	625,000
Motor Vehicles (incl. armd. recon. cars)	600,000
Tanks	3,350
Artillery Pieces	7,184

Estimate of Soviet Strength (June 1941)

Sources of Information

Radio intercepts were, the only reliable source of intelligence available to the Germans before the outbreak of hostilities. Intercept stations had been set up in Bulgaria, Romania, Hungary, Bohemia, Moravia, western Poland, East Prussia, and Finland. Because of insufficient personnel and inadequate equipment these stations did not reach very deeply into the interior of the Soviet Union, their range being limited to the territories west of the Desna and Dnepr, the Baltic States, and some of the border area near the Finnish frontier.

Reports from agents in Finland and Turkey proved valuable in tracing Russian troops movements.

Reconnaissance missions were flown by special high-altitude, longrange planes from bases in the Balkans, western Poland, and East Prussia. The picture obtained by air reconnaissance remained incomplete because of strong Soviet protests against such Luftwaffe activities.

Estimate of Red Army Dispositions

	Total Army Strength	Western Border Regions	Rest of European Russia	Far East
Infantry Divisions	170	118	27	25
Cavalry Divisions	33½	20	5½	8
Motorized and Armored Brigades	46	40	1	5

[For the distribution of the Red Army forces in the western border regions, see *map* 6.]

Estimate of Soviet Air Force Strength

The total strength of the Soviet Air Force was estimated at 8,000 planes, 6,000 of which were in Europe and the rest in Asia. The composition of the air forces in Europe was believed to be as follows:

800 obsolete close reconnaissance planes.
2,000 fighters, including 250-300 modern planes.
1,800 bombers, including approximately 800 up-to-date planes.
700 fighter-bombers, consisting of Stormoviks and obsolete planes.
700 naval planes of obsolete designs.

In the spring of 1941 a few Luftwaffe experts received permission to visit some airplane factories in the Urals. They saw six plants and reported that a large-scale aircraft production program was under way. These reports —just like all other warnings —were not heeded: Operation BARBAROSSA started according to plan.

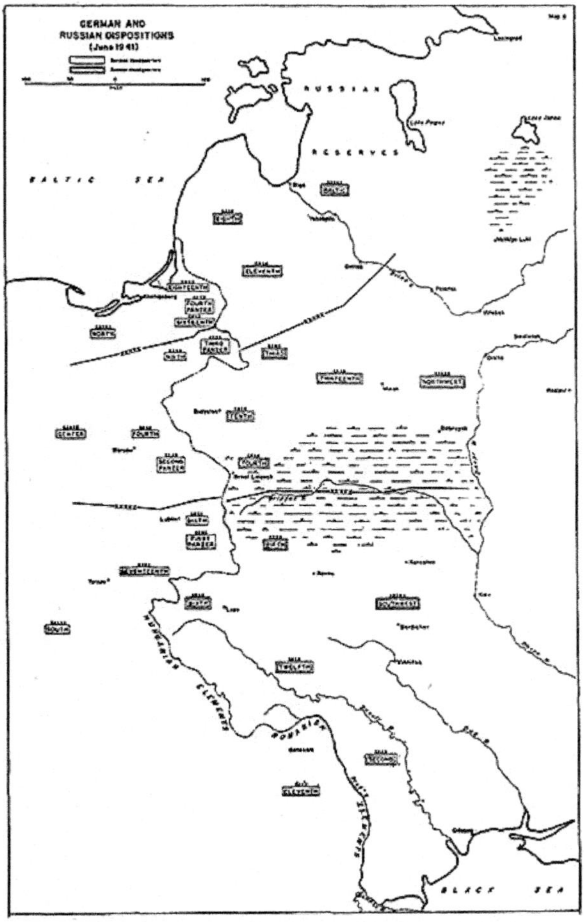

Map 6. German and Russian dispositions (June 1941).

PART TWO OPERATIONS IN 1941

Chapter 3 The Initial Operations (22 June-31 July 1941)

D Day

The German invasion of Russia began at 0300 on 22 June 1941. The Germans achieved complete tactical surprise. In some places the Russians were caught asleep in their billets, and in many instances Russian commanders proved helpless before the onslaught. In general, however, the Russian troops recovered quickly and offered strong local resistance.

The Situation on 30 June 1941

In the Army Group South area, the First Panzer Group had fought its way into the area east of Rovno, its advance having been repeatedly held up by counterattacks of skillfully led Russian units. Farther to the south the Seventeenth Army advance had progressed to the area around and especially south of Lvov but against strong resistance. The general impression was that the Russians facing Army Group South had recovered from their initial shock and, having realized the seriousness of the situation, were showing considerable skill in blocking the advance. Developments in the southern part of the theater were therefore not up to expectation.

In the Army Group Center area, the ring of encirclement around the Russian forces west of Minsk had been completely closed. The Second and Third Panzer Groups had linked up near Minsk according to plan. The Russians had been unable to prevent this maneuver or coordinate any countermoves. By the end of June the encircled units made uncoordinated efforts to break out of the pocket. Eventually, some 20 Russian divisions were destroyed in the Minsk pocket, and the Germans captured 290,000 prisoners, 2,500 tanks, and 1,400 guns. The situation in this area was so satisfactory that Hitler considered diverting forces to Army Group South to intercept and destroy the Red Army reserves being brought up from the rear.

In the Army Group North area the situation developed according to plan. The Dvina had been crossed at Dvinsk and Yekabpils, and the crucial step toward implementing the army group plan had thus been taken. In Lithuania and Latvia, the Russians were offering strong resistance in a series of delaying actions. By this time 12 to 15 Russian divisions had virtually been wiped out during the fighting west of the Dvina.

In general, the Germans had every reason to be satisfied with the progress of the first nine days. The Luftwaffe had gained complete air supremacy. The Russians had been forced to give battle on all fronts. An organized withdrawal opposite Army Groups Center and North was no longer to be feared, whereas in the Army Group South area the Russians could still evade the German envelopment. In view of the heavy losses suffered by the Soviet forces, the overall success of the German operation seemed assured. In a conference on 29 June Hitler stated that, instead of driving straight toward Moscow, he would prefer to divert forces for a thrust on Leningrad. The capture of Leningrad would drive the Russians from the Baltic and thus secure German shipments of ore across that body of water, enable the Finns to seize the initiative, and disengage the German left for a thrust on Moscow. Jodl interjected that the detour to Moscow via Leningrad would be beyond the capabilities of the panzer formations. After some discussion it was decided that the question would be reexamined at a later date.

Developments in Early July 1941

In a diary entry of 3 July General Halder expressed the justifiable optimism, shared at that time by most Germany military leaders, that the mission of destroying the Red Army west of the Dvina and Dnepr had been accomplished. He did not doubt the word of a captured Russian corps commander that east of these two rivers the Germans would encounter only isolated forces whose strength would be insufficient to hamper operations decisively. It therefore seemed to him no exaggeration to state that the Russian campaign had been won in less than two weeks. Of course, this did not imply that the campaign was completely terminated. It would take many more weeks to occupy the vast Russian theater and overcome the stubbornness with which the Soviets would continue to offer resistance.

Hitler's opinion on the same subject, as expressed on 4 July, ran as follows: "I constantly try to put myself in the enemy's position. For all practical purposes the enemy has lost this campaign. It is a good thing that we have destroyed the Russian armored and air forces right at the beginning. The Russians will be unable to replace them." At the same time the Fuehrer was preoccupied with the question of what was to happen after crossing the Dnepr-Dvina line. "Are we to turn north or south? This will probably be the most difficult decision of the entire campaign." He obviously did not consider driving straight on to Moscow.

The next day Jodl asked Halder to submit his plans and ideas for the continuation of the offensive to Hitler. In Jodl's opinion the significance of the next movements of the panzer groups was so great that Halder should consult Hitler before definitely committing these forces. Jodl added that two important questions preoccupied Hitler:

1. Would Army Group North be sufficiently strong to accomplish its mission singlehandedly or would the Third Panzer Group have to lend its assistance? In the latter case, should this panzer group be diverted northeastward immediately after crossing the Dnepr-Dvina line?

2. Should Second Panzer Group be diverted southward immediately after having crossed the Dnepr?

Brauchitsch and Halder reported to Hitler on 8 July. They indicated that out of 164 Russian rifle divisions so far identified by the Germans, 89 had been destroyed, 46 were still capable of commitment, 18 were employed in secondary theaters such as Finland, and the whereabouts of 11 divisions were unknown.

Brauchitsch then suggested that First Panzer Group immediately turn southward for a close-in envelopment and that a protective screen be built up west of Kiev. Hitler, however, preferred to capture Kiev first and then launch a wide envelopment along the east bank of the Dnepr with the assistance of strong Army Group Center forces. Brauchitsch objected to this plan, indicating that the logistical problems it involved seemed insuperable at that time. He did advocate, however, that the wide envelopment be carried out after the close-in one had met with success. No immediate decision was taken.

At that time the Army Group South operations hinged upon the progress made by Sixth Army and First Panzer Group. To achieve a decisive success the latter would have to penetrate the Red Army defenses that blocked the German axis of advance in the direction of Vinnitsa and Korosten. The mounting pressure, exerted by the Russian *Fifth Army* which was threatening the German north flank from the Pripyat Marshes, had to be eliminated at the same time. Moreover, the Eleventh Army would have to join the offensive and move northeastward toward Vinnitsa, where — despite its relative weakness — it was to assist First Panzer Group. This maneuver might pave the way to the encirclement of Russian forces southwest of Berdichev.

The next objective of Army Group Center was to bring about the collapse of the Russian defensive triangle anchored on Orsha, Smolensk, and Vitebsk. There, between the Dnepr and the Dvina, was the corridor that was vital for the continuation of the German thrust on Moscow. The Russians were apparently preparing an allout defense along this same corridor, using not only whatever forces had escaped from the Minsk pocket but also fresh ones then being moved up. Another Soviet concentration was being built up near Velikiye Luki for future commitment against Army Group Center or Army Group North.

To accomplish its next mission Army Group Center would have to make a sweeping double envelopment in the course of which Second Panzer Group was to advance in the general direction of Bobruysk-Roslavl and Third Panzer Group along the upper Dvina via Polotsk and Vitebsk. The infantry divisions of the Fourth and Ninth Armies would have to close up and constantly support the armor if the Orsha corridor was to be enveloped.

Army Group North was to drive toward Lake Ilmen, with Fourth Panzer Group in the lead, and then turn northward in the direction of Leningrad. Strong Russian resistance was to be expected at the former Russian-Estonian border, and Estonia proper would have to be mopped up by infantry divisions brought up in the rear.

At this stage the crucial problem confronting all three army groups was to keep the infantry from falling too far behind the armor. The infantry divisions with their horse-drawn vehicles could not help being delayed whenever they were engaged in completing encirclements or in mopping up pockets. To overextend the distance between the onrushing armor and the temporarily stalled infantry meant courting danger. The Army's low strength in motorized infantry divisions (because of the constant POL and materiel shortage, Germany had but 14 such divisions) proved to be a handicap. It is true that this deficiency was somewhat compensated for by the almost unbelievable march performances of the infantry divisions, which time and again succeeded in closing up even though they were denied the use of the few good roads reserved for the motorized units.

The question of determining the proper size for a ring of encirclement also preoccupied the Army. The lesson learned from the battle that had raged between Bialystok and Minsk was that it was unsound to try to envelop too much at one time; if the ring of encirclement was too large it would not be sufficiently strong to prevent a breakout of Russian forces.

For the time being, supply was no problem since the precautionary measures of establishing forward depots and new base sections guaranteed a satisfactory support of the projected operations.

The railroads functioned surprisingly well. By 3 July, for instance, the tracks from Brest Litovsk half-way to Minsk had been converted to European gauge, with the remaining section being reopened two days later for trains using captured Russian rolling stock. A few days later this section also had to be converted because the Germans had not captured any Russian tank cars. Fleets of German tank cars moved up the large quantities of POL needed to feed the offensive.

The Luftwaffe had achieved air superiority despite the surprising numerical strength of the Russian Air Force. An Armed Forces High Command communique, issued on 12 July, mentioned that 6,233 Russian planes had been destroyed against very minor Luftwaffe losses. Soviet communiques covering the same period spoke of 1,900 Russian planes lost against 2,300 German planes destroyed — 300 more than the total number of German planes committed in the Russian theater. Even though these figures are obviously exaggerated and differ so greatly, they do convey an idea of the impact of the initial air battles.

The Mid-July Estimate

On 14 July Hitler mentioned that Moscow would have to be bombed from the air if the center of Communist resistance was to be hit and the orderly evacuation of the Soviet Government prevented.

Three days later Hitler considered once against the diversion of Hoth's Third Panzer Group to the northeast and Guderian's Second Panzer Group to the southeast. For the latter maneuver, to be initiated immediately after the liquidation of the Smolensk pocket, Guderian's panzer forces were to be reinforced by strong infantry units of the Second Army.

In the Army Group South area, the efforts of Sixth Army and First Panzer Group were in danger of being dissipated. The pressure exerted by the Russian *Fifth Army* from the Pripyat Marshes against the army group's flank diverted more and more Sixth Army troops from their original mission. [See *map 7*.] Armored elements were arriving in the vicinity of Kiev where they protected the flank of the First Panzer Group. The latter was thrusting southeastward toward Uman in an attempt to envelop the Russian forces in front of Seventeenth Army. Despite stubborn Russian resistance and unexpectedly heavy rainfall, the Seventeenth Army had meanwhile penetrated into the Vinnitsa area, while the Eleventh Army had advanced as far as the Dnestr. Some German elements had pushed to Kishinev for the purpose of getting the Romanians started on the road to Odessa.

The Russians opposing Army Group South continued to fight a stubborn and skillful delaying action, meanwhile avoiding most German enveloping maneuvers. Marshal Semen Budyenny who commanded the Russian *Army Group Southwest* was Rundstedt's opponent.

Brauchitsch, Halder, and Rundstedt agreed that First Panzer Group would have to launch a wider envelopment than originally intended. The thrust toward Uman no longer complied with the existing situation, and the armored forces were therefore to drive deeper into the Dnepr bend and attempt to establish a bridgehead south of Kiev. :At the same time Rundstedt -stressed the necessity for offensive action to eliminate Russian forces threatening his left flank from the Pripyat region. While .Halder agreed in principle, he did not believe that combing out the Pripyat Marshes could be accomplished effectively without employing the proper forces. He felt that it would be more expedient to cut the lines: of communication of the Russian *Fifth Army* between the Pripyat and the Dnepr and let the army perish in the swamps.

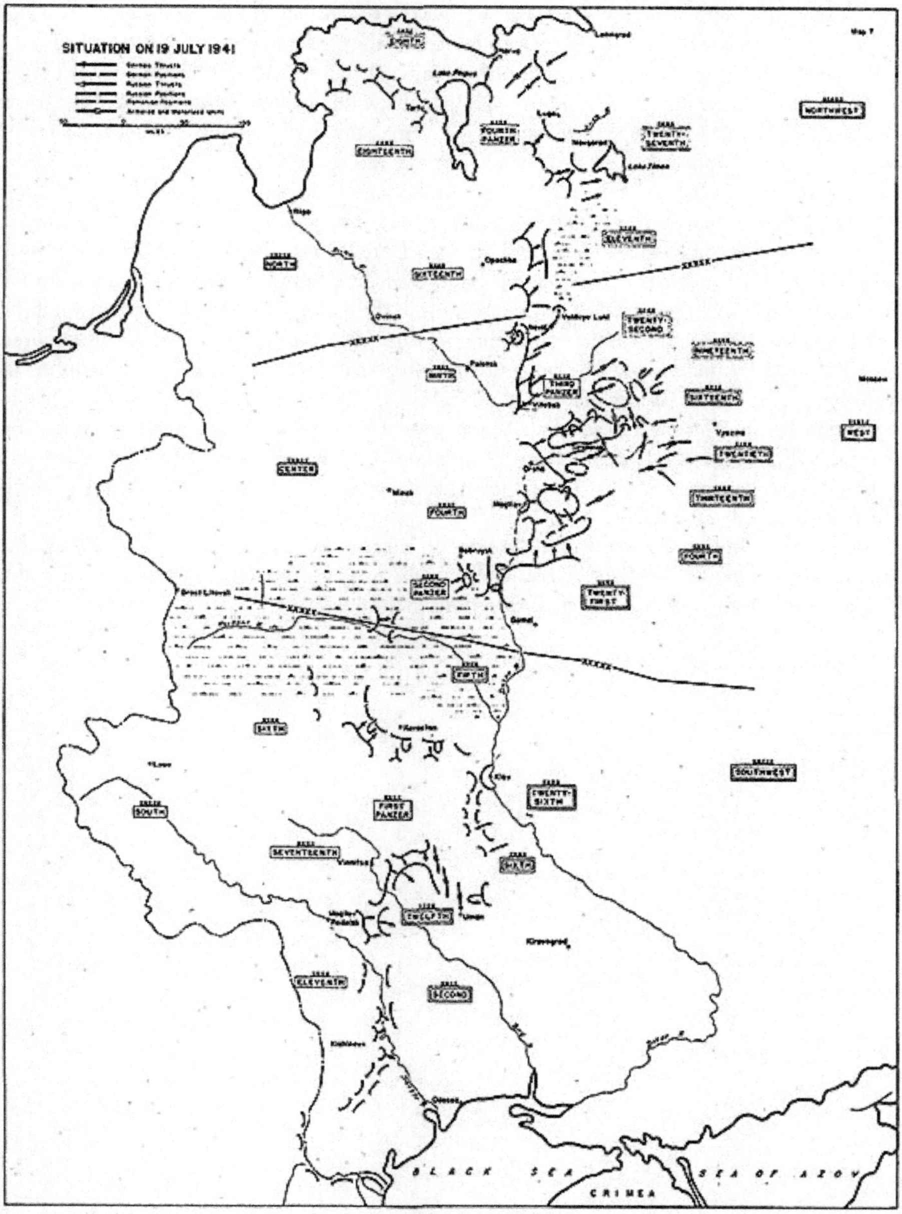

Map 7. Situation on 19 July 1941.

The situation of Army Group Center was far more far moreavorable. The Orsha-Smolensk-Vitebsk barrier had been pried open and the ring of encirclement near Smolensk closed. Another 100,000 prisoners, 2,000 tanks, and 1,900 guns had fallen into German hands. Russian attempts to build up a new front and to extend it to the north and south had failed. The Russians, although split into isolated and more or. less encircled groups, continued to stubbornly resist east of Mogilev, between Orsha and Smolensk, northeast of Vitebsk, and near Nevel.

There was a certain amount of Russian pressure from the Gomel area, but in general the Red Army had been badly shaken; two weeks would be needed for mopping-up operations. Marshal Semen Timoshenko's *Aray Group West* was receiving;a constant flow of reinforcements, improvised units were arriving from Moscow, and the Soviet Government was obviously using every possible means to stop the German advance on the Russian capital.

In the Army Group North area Sixteenth Army had fought its way eastward against stubborn resistance in the difficult terrain east of Opochka, while Fourth Panzer Group had turned northward, advancing between Lakes Ilmen and Peipus toward Leningrad. Marshal Klementi Voroshilov, who commanded. *Army Group Northwest,* was strongly resisting this German drive. The two armored corps, of Fourth Panzer Group became separated during the course of their advance. While the corps on the right was driving toward Novgorod to isolate Leningrad from the east, the other corps moved up the east shore of Lake Peipus, because the more direct route to Leningrad via Luga led through extremely difficult terrain that was ,unsuitable for armor. The latter corps .was to capture Narva, thereby closing the corridor between Lake Peipus and the Baltic, and then resume the advance on Leningrad from the west. The splitting of this armored force was a totally undesirable development since the Army, High Command had planned to keep the Fourth Panzer Group intact until it reached the area southeast of Leningrad. The city would thus be cut off from the east, and the way paved for the advance of the Finns approaching along the shores of Lake Ladoga. Leeb was reminded of the necessity of implementing this plan and was given specific instructions to move up infantry forces behind the panzer corps which had turned northward.

For the first time in the campaign the flow of Supplies became unsatisfactory. Delays occurred in the Army Group Center: area and to some extent also in the north. Increasing difficulties in rail transportation affected operations accordingly.

Directive No. 33 (19 July 1941)

The introductory paragraph of this directive, which carried the subtitle "Continuation of the Russian Campaign," enumerated the successes hitherto achieved. It also mentioned that Army Group Center would need some time to mop up the remaining Russian pockets and that the progress of Army Group South was hampered by Fortress Kiev in front and the Russian *Fifth Army* in the rear.

The twofold objective of future operations was to prevent the withdrawal of strong Soviet forces and to annihilate them. The measures to be taken for this purpose were as follows:

a. South. A concentric attack on the Russian *Twelfth* and *Sixth Armies* was to lead to their destruction west of the Dnepr. [See *map 7*]. The Russian *Fifth Army* was also to be destroyed through a joint effort of Army Group South and Center forces. The Second Panzer Group and strong infantry forces of Army Group Center were to be diverted to the southeast to cut off those Russian units trying to escape across the river.

b. Center Army Group Center was to mop up the numerous pockets in its area and then continue its advance on Moscow with a force exclusive composed of infantry divisions The Third Panzer Group was to thrust northeastward to cut the communications between Moscow and Leningard and simultaneously protect the right flank of Army Group North during its advance on Leningard.

c. NOrth The drive on Leningard was to continue as soon as the infantry divisions of Eighteenth Army had closed with Fourth Panzer Group and the Sixteenth Army had made contact with Third Panzer Group.

d. Finland The Finnish forces in the south, reinforced by the German 163d Infantry Division, were to place their main effort east of Lake Ladoga and coordinate their offensive with Army Group North. This mission of the German units committed in northern Finland remained unchanged.

e. Air Support. The Luftwaffe was to support the diversion to the southeast with all its available forces. The Second Air Force, temporarily reinforced by the transfer of forces from the West, was to bomb Moscow as retribution for Soviet air attacks on Bucharest and Helsinski.

f. Naval Support. The Navy was to safeguard supply convoys and prevent the escape of Russian naval units to neutral ports in-Sweden. After the Baltic had been cleared of the Soviet forces, some elements of the German Baltic Fleet were to be transferred to the Mediterranean. A few submarines were to be dispatched to the Norwegian Sea-to support the operations in Finland.

The last paragraph of the directive dealt with the redistribution of forces in western and northern Europe.

Two days after signing the directive Hitler visited Army Group North headquarters, where he discussed the implications of his orders with Leeb and his staff He pointed out that the capture of Leningrad — a symbol of Bolshevism since 1917 — might lead to a complete collapse of the already badly shaken Soviet regime. Because of the significance of the city it was to be expected that the advancing German troops would encounter strong resistance. The Third. Panzer Group was still engaged in liquidating the pockets near Smolensk, but the decision would have to be made within the next five days whether this force was to be diverted from the drive on Moscow. Despite having issued the directive, Hitler was still undecided as to its implementation. During the conference Hitler also stated that, to him, Moscow was simply a place name.

On 23 July Hitler attended a conference at Army High Command headquarters. General Halder reported the most recent information on Russian and German strength figures, as follows:

Estimate of Russian Strength (23 July 1941)

Russian Strength	Divisions			
	Total	Rifle	Armored	Cavalry
Totals	93	78	13	2
Opposite German Army Group:				
North	23½	20	3½	
Center	35½	32	3½	
South	34	26	6	2

After one month of fighting, the effective strength of then German infantry divisions had been reduced by approximately 20 percent and that of the panzer and motorized infantry divisions by 50 percent.

For future planning Halder estimated that Army Group South would be able to cross the Dnepr by the middle of August, but that Army Group Center could not possibly resume its advance before 5 August. The pockets would have to be mopped up, supplies moved up and distributed, etc. Very strong resistance was to be expected west of Moscow where the Russians were building up strength, including a formidable antiaircraft defense system. The Army Group North forces would probably have to be regrouped before the final drive on Leningrad could be launched.

Hitler emphasized that the basic principle in conducting the operations was to destroy enemy forces wherever they were encountered. In addition the three principal objectives to be attained were as follows:

1. The Leningrad region because of its industrial, naval, and political importance;
2. The Moscow area because of its war production facilities; and
3. The Ukraine because of its natural resources and industry. He repeated that after the fighting around Smolensk had subsided the Second and Third Panzer Groups would have to turn right and left respectively to support the adjoining army groups. Army Group Center would have to carry out its advance on Moscow without armored support.

As a result of this conference the Supplement to Directive No. 33 was issued on 23 July. This order specified the scope of future operations as follows:

a. South. All enemy forces remaining west of the Dnepr were to be defeated and destroyed. As soon as circumstances permitted, First and Second Panzer Groups were to be put under the command of Fourth Army and assembled west of the Dnepr. Reinforced by infantry and mountain divisions, this army was to seize the industrial region of Kharkov, cross ,the Don, and drive into the Caucasus.

b. Center. After having mopped up around Smolensk and stabilized the situation along its southern flank, Army Group Center was to defeat the Russian forces still remaining between Smolensk and Moscow and seize their capital, "using the infantry units of its two armies, which were sufficiently strong for this purpose."

The Third Panzer Group was to be temporarily attached to Army Group North, but would revert to Army Group Center as soon as its mission was accomplished. The armored forces would then take part in the subsequent drive from Moscow to the Volga River.

c. North. Receiving the support of Third Panzer Group, Army Group North would be able to commit its infantry in a direct assault on Leningrad while the mobile units would attempt enveloping maneuvers.

d. Redeployment. The Army High Command was to plan organizational measures for the transfer and reassignment of Army Group North forces after their mission to seize Leningrad had been accomplished.

The last two paragraphs of the Supplement dealt with air and naval reinforcements for the Finnish theater and with rear area security measures in occupied Russian territories. Greater security was to be achieved by "applying appropriate Draconian measures, not by requesting more security forces."

The Army vigorously protested against the contents of the Supplement to Directive No. 33, and Brauchitsch claimed that for the time being its implementation was impossible, particularly in the Army Group Center area. On 23 July he asked Keitel, who had signed the Supplement, to defer its application until current operations had been brought to a more conclusive point. After Keitel refused this request, Brauchitsch asked for another conference with Hitler, this time on the subject of the contents of the Supplement.

This conference apparently took place on the same day. Hitler listened to Brauchitsch's objections, then stressed that certain lessons on the conduct of mobile operations could be learned from the experience of the five weeks'-old Russian campaign. Because of the Soviet forces' stiff resistance, operations with far-reaching objectives would have to be deferred until the Russians no longer had the strength to counterattack. Close-in envelopments would have to be attempted instead, thus giving the infantry divisions an opportunity to directly support the spearhead units, which in turn would become available for their proper mission.

The Army's Letter to the Armed Forces High Command

The Army's ideas on the further conduct of operations were explained in a letter drafted by the Operations Division of the Army High Command and approved by Halder on 30 June. The letter was never sent because its contents were partly superseded by Directive No. 33 and because the entire Armed Forces High Command — with the possible exception of Keitel — seemed to share the Army's point of view.

After dealing with secondary problems in the initial paragraphs, the letter stated the Army's case as follows:

a. The Offensive against Moscow. After the transfer of the forces that were to be diverted to the north and south, the two remaining armies of Army Group Center would be composed of 20-22 divisions, including all reserves in rear areas. These forces would have to suffice for launching an offensive along an approximately 150-mile front against an estimated force of 19 Soviet divisions, of which 3 were armored and 2 motorized. The Russians could probably move up reinforcements from the immediate vicinity of Moscow.

The German attack forces would have to penetrate a fortified position behind which there would surely be some additional field fortifications. Such a maze of defensive positions could be overcome only by a proper massing of forces. The forces for the main effort in the south would have to be assembled near Yelnya, those in the north around Bely. The southern axis of advance would have to run somewhere between the Roslavl-Moscow and Smolensk-Moscow roads, and the northern one would lead from Bely via Rzhev to Moscow.

No quick advance toward Moscow could be expected without armored forces. On the contrary, the operation would certainly be costly and painstaking, and it might bog down altogether.

b. Critique.

1. According to present plans Army Group Center would be composed of three different forces. The Second Panzer Group would attack in the direction of Gomel and the Third Panzer Group northeastward to the Valdai Hills; by eliminating any possible threat to the flanks these two movements would pave the way for a third force thrusting toward Moscow.

2. A decisive offensive against Moscow could not get under way before the beginning of September, when the two panzer groups would become available to participate in the drive.

3. The Russians would thus have one extra month to organize and strengthen their defenses while warding off the weak German attacks launched with insufficient forces. They would have achieved their objective of splitting up the German forces by continually jabbing at their flanks. At the same time the immediate danger to Moscow would subside for several weeks. Aside from the political significance of this success, the Soviets would benefit from remaining in control of the industrial and communications facilities of their capital.

4. The effectiveness of air attacks on Moscow remained doubtful because of the long distance separating the German airfields from the target area. No immediate improvement was in sight.

c. General Suggestions. A reexamination of the plans regarding the redistribution of the Army Group Center forces therefore seemed warranted. Being unable to evaluate the political and economic factors that might have motivated the decisions of the Armed Forces High Command, the Army could base its suggestions only on military factors. These were as follows:

1. The Russians would probably try to build up a defense line between the Baltic and Black Seas, along which they would attempt to stop the German advance before the onset of winter. They would no doubt try to establish this line west of their major industrial centers. If the present war of movement developed into position

warfare, the Russians would probably be able to organize and train strong units by next spring. This in turn would force the Germans to divert even more forces to the Russian theater. Such a course of events would, however, be contrary to the military objective of the Russian campaign, which was to quickly knock out one adversary and then turn all the power against the other one — Great Britain.

2. To forestall the Russian intentions, the Germans would have to keep their adversaries off balance. This could best be achieved by smashing the Russian resistance by a direct thrust on Moscow. Since possession of the Russian capital was vital from a military, political, and economic standpoint, the Soviet leaders would commit every available soldier to defend the city. By attacking Moscow the German Army could therefore destroy the bulk of the Red Army, split the Russian theater in two parts, and seriously impair the Soviet unity of command.

3. All secondary operations, having as the objective the destruction of individual Russian groupings, would have to be abandoned unless such operations could be integrated into the overall plan for a powerful offensive against Moscow.

d. Specific Suggestions.

1. Two armies composed of infantry divisions would launch a frontal attack on Moscow. The axis of advance of the southern army would be the Roslavl-Moscow road, that of the northern the line Bely-Rzhev-Dmitrov.

2. On the right of these two armies Second Panzer Group would thrust into the area south of Moscow, cut the railroads leading to the capital from the south, and support the right wing of the southern army. On the left Third Panzer Group would drive in the direction of Kalinin, cut the lines of communications between Moscow and Leningrad, seize the area north of Moscow, and support the left wing of the northern army.

3. Another army composed of infantry divisions would move up behind the Second Panzer Group, dislodge the Russian forces north of Gomel, and establish flank security along the line Bryansk-Pogost.

4. The offensive could probably begin on 12 August after the rehabilitation of the armored and motorized units. If the operations proceeded at all well, it could be assumed that Moscow would be reached by the beginning of September.

5. The essential difference between this and the previous plans was that the Russian forces around Gomel would not be encircled and destroyed by the Second Panzer Group but simply driven southeastward by an infantry army. Moreover, the Third Panzer Group would not be diverted to Army Group North; on the other hand, the principal mission it was supposed to accomplish during its temporary attachment to Army Group North — that of cutting the lines of communications between Moscow and Leningrad-would also be achieved according to this plan.

6. By assembling Second Panzer Group west of Roslavi and Third Panzer Group southwest of Bely, this or any alternate plan could be carried out without delay.

7. The decision on which the plan of operation for Army Group Center was to be adopted would not have to be made until 4 August; this delay would make it possible to take into account any further developments in the enemy situation.

This letter expressed the Army's anxiety over Hitler's plans, the implementation of which would be the first step toward dissipating the momentum of the powerful German offensive. Involvement in a series of local operations would eventually lead to a loss of initiative. Instead of applying the principles of grand strategy, the Army would be using grand tactics; and attempts to eliminate a local threat here and close a gap there, without considering strategic factors, would inevitably lead to position warfare.

During a visit to Army Group Center headquarters on 25 July, Keitel explained Hitler's contrasting viewpoint as follows: Instead of the sweeping enveloping maneuvers that had been successful during the preceding campaigns, the Germans would have to conduct small-scale battles of annihilation leading to the complete destruction of the encircled forces. In Russia the execution of too far-reaching envelopments had invariably resulted in the escape of major Soviet elements, which eventually were reintegrated into the opposing forces. This tactic also had the disadvantage that the precious armor was being decimated by Russian flank attacks. The distance between the armored and infantry units would have to be shortened, both to protect the armor and to tighten the rings of encirclement. The latter improvement was all the more necessary because air reconnaissance reports indicated that streams of Russian columns had been escaping for days from the Smolensk pocket through a gap on the eastern side. Keitel continued by enumerating Hitler's plans for future operations which corresponded to the contents of the Supplement to Directive No. 33.

On 27 July Jodl asked Hitler to reconsider his plans. The drive on Moscow ought to be envisaged after all, he stated, not because the city was the Soviet capital, but because the Russians would scrape together their last forces for the defense of Moscow. Moreover, the plan to attack Moscow was in conformity with Hitler's own concept of destroying the main Soviet forces. Hitler replied that the Germans would have to seize the Donets Iasin as soon as possible to deprive the Russians of their armament production facilities and cut off their oil supplies. The next day Hitler gave another reason for his refusal to drive straight toward the Soviet capital — that the industrial region around Kharkov was more important to him than Moscow. Finally, on 29 July, he suddenly explained that the successes hitherto attained in Russia went far beyond his most optimistic expectations, so far as both territorial acquisitions and the destruction of Russian forces were concerned. He had believed that the question of diverting the two panzer groups from the drive on Moscow would arise much sooner in the campaign. In the case of Army Group North, for instance, he had thought that the first major delay would occur along the Dvina and that the Third Panzer Group would have to be diverted at that time. By this last utterance Hitler made it obvious that the idea of diverting forces from the center to the wings went back to the early planning stage and had found expression in the first changes to Directive No. 21, Operation BARBAROSSA, made on 17 December 1940.

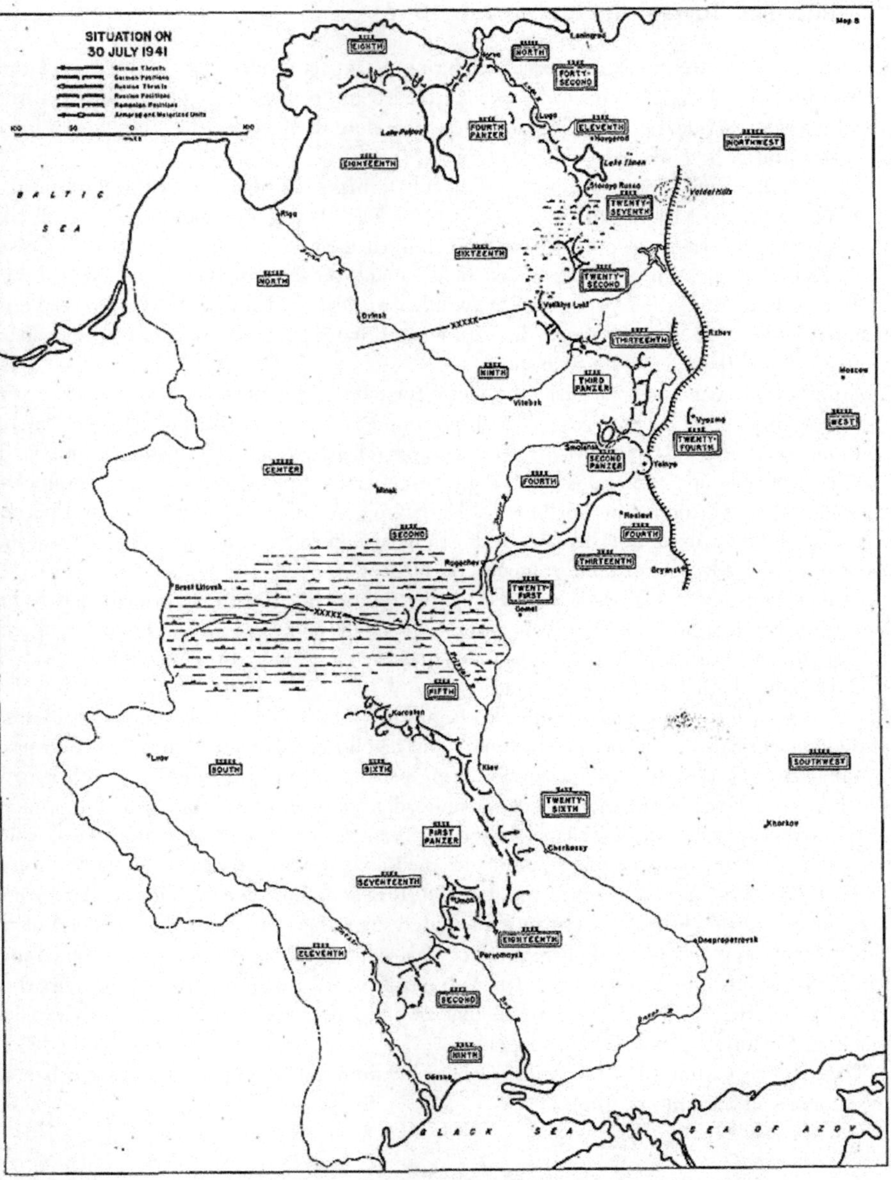

Map 8. *Situation on 30 July 1941.*

The Situation Toward the End of July 1947

No radical changes in the situation occurred during the second half of July. In the Army Group South area, First Panzer Group had finally succeeded in breaking through the Russian front and driving to Pervomaysk. [See *map 8.*] It was therefore to be hoped that large Soviet forces would eventually be encircled in the Uman area.

On the other hand, Sixth Army was still unable to make headway against the Russian *Fifth Army* in the Pripyat Marshes and was stalled west of Kiev. It was to be assumed, however, that the threat to the army group flank would be eliminated as soon as all the elements of Sixth Army had closed up. Then, a main effort could be built on the army's right and the Russians could be driven out of the Dnepr area. Bad weather marked by cloudbursts and torrential rains hampered all movements. Although the Russians continued to defend stubbornly, the general impression was that they were weakening.

Army Group Center had practically completed the mopping up of the numerous pockets with the exception of one near Smolensk. The disposition of forces was revised so that the armored divisions could be pulled out and sent to the rear for rehabilitation. The Russians continued to exert considerable pressure against both army group wings, from the area north of Gomel on the right and from the region northeast of Vitebsk on the left. Opposite the central portion of the army group front the Russians made strenuous efforts to build up a new defense line, moving up a steady flow of reinforcements via Moscow.

Army Group North had made progress on the right, while most of the infantry divisions had succeeded in closing with the two panzer corps along the Luga River and near Novogorod. Taking advantage of the delay in the German advance, the Russians had worked feverishly at strengthening the defenses of Leningrad.

Offensive operations had meanwhile also begun in Finland. The northernmost attack force of the Army of Norway had occupied Petsamo, but had bogged down near the Litsa River upon encountering superior Russian opposition during its advance on Murmansk. The other forces which were driving toward the Murmansk railroad made very slow progress in the primeval forests and swamps of central Finland. In the southern part of the theater of operations, which was under the Finnish Army High Command, the Karelian Army, advancing along the eastern shore of Lake Ladoga, had reached the pre-1940 Russo-Finnish border. However, the Finns were unable to comply with a German request to resume their advance in the direction of the Svir River without delay, because Russian forces massed in the Lake Onega area threatened their flank. The Finnish forces on the Karelian Isthmus launched their offensive against Viipuri on 31 July, after the Russian contingents in that area had been weakened by the withdrawal of units needed for the defense of Leningrad.

The supply situation of Army Group Center, far from having improved, began to hamper the progress of current operations.

Chapter 4 Planning for Future Operations

The conflict over the continuation of operations became acute when Hitler overrode all his advisers — except Keitel — and imposed Directive No. 33 and the Supplement upon the Army. Once Hitler made a decision, its execution was mandatory: therefore on 28 July the Army High Command issued an order implementing the Fuehrer's directives. By that time, however, Hitler apparently felt less sure of himself and drafted another directive which was actually a compromise between his viewpoint and that of his military advisers. Whereas in the Supplement to Directive No. 33, dated 23 July, Hitler had envisaged drives into the Caucasus and beyond Moscow to the Volga River, in Directive No. 34, issued seven days later, he set aside these operations with their distant objectives. Actually, these were secondary issues compared with the basic problem: was the drive on Moscow to be continued or not?

At this moment Hitler was at the zenith of his military triumphs. Starting with the remilitarization of the Rhineland in 1935, an uninterrupted series of successes seemed to have vindicated his intuition whenever he had come into conflict with his military advisers. More than logic or strength of character was needed to make a successful stand against a man who had been so consistently lucky.

If on this occasion Hitler was vacillating and inclined to adopt some of the Army's suggestions, this would simply imply that he realized the importance of his decisions for the future course of the Russian campaign. The following steps, reconstructed and juxtaposed, led to Hitler's final decision.

The Army's Order of 28 July 1941

In the first part of this order the Operations Division of the Army General Staff analyzed the Russian capabilities, arriving at the conclusion that the bulk of the regular Red Army forces had been destroyed. The Russians were trying to obstruct the German advance by throwing in strong reinforcements and even improperly trained personnel, but it was believed that their military strength would prove insufficient. In continuing the operation, the Germans would have to take advantage of every opportunity for isolating and destroying individual Soviet groupings. These tactics were to be employed to (1) prevent the Russians from building up a continuous defense line; (2) safeguard the German forces' freedom of maneuver; and (3) seize the Soviet armament production centers.

All plans for conducting far-reaching operations would have to be abandoned. The immediate objective was to destroy the Russian forces west of the Dnepr, north of Gomel, and south of Leningrad. In addition, Army Group South would employ the armored and infantry forces that were to be transferred from Army Group Center for a thrust into the Donets Basin. Army Group Center was to commit its remaining forces for an advance in the direction of Moscow; and Army Group North was to encircle Leningrad, establish contact with the Finns, and occupy the remainder of the coastal areas of the Baltic States.

The contents of the order then defined the mission of each army group, outlining such details as assembly areas, direction of attack, coordination with adjacent units, etc. Because of the Russian combat methods, particular attention was drawn to forming points of main effort, protecting flanks by mine fields, and maintaining contact between armored and infantry units. Rear areas and the lines of communications leading through them would have to be properly secured.

Attached to this order was an intelligence summary dated 27 July. The 150 infantry, 25 armored, and 5 cavalry divisions identified along the German front to date were estimated to have suffered an average reduction in strength of 50 per cent. The 25 newly organized Soviet divisions were understrength and were short of artillery and heavy weapons. Their personnel were barely trained and the shortage of cadre, drivers, and radio operators was particularly noticeable. Because of the inadequacy of the corps commanders, the Soviet army group staffs had to rely more and more on army command staffs composed of a nucleus of trustworthy and experienced individuals.

The estimate of Russian strength given in this report differed with the figures of 23 July only insofar as it mentioned the presence of 10 newly formed divisions in the area around Moscow. Another major body of troops stood west of Vyazma where 10 divisions blocked the road to Moscow. A Soviet force of 9 infantry and 2 armored divisions was attacking the southern flank of Army Group Center northwest of Gomel. Out of 20 divisions defending Leningrad, 6 were facing the Finns and 14 stood opposite Army Group North.

In summary, the Red Army command was making every effort to stabilize the situation. Russian morale was far from broken, and no signs of internal disintegration had so far appeared.

Directive No. 34 (30 July 1941)

In this new directive Hitler stated that the distant objectives designated in Directive No. 33 of 19 July and in the Supplement, dated 23 July, would be temporarily set aside because of recent developments: the appearance of strong Soviet forces in front of and along the flanks of Army Group Center, the precarious supply situation, and the panzer groups' urgent need for rehabilitation, which would take about 10 days. Instead he ordered:

a. Army Group North to, continue its offensive against Leningrad while taking the necessary precautions to protect its flank south of Lake Ilmen.

b. Army Group Center to switch to the defensive so that its two panzer groups could be withdrawn and rehabilitated; the Third Panzer Group thrust toward the Valdai Hills to be deferred for the time being.

c. Army Group South to receive no additional forces for accomplishing its previously designated missions of destroying the Russian forces west of the Dnepr, establishing bridgeheads near Kiev, and neutralizing the Russian *Fifth Army.*

d. In *Finland* the German attack in the direction of Kandalaksha to be stopped, but attempts to sever the Murmansk railroad to be continued, especially at Loukhi.

e. Air Support: The Luftwaffe to shift its main effort from Army Group Center to Army Group North by 6 August at the latest; bombing attacks on Moscow to continue; essential air support to be given to ground operations in all other parts of the theater.

On 31 July the Army issued an order implementing Directive No. 34, in which special emphasis was put on the rehabilitation of Second and Third Panzer Groups and their eventual commitment in the direction of Gomel and the Valdai Hills respectively.

Hitler's Vacillation Over Strategy

Directive No. 33, the Supplement, and Directive No. 34 may be considered as manifestations of Hitler's hesitancy with regard to the continuation of operations. Feeling none too sure about the advisability of diverting forces from Army Group Center, Hitler made strenuous efforts to inform himself on the subject by personal visits to two army group headquarters. The first of these conferences took place on 4 August, when Hitler and his staff visited Army Group Center headquarters. The Army group commander, Field Marshal von Bock, began the conference by reporting on personnel and equipment matters. Then both Generals Guderian and Hoth, his subordinate panzer group commanders, emphasized that major operations would be feasible only if an adequate number of spare engines could be delivered in time to replace the wornout ones.

Hitler replied that the bulk of the current production of tank engines was needed for equipping newly formed armored divisions. Nevertheless, 400 new engines might be made available to the two panzer groups. Guderian immediately objected that this number would prove unsatisfactory because he alone needed 300 engines for the Second Panzer Group. Hitler thereupon quickly changed the subject to the future conduct of operations. Going into great detail, he reemphasized how important it would be to capture Leningrad, the Donets Basin, and the Crimea. To him, all these objectives had priority over Moscow.

Before the conference was brought to a conclusion, Guderian and Hoth stated that, if withdrawn from the line by 8 August, their panzer groups would be operational by 15 and 18 August respectively. Whether they would be capable of executing far-reaching maneuvers or only operations with limited objectives would depend on the number of tank engines that could meanwhile be made available.

In concluding Hitler stated that the Soviets rated the Moscow area third in importance after Leningrad and the industrial regions of the south. Reports by experts on Russian weather tended to prove the soundness of his plans, since in southern Russia the rainy period in autumn usually started in mid-September, whereas in the Moscow area it did not begin until one month later. Hitler continued that he had also "briefly considered" the possibility of a limited thrust toward Moscow. Bock interjected that such an offensive could have decisive results, if it were properly staged and supported. But Hitler needed more time to arrive at a definite decision.

On 6 August during a conference at Army Group South headquarters Rundstedt emphasized the significance of the possession of Moscow in achieving a quick victory over the Soviet Union. Hitler, however, refused to listen to his arguments, enumerating the most important objectives of the campaign in their former priority: Leningrad, eastern Ukraine, and Moscow.

On the next day Halder asked Jodl whether Hitler's primary objective was to defeat the Soviet Union or to acquire economic assets in the Ukraine and the Caucasus. Jodl expressed the opinion that Hitler was attempting to attain both objectives simultaneously. Halder then stated that Leningrad could be seized without diverting any forces from Army Group Center that would be needed for the drive on Moscow. If the Russians were to be defeated by autumn, the offensives against Moscow and the Ukraine would have to be conducted simultaneously.

Halder also stressed that German strategy should not be influenced by Russian tactics. By trying to eliminate threats to their flanks the Germans would dissipate forces instead of concentrating them for decisive operations. Jodl seemed impressed by these arguments and submitted them to Hitler on 10 August in an Armed Forces Operations Staff memorandum.

This document restated that according to all available intelligence the bulk of the Russian forces were massed in front of Moscow. Their destruction and the seizure of the Russian capital were therefore the primary objectives for the German Army. Tempting diversions to the north or south would have to be ignored for the time being. On the other hand, the flanks of Army Group Center would have to be secured by limited-objective attacks — some of which were already underway — before the army group committed its forces to an all-out drive on Moscow.

If the maneuvers to secure the flanks could be successfully concluded within the next two weeks, the Moscow offensive could be launched by the end of August. During the initial stage of the offensive Army Groups South and North would have to get along as best they could, but would be certain of support from Army Group Center as soon as the latter launched its pursuit.

The memorandum continued by outlining the missions of the different armies operating in the north and south of the theater and stressed that the VIII Air Corps would support Army Group North only until around 20 August, by which time the forces of Army Group Center would be concentrated.

In summarizing, the Armed Forces Operations Staff recommended that Army Group Center prepare an offensive against Moscow for the end of August. Once the advance had reached the pursuit stage, Guderian's panzer forces could be diverted southeastward in the direction of the Don bend.

Halder noted in his diary on 11 August that the Germans had reckoned with 200 Russian divisions at the start of the campaign, but that by 10 August 360 divisions had already been identified. Even though these divisions were not as well organized, equipped, and led as the German ones, they nevertheless existed and had to be defeated. Each time the Germans destroyed a dozen of them, the Soviets simply moved up 12 more. The German frontline was overextended, and there were no reserves. As a result, German troops were exposed to Russian counterattacks, some of which were successful because the Germans were unable to close all the gaps in their lines in so vast a theater of operations.

The Supplement to Directive No. 34 (12 August 1941)

The effect of the Armed Forces Operations Staff memorandum and the personal impressions gathered by Hitler during his visits in the field were reflected in the contents of the Supplement to Directive No. 34, issued on 12 August. The latter defined the missions of Army Group South as follows:

1. To prevent the establishment of a continuous Russian defense line along the Dnepr;
2. To seize the Crimea; and
3. To capture the Donets region and the industrial area around Kharkov.

The attack on the city of Kiev proper was to be stopped; instead the city was to be annihilated by fire bombs and artillery shells as soon as a sufficient quantity of these means of destruction would become available. The Luftwaffe was to give every possible support to the ground forces.

Army Group Center's primary mission was to eliminate the Russian salients that were protruding far into its flanks. After this had been successfully accomplished and the armored groups had been rehabilitated, the army group forces were to jump off for the Moscow offensive on a wide front. However, the operation against Leningrad had to be brought to a conclusion and VIII Air Corps had to revert to Second Air Force before the offensive against Moscow could be undertaken.

The current attacks in the Army Group North area were to lead to the encirclement of Leningrad and a link-up with the Finnish forces. Air support units were to pinpoint their missions on selected targets to achieve maximum effectiveness.

The Supplement did not mention any diversion of Army Group Center forces to the south and made only a very indefinite reference to shifting of divisions to strengthen Army Group North. On the other hand, even though the Supplement authorized an offensive against Moscow, the launching of the offensive was to be contingent upon the success of the Leningrad drive.

This priority was even more clearly expressed in a conference note signed by Jodl and dated 15 August. It referred to Brauchitsch's verbal report of the same date, following which Hitler had ordered that all further attacks in the direction of Moscow be stopped. Army Group Center was to switch to the defensive and hold the line without major air support. The Army Group North attacks would have to be brought to a successful conclusion with a minimum of delay. As many Third Panzer Group divisions as could be employed and supplied by Army Group North were to be transferred from Army Group Center to eliminate the threat to Army Group North's flank. Moreover, a breakthrough achieved by several Russian divisions south of Staraya Russa prompted Hitler to issue a direct order for the transfer of one armored corps to Army Group North.

Developments to Mid-August 1941

During the first half of August Army Group South partially succeeded in destroying the Russian forces that were left west of the Dnepr. By 5 August, First Panzer and Seventeenth Armies encircled 16 to 20 Russian divisions near Uman and destroyed them despite repeated delays caused by bad weather. Subsequently, the entire Dnepr bend was cleared of Russian forces, their remnants withdrawing across the river wherever they were able to do so. The Sixth Army was in a less favorable situation, since it had been unable to seize Kiev or score a decisive success against the Russian *Fifth Army*. On the contrary, several relatively strong Russian counterattacks had led to critical situations, particularly around Kiev and south of that city.

On the whole, Army Group South had concluded the initial phase of the operation without fully attaining its objective. The weather had seriously hampered operations. Rundstedt next intended to establish bridgeheads at Dnepropetrovsk, Kremenchug, and Cherkassy.

In the Army Group Center area the first days of August were characterized by furious Russian local attacks. Strong Soviet counter-thrusts near Yelnya were held off during heavy fighting lasting until 8 August. At the same time German local attacks near Rogachev and Roslavi eliminated immediate threats and relieved the pressure against the southern flank of the army group and against Yelnya. The entire Second Panzer Group was pulled out of the line by 8 August, and the Third Panzer Group followed two days later. It was anticipated that the rehabilitation of these armored units would be completed between 15 and 20 August.

Up to 8 August the Russians seemed intent upon forcing a withdrawal of Army Group Center; at that time they apparently decided to switch to the defensive with the intention of preparing the line Bryansk-Vyazma-Rzhev for an all-out defense.

The Army Group North drive began on 10 August with a three-pronged attack on Leningrad. One force thrust northward from Lake Ilmen, a second one from the Luga area, and a third one approached Leningrad from the west. All three forces encountered stubborn resistance, and their progress was therefore slow.

The Army Memorandum of 18 August 1941

On 18 August General Halder sent Hitler a memorandum that presented the viewpoint of the Army as follows:

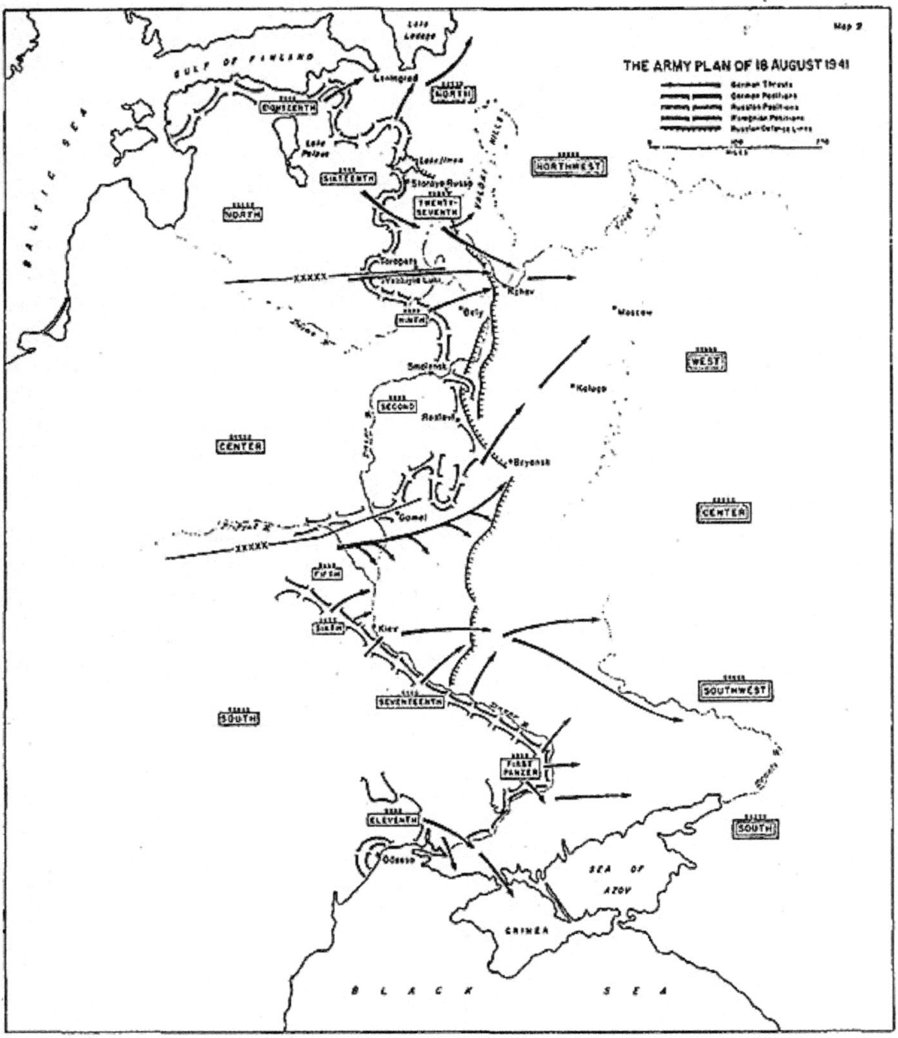

Map 9. The Army Plan of 18 August 1941.

a. Summary of the Enemy Situation. The Russians were massing their forces opposite Army Group Center in anticipation of a German drive on Moscow. They were exploring every possible method of strengthening the Moscow sector. Russian forces then stationed in salients protruding into the German lines, such as those near Gomel, would probably be withdrawn to shorten the lines in view of the noticeable shortage of Soviet units. [See *map 9.*]

b. The Next Objective. Whereas the objective of a German offensive in the north or south would he either to eliminate the Russian Baltic Fleet or to seize important industrial areas in the Donets Basin, an offensive in the center would lead to the destruction of strong Soviet forces and the laceration of the Russian front. That in turn would result in the German seizure of

Moscow which, together with the losses suffered in the north and south, would prevent the Soviets from offering any further coordinated resistance.

The decision of selecting Moscow as the next objective of Army Group Center was based on the following considerations:

(1) The Time Element. Because of Russian weather conditions the offensive against Moscow would have to be carried out during September and October. In view of the distances to be covered and the strong resistance the Russians were bound to offer, two months would be the minimum time requirement for executing the operation.

(2) Combat Efficiency. After emergency rehabilitation, the armored and motorized infantry units would be capable of covering only limited distances. Because of their reduced combat efficiency, these units would have to be reserved for decisive actions exclusively.

(3) Massing of Forces. The offensive against Moscow could meet with success only if the forces of Army Group Center were properly massed to attain this one objective to which all other operations would have to be subordinated. Otherwise, Army Group Center could not achieve a decisive success during the current year. In any event, the two other army groups would be sufficiently strong to accomplish their missions without outside assistance.

c. Plan of Operations. The main effort should be placed on both extremities of the Army Group Center front. There, strong forces would carry out enveloping attacks while the center of the front tied down the opposing forces. The southern attack force would advance via Bryansk and Roslavl toward Kaluga, and the northern one from southwest of Bely and west of Toropez via Rzhev to the east. An entire army — including some motorized units capable of smashing any threat from enemy forces without delay — would have to cover the south flank of Army Group Center. A similar flank cover would be provided for the northern force once the situation south of Lake Ilman had been cleared up. Both attack forces would have to break through the Russian defense lines because any effort to envelop the Russian positions would involve too great a detour. Whether the attack groups were to continue their advance north and south of Moscow or initiate enveloping maneuvers immediately after having broken through would depend on the situation and the punch they would be able to deliver at that time.

d. Distribution of Forces. For the execution of the operation Army Group Center would have 42 infantry, 1 cavalry, and 12½ armored and/or motorized infantry divisions. After both army group flanks had been secured 'by preliminary operations, the Red Army forces opposing the German drive would number approximately 42 divisions to which should be added about 20 divisions that were in the process of activation. Russian numerical superiority would be outmatched by German combat efficiency and excellence of equipment. The suggested distribution of forces was as follows.:

(1) *Southern Attack Force.* This force would be composed of 12 infantry and 6 armored and/or motorized infantry divisions deployed along an 80-mile front extending from Bryansk to Roslavl.

(2) *Central Front.* East of Smolensk, 10 infantry divisions would cover a defensive sector 95 miles wide.

(3) *Northern Attack Force.* This force would consist of a southern group composed of 6 infantry and 2 armored and/or motorized infantry divisions jumping off from the area southwest of Bely and a northern group assembled west of Toropez and composed of 7 infantry and 2 armored and/or motorized infantry divisions. The latter group would have to eliminate the Russian salient around Velikye Luki in a preliminary move.

(4) *Flank Protection Army.* An army consisting of 1 cavalry, 5 infantry, and 2 armored and/or motorized infantry divisions would advance into the area east of Gomel and leave 2 additional divisions to cover the Pripyat flank.

e. Assembly of Forces.

(1) The assembly of the southern attack force by the beginning of September would present no major difficulties, if the fighting around Gomel were brought to a successful conclusion by 23 August.

(2) The attack group assembling west of Toropez would also be ready to jump off by the beginning of September if the attack on Velikye Luki started no later than 21 August.

(3) Regrouping of the other army group forces could also be accomplished by the beginning of September.

(4) The armored and/or motorized infantry divisions assigned to the attack forces would be rehabilitated by the end of August at the latest. The two divisions that might not be ready in time could be used for flank protection.

f. Projected Course of Events

(1) Army Group Center would be ready to jump off at the beginning of September to carry out the operations outlined above.

(2) Army Group South would begin its attack against the Russian *Fifth Army* by 23 August. By early September elements of Sixth Army were to reach the Dnepr north of Kiev and Seventeenth Army was to force river crossings farther to the south. With these operations in full swing, it would be unlikely that the Russians could shift forces to the north.

(3) Army Group North was to complete the encirclement of Leningrad by the end of August, and its forces would then attempt to establish contact with the Finns. The Army group forces south of Lake Ilmen were to eliminate the Russian penetration south of Staraya Russa and start their advance to the Valdai Hills simultaneous with the offensive of Army Group Center. If these forces could advance far enough toward the southeast, it might be possible to integrate their advance into the drive of the northern attack force.

The operations of all three army groups would therefore be coordinated. To assure the success of the offensive, the necessary orders would have to be issued without delay.

On 18 August General Warlimont wrote an Armed Forces Operations Staff estimate that fully endorsed the Army memorandum of the same date. He stated that to attain the objectives of the Russian campaign before the outbreak of winter the forces operating in the north had only 8 weeks at their disposal and those in the south just 13. Because of the long distances, the relatively short time, and the high attrition of automotive vehicles, the operations conducted during the coming months would have to be driven straight toward the primary objective without any deviation. In determining whether the Army Group Center forces — less the panzer corps recently transferred to Army Group North — were to be kept together for the thrust on Moscow or whether the Second Panzer Group was to be diverted to the southeast to take advantage of the very favorable opportunities in that area, Warlimont arrived at the same conclusion as the Army: Army Groups North and South were sufficiently strong to accomplish their missions with their own forces while Army Group Center conducted the offensive against Moscow. In summarizing he restated that, to guarantee the success of the latter operation, no forces should be diverted to such secondary operations as the southeastern thrust of Second Panzer Group. Moreover, if necessary, critical situations along the flanks or in the rear should be ignored so that the attack forces could concentrate on the essential drive toward Moscow.

Hitler's Decision (20 August 1941)

On 20 August Hitler declared that he disagreed with the contents of the Army memorandum. He was not interested in Moscow and the forces assembled in the vicinity of the Soviet capital. His ideas found their expression in an order issued to the Commander in Chief of the Army on 21 August which ended the controversy over the continuation of the operations. Among the significant points were the following:

a. The most important objective was not the capture of Moscow; top priority was to be given to seizing the Crimea and the industrial region in the Donets Basin, to cutting off the Russian oil supply from the Caucasus in the south, and to encircling Leningrad and linking up with the Finnish forces in the north.

b. The situation was favorable for a concentric attack executed by the contiguous fronts of Army Groups South and Center against the Russian *Fifth Army* to prevent the latter from withdrawing. Regardless of subsequent operations Army Group Center was to assign to this mission all the forces necessary for the destruction of the Russian *Fifth Army,* because the liquidation of this force was the only means of assuring that Army Group South could resume its advance toward Rostov and Kharkov.

c. The seizure of the Crimea was of utmost importance for safeguarding the German oil supply from Romania against air attacks. A rapid advance into the Caucasus would be desirable to exercise pressure on Iran.

d. Only after *a* and *b* had been accomplished would the necessary forces be available to attack and defeat the Russians defending Moscow in accordance with the instructions issued in the Supplement to Directive No. 34.

General Guderian, the commander of Second Panzer Group, made one last attempt to change Hitler's mind by explaining the difficulties involved in pivoting his force southeastward. His arguments failed to impress the Fuehrer, and the Army High Command was forced to implement Hitler's order.

A Russian general, captured by the Germans in the spring of 1942, stated that the German failure to drive home the offensive against Moscow in the early fall of 1941 impressed the Soviet High Command as being a second "miracle of the Marne," which saved the Soviet capital in 1941 in much the same way the first one had spared Paris in 1914.

Chapter 5 The Diversion and Reassembly

The Personnel Situation (End of August 1941)

The German Army suffered a total of 409,998 losses, or 11.05 per cent of the average strength figure of 3.78 million men employed in the Russian theater, from 22 June-31 August 1941. These losses were broken down as follows:

German Army Losses	(22 June-31 August 1941)		
	Total	Officers	EM
Totals	409,998	14,457	395,541
Killed in Action	87,489	4,006	83,483
Wounded in Action	302,821	10,080	292,741
Missing in Action	19,688	371	19,317

To compensate for these losses, the Army High Command **assigned** 317,000 replacements from the Zone of Interior to the Russian theater, distributing them as follows:

Replacements Transferred to the Russian Theater

Period	Total	Army Groups		
		South	Center	North
Totals	317,000	119,000	131,000	67,000
22 Jun-25 Aug 41	146,000	52,000	66,000	28,000
25-31 Aug	71,000	27,000	25,000	19,000
Expected to arrive after 31 Aug	100,000	40,000	40,000	20,000

As of 31 August, however, only 217,000 men had arrived in the Russian theater to compensate for the 409,998 losses, and the personnel shortage in the theater therefore amounted to about 193,000 men.

A total of 21 out of 24 divisions, constituting the Army High Command reserves at the beginning of the campaign, had reached the front by the end of August and had been distributed as follows:

Distribution of Forces, September 1941

Type	Total Divisions	Divisions assigned to Army Groups		
		South	Center	North
Totals	21	10	8	3
Infantry	20	9	8	3
Motorized Infantry	1	1	--------	--------

Only three divisions were left in the hands of the Army High Command.

Increasing Logistical Difficulties (Early September 1941)

POL

The POL shortage was serious except in the Army Group North area. Stock piles were exhausted and newly arriving shipments were immediately distributed to the front-line units, particularly those of Army Group South, where occasional shortages hampered operations. In calculating the requirements for the offensive in the direction of Moscow the planners found that the daily rate of POL trains arriving in the theater would have to be stepped up from 22 to 27 for the period 17 September to 2 October and to 29 as of 3 October.

Track-Laying and Wheeled Vehicles

On 4 September the following breakdown of tank strength in the Russian theater was given by the Army High Command:

Available for employment	47 percent
Deadlined for repair	23 percent
Disabled	30 percent

Compared with the tank status report of 4 August, the percentage of disabled tanks had increased from 20 to 30 percent. On the other hand, the percentage of deadlined vehicles had been reduced from 30 to 23 percent because of the arrival of spare parts and the possibility of allocating time for maintenance and repair. However, the repair facilities were inadequate and the shortage of tank engines continued. Moreover, the repaired tanks had been so overtaxed by previous employment that their future usefulness was bound to be short. It was estimated that the percentage of tanks available for employment at the start of the Moscow offensive could be increased to 60.5 of T/E strength if all new tanks then in the hands of the Army High Command were distributed to the field forces.

The number of trucks in operating condition had dropped to 77.65 percent of T/E strength, that of prime movers to 67.90 percent, including repaired vehicles. Only emergency repairs were being performed so that the complete loss of the vehicles after 200-250 additional miles had to be anticipated. The combat efficiency and mobility of the ground forces would therefore be greatly reduced at the decisive moment of the offensive — when they were approaching Moscow.

Halder suggested that all newly produced tanks and trucks be allocated to the Russian theater as replacements, instead of being used to equip new divisions. He believed that under such conditions the situation could be remedied. Immediate steps would have to be taken since the arrival of the vehicles could not be expected before three to four weeks. All possible disadvantages that might result from this suggestion would be of far less consequence than a sudden bogging down of the Moscow offensive at the beginning of winter.

Developments to Mid-September 1947

The implementation of the order issued by Hitler on 20 August resulted in the following developments:

Army Group South had succeeded in carrying out its enveloping maneuver with the assistance of Second Army and Second Panzer Group, even though the pivoting movement of the latter had encountered some difficulty. Several Russian armies, among them the *Fifth* which had finally been forced to withdraw to the east bank of the Dnepr, were facing annihilation east of Kiev. [See *map 10*.] When this gigantic pocket was finally mopped up, the Germans took 665,000 prisoners and a tremendous amount of booty. The original strategic objective in the Army Group South area had thus been attained, but only by diverting strong forces from Army Group Center. In any event, the way was open for a sustained eastward drive in the southern part of the Russian theater. At the same time the advance in the direction of the Crimea had made good progress and German forces were approaching the gateway to the peninsula.

In early September Army Group Center had been engaged in heavy defensive battles during which a number of critical situations had arisen in the central sector of the army group front. At the same time, the northern attack force of Army Group Center operating in conjunction with Army Group North had penetrated into the area east of Toropets. Bock was greatly weakened by heavy transfers of forces to the adjoining army groups. His front was overextended, and he had almost no reserves.

Army Group North had completed the encirclement of Leningrad. A direct attack on the city proper was expressly forbidden by Hitler, who wanted to avoid the heavy casualties of house-to-house fighting and who refused to assume the responsibility for feeding the city's millions. He considered throwing a ring around the city sufficient. One of the difficulties in carrying out this plan was that the flank protection forces along the Volkhov were very weak. South of Lake Ilmen, the Sixteenth Army was spread over a wide area in the difficult terrain at the foot of the Valdai Hills and was making little headway.

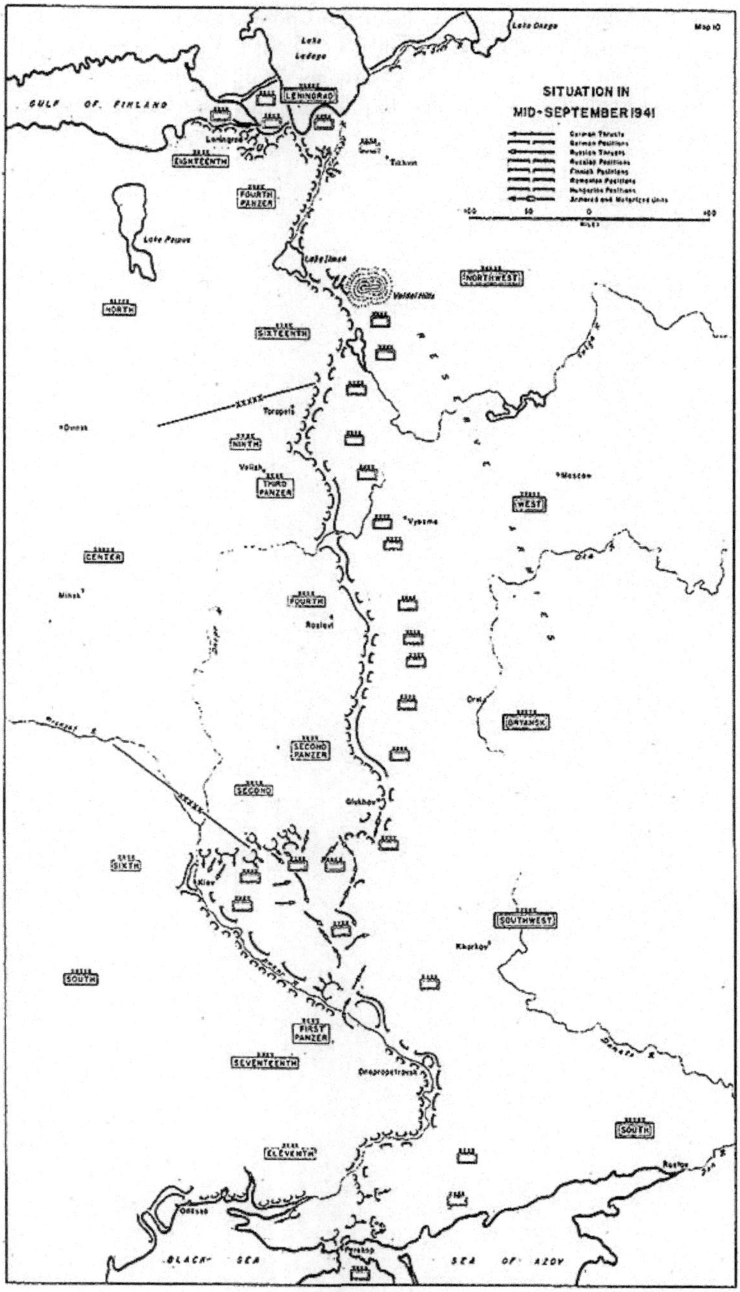

Map 10. Situation in mid-September 1941.

For the time being, Army Group North could not continue to advance into the area east of Lake Ladoga since it was forced to employ large bodies of troops to close the ring of encirclement around Leningrad. The planned linkup between German and Finnish forces east of Lake Ladoga could therefore not be realized. This in turn compelled the Finns to commit sizeable forces on the Karelian Isthmus so that Leningrad could be sealed off from the north.

In the north the war of movement had degenerated into position warfare. The Army of Norway, stopped or bogged down in all three attack zones, had failed to reach its objectives.

At the request of its government, the Finnish High Command had limited the advance of its troops to a line approximating the Russo-Finnish border of 1939 on the Karelian Isthmus, and to the Svir River east of Lake Ladoga. The uncertainty regarding further developments around Leningrad induced Finnish political leaders to prosecute the war against Russia with restraint.

Directive No. 35 (6 September 1941)

On 6 September Hitler issued a new directive based on recommendations made by the Army High Command. The prerequisites for a decisive offensive existed in the Army Group Center area now that Leningrad was encircled and the early destruction of the Russian forces facing Army Group South could be anticipated. The plan called for the envelopment of the Soviet units west of Vyazma by a pincers attack that was to be launched at the end of September. For this purpose two armored forces were to be concentrated near Roslavl and east of Velizh. Only after the bulk of Timoshenko's forces had been annihilated were the attack forces to launch a pursuit in the direction of Moscow along a front extending from the Oka River on the right to the upper Volga on the left. Army Group South was to conclude the battle east of Kiev as soon as possible so that Second Panzer Group and Second Army would revert to Army Group Center without delay. Similarly, as soon as Leningrad had been cut off from the east, Army Group North was to return those air force and armored units which had previously been detached from Army Group Center. The Navy was to concentrate a sizeable fleet near the Aaland Islands to prevent the Russian Baltic Fleet from escaping. Mine fields were to be laid in the Gulf of Finland.

The directive conformed to the recommendations of the Army High Command, except for the deadline. The Army felt doubtful whether the mobile elements of Second Panzer Group could be moved up by the end of September. To avoid any delay, it was decided that the armored force whose assembly was near Roslavl would be controlled by Fourth Panzer Group headquarters, which was to be transferred from Army Group North. . This attack force was to consist of the 10th Panzer Division, in the Roslavl area, the 2d and 5th Panzer Divisions, to be transferred from the Army High Command reserve, the 11th Panzer Division, to be transferred from Army Group South, and the 19th and 20th Panzer Divisions, to be transferred from Army Group North.

The armored force, to be concentrated near Velizh, was to be led by Third Panzer Group, whose headquarters had already been established in the area. This force was to be composed of the 7th Panzer Division, in the Velizh area, and the 1st and 6th Panzer Divisions, to be transferred from Army Group North.

Many difficulties were encountered in performing the lateral displacements necessitated by the assembly of the Third and Fourth Panzer Groups, some elements of which had to be moved several hundred miles.

As soon as it reverted to Army Group Center, Guderian's Second Panzer Group, composed of the 3d, 4th, 9th, 17th, and 18th Panzer Divisions, was to make a wide enveloping sweep from Glukhov toward Orel. If this maneuver proved successful, the Second Panzer Group would be well placed to continue its advance in the direction of Moscow.

To the uninitiated, the halt and diversion of strength, imposed upon Army Group Center at a decisive moment, appeared of little significance. In reality, however, and entirely apart from the time consumed in shifting the armored units, the Germans had lost six precious weeks, and this loss could be decisive in view of the advanced season. The Second Panzer Group had to march 400 miles before it could reestablish contact with Army Group Center. Its equipment was heavily overtaxed, and it was doubtful that it could withstand the wear and tear of another 300-mile thrust before reaching Moscow.

The mission of Army Group South was clear cut: after the battle at Kiev, it was to advance toward Rostov and Kharkov. During this drive the northern wing had to be so strengthened that it could provide flank protection for the advancing Army Group Center.

Army Group North was to tighten its grip on Leningrad and at the same time reinforce its flank along the Volkhov River and south of Lake Ilmen. The latter flank was particularly important in that its reinforcement provided simultaneous protection for Army Group Center.

The Situation at the End of September 1941

Army Group South continued its operations according to plan. On 26 September a breakthrough into the Crimea was attempted across the Perekop Isthmus. Toward the end of the month the armies that had participated in the battle of Kiev resumed their drives in the direction of Rostov and Kharkov respectively. The mopping up of the various pockets east of Kiev had caused considerable delay. Behind the army group front Odessa alone remained in Russian hands, and German forces had to be moved up to assist the Romanians besieging the city.

On 20 September Second Panzer Group began to regroup its forces for their next mission, the thrust on Orel. After overcoming the manifold difficulties involved in turning its axis of advance almost 1800, the panzer group jumped off 10 days later.

An estimate of the Russian intentions indicated that in the southern part of the theater the Russians were improvising a new defense line and moving up reinforcements, particularly west of the Donets salient and around Kharkov. The supply situation of Army Group South was considered serious because all railroad bridges across the Dnepr had been demolished.

Army Group Center had to overcome many obstacles in preparing for the new offensive. In order to meet the deadline, the Army High Command had to assume control over the movement of those armored divisions that were to be transferred from Army Group North. Deceptive measures were to conceal the shifting of ground and air force units. Whenever possible, movements were to take place during the hours of darkness.

West of Moscow the Russians were strengthening their defensive preparations, channeling reinforcements through their capital and building one defensive position behind another. Partisan activities against the road and rail nets in the rear areas became more and more effective, forcing the Germans to divert a large number of troops to security missions. The German supply situation was becoming precarious, but Bock's chief of supply was able to issue fairly adequate quantities of gasoline and ammunition to the spearhead divisions. It was evident, however, that the consumption of large quantities of POL would create a serious problem and lead to drastic rationing in other parts of the theater.

After Army Group North had transferred the armored forces, its offensive slowly ground to a halt. Having attained his immediate objective, Leeb had only to tighten the ring around Leningrad, strengthen his eastern flank near the Valdai Hills and along the Volkhov River, and close in on Leningrad by a series of local attacks. An attack via Tikhvin, for the purpose of linking up with the Finnish forces east of Lake Ladoga, was planned for a later date. By midSeptember the first bad-weather period set in, hampering all operations.

The Russians appeared to be moving reinforcements into the Valdai Hills and toward the Volkhov River with the obvious intention of relieving Leningrad in the near future. It was therefore to be expected that they would exert pressure in these two areas, where relatively weak German forces were thinly spread and critical situations might easily arise. This threat had to be watched the more carefully because it could develop into an acute danger for the left flank of Army Group Center as the latter gradually became exposed during the eastward drive on Moscow. The Valdai Hills region therefore assumed a primary strategic importance and was kept under constant observation by the Army High Command.

To the rear, the struggle for the islands in the Gulf of Riga continued. Despite local shortages caused by the high rate of ammunition expenditure in the fighting around Leningrad, the overall supply situation of Army Group North was satisfactory.

In general, however, the German lines of communications had become very strained during the first three months of the campaign. Despite considerable effort less than 10,000 of the 15,000 miles of rail lines in use had been converted to normal European gauge. Army Group North was in the most favorable position because it also received supplies via Baltic sea transport.

In summary, no major surprise had occurred during the month of September. An analysis of Russian combat methods revealed that the Red Army continued to offer strong resistance and exploit every opportunity to counterattack. What did astound the Germans was the strength still displayed by the Russians, their ability to improvise quickly in any given situation, the apparently inexhaustible flow of new divisions arriving at the front, and the absence of any true symptoms of disintegration.

Despite the tremendous losses it had suffered, the Red Army was still a powerful adversary. The early collapse expected by the German military leaders had not materialized, and the elements of space and time thus assumed increasing strategic significance. Whether the Germans would be able to reach their objectives before the onset of winter remained to be seen.

Military-Economic Survey (2 October 1941)

On 2 October General Thomas submitted a survey of the militaryeconomic situation of the Soviet Union for the following four hypothetical cases:

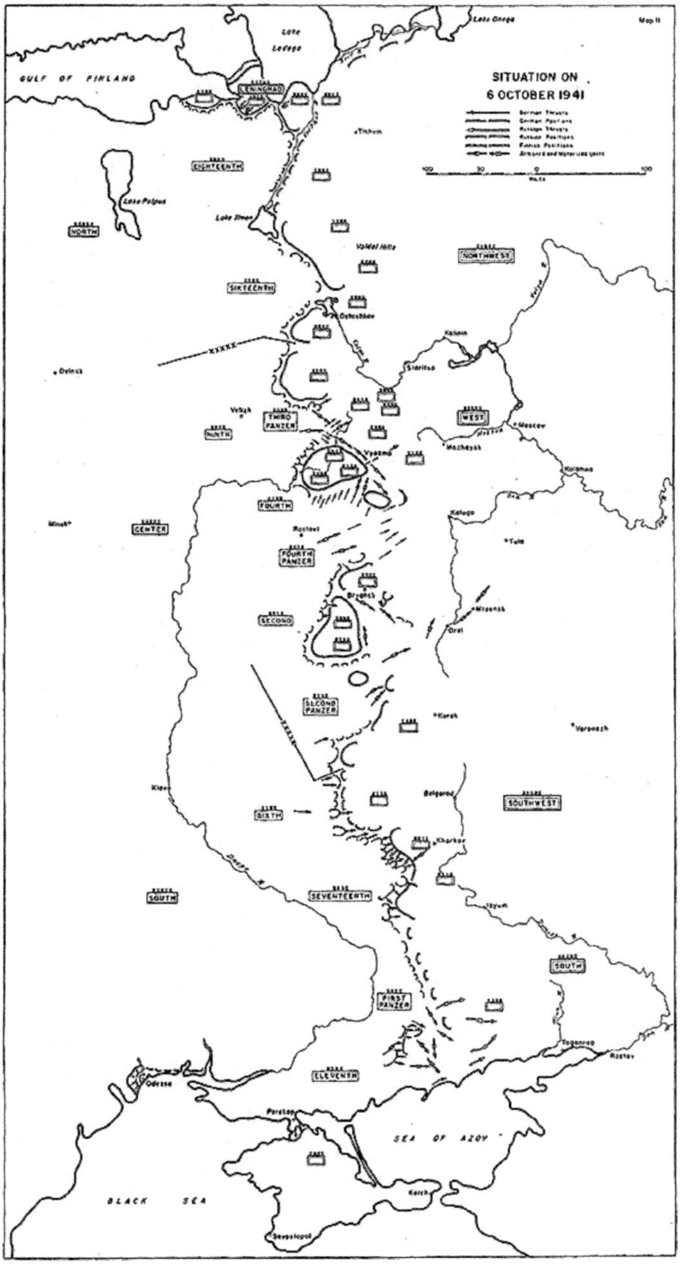

Map 11. Situation on 6 October 1941.

1. If all territory west of the line Crimea-Diepr-Kharkov-Tula-Moscow-Leningrad-Kandalaksha (including the cities proper) were seized by the Germans, the Soviets would lose approximately two-thirds of their steel and aluminum production facilities. Suuh a loss would

preclude any increase in the industrial capacity still available to the Soviet Government, probably making its full utilization impossible. As a result, the Red Army would be incapable of fully equipping its forces during a winter lull in operations; the Russians might, however, be able to produce the most urgently needed equipment, enabling them to continue resistance in the spring of 1942.

2. If, in addition, the Soviet Union lost the Maikop oil fields and the Donets Basin, its economic potential would be so greatly impaired that by the summer of 1942 the Red Army would lack the necessary equipment to resume the struggle west of the Urals.

3. Assuming that the USSR would suffer the above losses plus that of the industrial area of Gorki, the effect would be the almost complete stoppage of truck and passenger vehicle production. The aircraft industry would lose one of its key fuselage construction plants which in turn would lead to a further reduction in airplane output. In general, however, the military-economic situation would be no worse than predicted in Case 2.

4. In the event that all territory west of the Volga was seized by the Germans, the Soviet armament potential would be greatly weakened without necessarily collapsing. A complete economic breakdown of the Soviet system was not to be expected unless the industrial area of the Urals was occupied by the Germans.

In General Thomas' opinion the military-economic potential of the Soviet Union had not been decisively affected by the German operations conducted up to the end of September. Moreover, his analysis indicated that the seizure of Moscow and Leningrad, even if achieved before the onset of winter, would by no means guarantee the collapse of Soviet resistance. Hitler and his military advisers failed to draw the proper conclusions from this survey.

The Muddy Period and Its Effect on Operations (October 1941)

In compliance with Directive No. 35 Bock launched the Army Group Center offensive on 30 September when Second Panzer Group jumped off, followed two days later by the two enveloping forces from Roslavl and Velizh. By the beginning of October Bock attained his immediate tactical objective. The rings of encirclement around the Russian forces southwest of Moscow were closed near Vyazma and Bryansk. [See *map 11.*] The liquidation of these two pockets was time-consuming (but it yielded another 658,000 prisoners) and Bock grew anxious to prevent his armored forces from losing their momentum or getting bogged down. To this end it was important that Second Panzer Army (First and Second Panzer Groups had been redesignated panzer armies as of 5 October), whose lead elements were approaching Mtsensk against light opposition, advance rapidly toward Tula in order to break through to Moscow from the southwest. The Third Panzer Group was to cut off the main railroad connecting Moscow with Leningrad, drive to the Volga River, and thence descend upon the capital from the northwest. These two enveloping drives would simultaneously protect the flanks of those army group elements which were to launch the secondary frontal attack in the center. Army Group North was to support the offensive by seizing the area east of Ostashkov, while Army Group South was to assist by advancing into the region west of Voronezh.

Moscow, the final objective, seemed close at hand. Then, on 7 October, the autumn rains began turning the ground into a sea of mud. While it handicapped every movement in the Army Group Center area and slowed down Guderian's vital thrust, some of the latter's forces were able to push eastward. By 20 October Fourth Army and Fourth Panzer Group reached the area east of Kaluga and Mozhaysk, and Ninth Army and elements of Third Panzer Group captured Kalinin and Staritsa; but Guderian's Second Panzer Army remained bogged down. Closing with Second Panzer was Second Army whose mission it was to provide flank protection along the upper Don River and maintain contact with Army Group South.

In general, the period from 7 to 20 October was marked by heavy fighting; hot pursuit of a defeated enemy gradually turned into a desperate effort to make headway in rain, snow, and mud. Realizing the imminent threat to their capital the Soviet leaders threw all available resources into the battle.

Up to the beginning of November the situation was generally unchanged. Only Second Panzer Army had gained some ground and, advancing into the Tula area, had reached its designated jump off area for the thrust on Moscow. Its exposed east flank practically invited counterattack, if the Russians were still strong enough to make one. For the time being there was no indication that such an attack was being prepared by the Soviets. The other elements of Army Group Center had made a few local gains; the area west of Kalinin seemed sufficiently secure, and the northern flank thus appeared protected.

During October Army Group South steadily gained ground in the direction of Rostov. Encountering only sporadic Soviet resistance, First Panzer Army had advanced into the Taganrog area by 20 October. Stronger Russian resistance, coupled with the effects of the mud, delayed Seventeenth Army and, even more, Sixth Army. In the Crimea, the struggle to force the Perekop Isthmus went on, the weak German forces meeting stubborn resistance. By 8 November the Russian defenders were split into two groups and thrown back toward Sevastopol and the Kerch Peninsula. At the same time First Panzer Army reached the western edge of the industrial Donets Basin, Seventeenth Army stood astride the Donets River at Izyum, and Sixth Army captured Kharkov and Belgorod. Sixth Army reported a particularly high materiel attrition rate and a lowering of its combat efficiency.

During the same period Army Group North had succeeded in establishing contact with Army Group Center at Ostashkov as planned. The ring around Leningrad had been strengthened and the islands in the Gulf of Riga had been seized by the Germans. By 20 October, all preparations were made for a thrust on Tikhvin. There, German forces were to link up with the Finns, who by the beginning of September had reached the Svir River east of Lake Ladoga. Tikhvin was also important to the Germans because of the bauxite deposits located in the vicinity. The attack, started on 21 October, led through difficult terrain where there was but a single road. On 8 November, after overcoming great difficulties, the German forces penetrated into the Tikhvin area.

In summary, the muddy season of October 1941 did more than deprive the Germans of the fruits of victory after the battle of Vyazma. The change in ground conditions eventually proved to be one of the major reasons for the German failure to capture Moscow.

Hitler's Plan for the Seizure of Moscow (12 October 1941)

Hitler's ideas on the future destiny of Moscow and its population were explained in an order issued on 12 October. According to this order the capitulation of Moscow was not to be accepted if the Russians decided to surrender the city. Time bombs and booby traps had endangered German lives during the seizure of Kiev, and no risks were to be taken at Moscow or Leningrad. Another reason for caution was the serious danger of epidemics that might break out in these two cities. The lives of German soldiers were not to be sacrificed for the sake of preserving Russian cities. For these reasons no German soldier was to enter Moscow or Leningrad.

Russian civilians trying to escape toward the German lines were to be turned back with fire. Their mass migration into the interior of Russia was considered desirable. No Russian civilians were to be fed at the expense of the German economy. As a general rule, Russian cities under siege were to be softened up by artillery fire and air attacks, and their civilian population was to be put to flight. The greater the chaos in unoccupied Russia, the easier the exploitation of German-occupied territories.

In the letter of transmittal to Army Group Center, the Army High Command added that every effort was to be made to close the ring around Moscow without delay.

Four days later, on 16 October, the Operations Branch of the Army High Command sent to the three army groups a memorandum containing an estimate of the situation. Apparently, a certain number of sources seemed to indicate that the Russians had decided to make a large-scale withdrawal preceded by thorough destruction of industrial facilities. According to this information the Soviets planned to withdraw the maximum number of their remaining units in order to use them as cadres for new divisions that were to be activated during the winter, thus improving their chances for successfully continuing the war in the spring of 1942.

In addition to their previously designated missions the three army groups were to tie down as many Soviet units as possible and destroy them. Wherever Russian units attempted to retreat, improvised pursuit forces — amply provided with gasoline — would have to follow and envelop them. The rest of the memorandum defined specific missions based on the above premises.

The contents of this memorandum indicated that the German estimate of Soviet strength and intentions was faulty at the crucial moment, when decisions regarding the continuation of the Moscow offensive had to be made.

Chapter 6 The German Attack on Moscow

Strategic Factors

At the beginning of November 1941 the question of whether the offensive on Moscow was to be resumed at the close of the muddy season was submitted to a thorough examination. The principal arguments against such an offensive were as follows:

1. Weather Conditions. A relatively short period of suitable weather with only light frosts could be expected immediately after the muddy season. The Russian winter was close at hand. Around Moscow it usually set in by mid-December at the latest, and its full impact would make itself felt by the end of the year. By then the German forces would have to be redistributed and billeted in such a manner that they could withstand the rigors of winter.

2. The Condition of the Combat Forces. The combat efficiency of the infantry divisions had dropped by 35 percent, that of the armored divisions by 40 to 50 percent. The tank attrition rate varied from 65 to 75 percent. 65 to 75 percent. was striking. Approximately one-third of the officer casualties had been killed in action. On the basis of the above figures it was estimated that the real combat value of the 136 divisions employed in the Russian theater was equivalent to that of only 83 full-strength divisions.

3. The Rail Transport and Supply Situation. The flow of supplies was disrupted and only the most urgently needed rations, ammunition, and gasoline could be moved forward, and then only with difficulty. The situation could hardly be expected to improve soon. It would require considerable time to overcome the obstacles caused by the destruction of rail lines and installations, to change the gauge of the tracks, and to repair the damage resulting from various causes. Meanwhile, the German forces would have to live a hand-to-mouth existence that was not conducive to launching an all-out offensive. Because of the transportation difficulties practically no winter clothing and equipment for Army units would become available for distribution before early January.

4. Flank Protection. The southeast flank of Army Group Center in the area east of Kursk and Orel was very exposed. Here weak forces of Second Army were scattered over a wide area, having only occasional contact with Army Group South. If the Russians were still capable of exploiting such an opportunity, this latent threat might develop into an acute danger.

5. Change in Tactics. All the forces of Army Group Center were deployed along the front without any units being held in reserve. Any major reverse could have disastrous consequences, and launching an offensive under such circumstances would be a desperate gamble. Far more promising would be a temporary switch to elastic defensive tactics allowing even for major withdrawals, if necessary. By adopting such tactics, the front line could be held with relatively small forces. Meanwhile, such strong reserves of manpower and materiel would gradually be built up that a decisive offensive could be launched as soon as there was a favorable opportunity.

By contrast, the proponents of the offensive advanced the following arguments:

1. Russian Exhaustion. The Russians had apparently exhausted their strength. The Soviet Government was scraping together every man and machine and throwing them into the defense of Moscow. The Red Army had uncovered wide sectors of the front and, having run short of trained combat troops, was using hastily improvised units on a large scale.

2. The Knock-Out Blow. There seemed a good chance that an all-out effort before the winter would knock the Soviets out of the war. On the other hand, if the attack was postponed until spring, the Russians would be given time to reorganize their forces.

3. The Missed Chance. This last offensive would have to be risked, if only because one could not possibly give up within sight of the goal. In any event the German mistake at the Marne in 1914, when victory was conceded although the battle was far from lost, was not to be repeated.

4. The Closeness of the Objective. Moscow was but 40 miles away. Thus, even though there were only a few weeks of relatively favorable weather ahead, the objective was so close that it seemed within reach. Under these circumstances there was no doubt that the troops would once again make every effort to take Moscow.

5. Political Significance. The political effect would be resounding if the German Army succeeded in capturing Moscow despite all obstacles.

After carefully weighing the pros and cons, the Army High Command decided that the offensive had to be risked. However justified this decision may have been on the basis of the estimate of the situation and available intelligence, it did not take into account the demands which the offensive would make upon the German troops and the shortage of manpower and equipment that beset Army Group Center. To make matters worse, more and more fresh and well-trained Russian divisions were arriving at the front from Siberia, apparently unobserved by German air or ground reconnaissance.

Before the decision to launch the offensive was made, Gen. Friedrich Fromm, Commander, Replacement Army, suggested to Brauchitsch that a peace offer be extended to the Soviets. Since the plan "to crush the Soviet Union in a lightning campaign" had not materialized, he urged that the opportunity of extricating Germany from the risk of a two-front war be exploited — now that the fortunes of the Wehrmacht looked most promising and the threat of losing Moscow loomed large before the Soviet Government. Whether such a peace proposal would have had any chance of success will have to remain a point of conjecture. There is little doubt, however, that Hitler would have sharply rejected such a recommendation.

Last-Minute Planning and Operations to 13 November 1941

The offensive was to start with another attempt at double envelopment as soon as the weather and the supply situation permitted. The immediate objectives were to be the Moskva River and the Volga Canal, and the continuation of the operation would depend upon the prevailing situation. Second Panzer Army was to drive northward from Tula, enveloping Moscow from the southwest. The enemy situation in front of Guderian's armor was obscure, but it seemed probable that the Germans would eventually be faced by strong Russian forces. Guderian's right flank grew longer and longer so that more and more forces had to be diverted from the main thrust to cover the flank. The frontal attack from the west was to be delivered by Fourth Panzer Group as well as by Fourth and Ninth Armies, and the enveloping thrust from the northwest by Third Panzer Group. With its left anchored on the Volga River, the latter was to drive on Moscow from the north. Fierce resistance, mostly by improvised units, could be expected.

On 13 November General Halder presided over a meeting of the chiefs of the army group and army staffs which was held at Orsha. The discussions covered intelligence information, organization matters. and tactical and logistical problems on the theater and army group level. A review of current operations showed that the situation had meanwhile developed as follows:

Army Group South: In the Crimea, the Kerch Peninsula had been almost cleared of Soviet forces. First Panzer Army was slowly closing in on Rostov. Seventeenth Army had consolidated its front along the Donets, while Sixth Army, despite repeated orders to do so, was unable to resume its advance. This delay was particularly inopportune because Russian intentions at the army group boundary were obscure; in this area the Soviets appeared to be withdrawing forces to bolster the defense of Moscow.

Army Group Center: Few changes had occurred on the Second Army front, which extended over a wide area between Kursk and Orel. Here, too, the Russian intentions were unclear. Major troop movements in the direction of the Soviet capital were apparently under way. Seven concentric rings of antiaircraft defenses, established two to three miles from one another, surrounded Moscow and made the city almost invulnerable from the air. For the first time since the early days of the invasion the Soviet Air Force intervened actively.

Army Group North: Tikhvin was captured on 11 November after a hard struggle; at the same time other forces drove a wedge across the Volkhov River toward Lake Ladoga. The Finns were expected to exploit the German thrust on Tikhvin by launching an offensive during which the Karelian Army was to link up with Army Group North. But this hope was not fulfilled becauses political considerations modified the Finnish military plans. One German division, reinforced by Finnish troops, attempted to advance on Tikhvin from the lower course of the Svir River, but was stopped by numerically superior Russian forces.

The Course of the Offensive (14 November-5 December 1941)

The three weeks from 14 November to 5 December 1941 marked the turning point in the Russian campaign. The German offensive ground to a halt along the entire front. At the same time the Russians began to seize the initiative.

The first warning came in the south, where Kleist's First Panzer Army attempted to seize Rostov by a *coup de main* and succeeded in entering that city from the east on 20 November. [See *map 12.*] The German propaganda agencies celebrated this success in such enthusiastic terms that Kleist felt obliged to hold Rostov despite mounting Russian pressure. His position, however, became so precarious that Rundstedt requested the authorization for Kleist's evacuation of Rostov. When Hitler refused, Rundstedt asked to be relieved of his command. His successor, Field Marshal Walter von Reichenau, was forced to abandon Rostov, when the Soviet forces began to assault the city from three sides on 28 November. (Halder noted in his diary that the people at the Fuehrer's headquarters had no idea of the true condition of the German troops, their plans being conceived in a vacuum.) On 1 December Hitler finally agreed to a withdrawal to the Mius, where the German troops were able to dig in. They had to summon all their strength to stop the Russian counterattack and stabilize the front. The other sectors of Army Group South remained quiet during this period, but it became obvious that the Russians were ready to stop any German advance toward the Caucasus or Stalingrad with every means in their power, and that they had concentrated strong forces for this purpose.

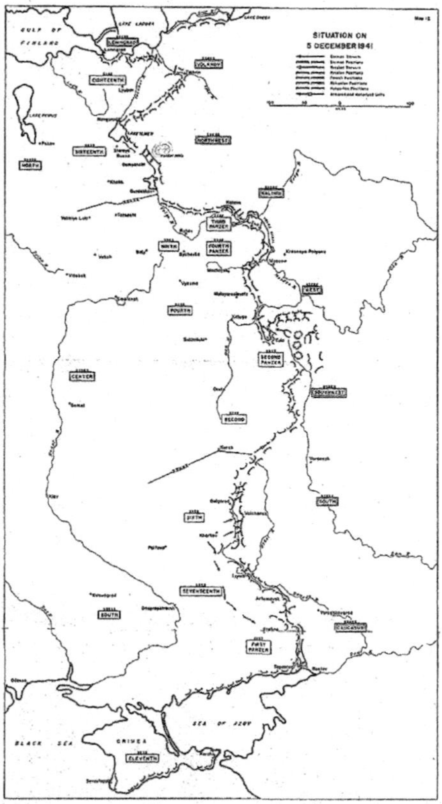

Map 12. Situation on 5 December 1941.

In the Army Group North area no gains could be made beyond Tikhvin or in the direction of Lake Ladoga. Here, too, the Russians were pouring in reinforcements for a series of counterattacks which started in early December. Along the front south of Lake Ilmen the Soviet forces had been counterattacking intermittently since the end of November. Similar attacks were also launched by the Leningrad garrison in an attempt to relieve the pressure on the Moscow front.

In the all-important zone of Army Group Center, Third Panzer Group and Ninth Army had jumped off on 15 November, with Second Panzer Army following shortly afterward. While the Russians offered stubborn resistance in front of Ninth Army, they seemed to give way opposite Guderian's forces in the south. This also appeared to be the case in front of Second Army whose eastward drive began to gain momentum, thereby removing any immediate threat to the exposed right flank of the army group. The Russians apparently lacked the strength to exploit their opportunity for a counterthrust. On the central portion of the army group front, however, the Russians began to launch heavy attacks as early as 16 November, thus preventing Fourth Army from joining the offensive.

Despite these inauspicious developments the Army High Command and Bock, feeling confident that the greater stamina of the Germans would carry the day, agreed that the offensive had to be continued. By the end of November the two enveloping forces had scored further **successes,** even though they advanced but slowly against stiff opposition. The Fourth Army, however, was engaged in a defensive see-saw battle which greatly sapped its strength. Newly organized and freshly equipped Russian forces, such as an armored brigade almost exclusively equipped with British tanks, appeared unexpectedly all along the army group front. Not until 1 December could the divisions forming the center of Fourth Army switch to the offensive, and then they scored only local gains. From 1 to 5 December the entire offensive gradually bogged down. Winter came suddenly with temperatures down to -400 F. The German troops were in a state of almost complete exhaustion. Orders to halt the offensive had to be issued — first to Fourth Army, then to the spearhead units. The Fourth Panzer Group came to within 25 miles of Moscow when it was stopped at Krasnaya Polyana. Frostbite casualties were more numerous than those resulting from enemy action. To continue was beyond human endurance. Thus the last German all-out effort to force a decision in 1941 ended in failure.

The Personnel Situation (End of November 1941)

At the end of November the German ground forces in the Russian theater were short 340,000 replacements. With infantry companies at half strength, the average number of men available for combat duty varied from 50 to 60 per company. Day-to-day losses were about equal to the number of convalescents returning to duty. The shortage of replacements could not be compensated for by transfers from the Zone of Interior, where only 33,000 trained replacements were available. The only possible solution was to disband a number of units and use their personnel as replacements. Hitler, however, refused any such suggestion.

The official casualty reports as of 26 November 1941 read as follows:

Casualties	German Losses (From German Sources)	Russian Losses (From Russian Sources)
Totals	*743, 112	2, 122, 000
Killed in Action	156, 475	490, 000
Wounded in Action	555, 685	1, 112, 000
Missing in Action	30, 952	**520, 000

*23.5 per cent of the average strength (3.2 million men) employed in the Russian theater from 22 June to 26 November 1941.

**Against 3,006,867 prisoners of war claimed by the Germans as of 1 December 1941.

Critique

The German objectives for the Russian campaign in 1941 had not been attained. The Soviet military forces had not been destroyed and the Communist government had not collapsed. The danger of another two-front war loomed larger than ever. Instead of eliminating this threat, the invasion of Russia had actually brought it about.

Some of the basic mistakes that caused the German failure seemed to be the following:

a. Political Mistakes. Hitler had underestimated the internal political stability of the Communist regime. The average citizen's innate readiness to defend Mother Russia against any invader was stronger than his assumed aversion to the Communist dictatorship. Moreover, German failure to formulate and apply a satisfactory policy in the occupied territories, particularly in the Ukraine and the Baltic States, had intensified the spirit of resistance.

b. Underestimation of Russian Strength. The Soviet Union's economic foundations were more solid than Hitler had anticipated. The Germans were surprised by the Russians' ability to transfer and decentralize war plants. As to the Soviet armed forces, their unwavering determination, their unwillingness to admit defeat, and their capability to improvise astounded the Germans. Time and again these qualities compensated for the ineptitude of the Russian intermediate command.

c. Faulty Strategy. The change in German strategy decided upon in August 1941, when the main effort was shifted from Army Group Center to Army Group South and — to some extent — to Army Group North, was a crucial mistake. By making this decision the Germans may have lost their opportunity of knocking the Russians out of the war by a direct thrust on Moscow. There is, however, no way of proving the validity of this hypothesis, especially since a number of other, equally fundamental mistakes have to be considered in this connection.

d. Inadequate Mobility. The German Army did not have sufficient motor vehicles, planes, and POL reserves for operations in so vast a theater as European Russia. Instead of being able to take full advantage of their maneuverability, the panzer divisions were forced to halt time and again to permit the infantry to close up. Moreover, the inadequacy of the roads and the shortage of suitable air fields made the logistical support almost completely dependent on the damaged railroads, the operation of which was so difficult in Russia.

e. Wrong Space Calculations. During the planning stage the vastness of the Russian theater had not been fully taken into consideration. When the German Army failed to destroy the Russian armed forces in the initial onslaught, the space factor gave rise to problems which the Germans with their limited resources were not able to master.

f. Bad Timing. The time element became an increasingly important factor once the operation got under way. The initial delay in launching the offensive, the month lost in vacillating over the continuation of the offensive, and finally the diversion of forces to the south and north cost the Germans dearly.

g. The "Russian" Weather. The Germans did not make proper use of the information on Russian weather conditions that was available to them. The effect of the weather on the conduct of military operations in Russia was no secret, and the German military leaders should not have been surprised by muddy terrain in the autumn or low temperatures in the winter. It seems almost inconceivable that the German troops in Russia were caught unprepared by the sudden outbreak of winter. The explanation is that Hitler and his military advisers were convinced that the campaign would end before the onset of bad weather; winter clothing had been ordered for only those 60 divisions that were to remain in Russia and form the military occupation force after Germany's victory.

h. Erroneous Air Warfare Concepts. The faulty concept of a short war was also the reason why the Luftwaffe's mission was mainly to lend tactical ground support. Strategic bombing was to be envisaged only after the war of movement had been brought to its conclusion, i. e. after the campaign in European Russia had been won. Hitler and his military advisers deemed it unnecessary to smash the Soviet armament potential or even interfere with production schedules.

Nor was it considered important to disrupt rail communications to the Urals and Central Asia, a course of action that might have prevented the subsequent evacuation of Soviet war industries and the moving up of reinforcements.

The fact that the Luftwaffe had no specific strategic air force probably contributed to these crucial decisions. Whatever strategic air units the Germans had left after the Battle of Britain were eventually dissipated in tactical fighting, probably because both strategic and tactical units operated under the same tactical headquarters.

i. Lack of Self-Restraint. As stated in the various plans prepared for the invasion of Russia, German strategy was based on the assumption that the bulk of the Red Army would be destroyed in western Russia. The decisive initial blows were to be delivered west of the Dnepr-Dvina line. The pursuit to the Volga, which was to be launched during the following phases, was to be contingent upon the successful accomplishment of the initial maneuvers.

In their attempt to implement those plans, the Germans realized by the end of July that they, had been unable to destroy the bulk of the Red Army in western Russia. They had captured a great number of prisoners and booty, but the Soviets had been able to withdraw sufficient forces to continue active resistance. Instead of revising their plans, the Germans plunged into the depth of the Russian theater as if the prerequisites for the initial phase had been entirely fulfilled. It was therefore not really surprising that in December 1941 the Red Army succeeded in stopping the Germans short of their principal objectives — Moscow and Leningrad.

PART THREE 1942 — THE YEAR OF INDECISION

Chapter 7 The Russian Counteroffensive (December 1941 - February 1942)

The First German Reverses

The true situation of the German troops in front of Moscow was not understood at Hitler's headquarters, where victories had been the order of the day for more than two years of war. It took a great number of oral and written reports to bring home the dimensions of the German reverses along the entire Russian front.

One of the first sober notes was struck in the intelligence summary of 1 December 1941 originating from the Eastern Intelligence Division of the Army High Command. The mobilization of so many divisions by the Soviet Government was considered less surprising than the tremendous quantity of materiel encountered — especially tanks and guns — which exceeded anything hitherto known. Contrary to previous estimates it was now believed that Russian war production capacity had been expanded so much that the output of materiel would remain sizeable even after the loss of many important areas.

In November 1941, the report continued, the Soviets had launched their first coordinated offensive, involving as many as 20 divisions in the successful recapture of Rostov. Up to that time Soviet tactics had consisted of simply contesting every inch of ground.

Among the unexpected qualities demonstrated by the Red Army leaders during the first months of fighting was their organizing ability in the spheres of supply, activation and rehabilitation of units, and rapid construction of rear area defense lines with mass employment of civilian labor. The Russians had also shown great skill in using rail communications for troop transfers, efficiently repairing tracks, and evacuating the bulk of the rolling stock without too greatly impairing the capacity of the remaining net. The infantry excelled in defensive fighting. The Russian soldier was naturally gifted in using favorable terrain features, skillfully digging in and constructing fortifications, and camouflaging himself. His willingness to hold out to the bitter end seemed to be a natural trait. This estimate differed considerably from the somewhat disdainful opinion of the Russian soldier held before the start of the campaign.

On 6 December Halder reported to Hitler that the troops committed in Russia had to be rehabilitated. Hitler agreed on principle, but immediately changed the subject, pointing out that the objective in the south remained the Donets bend, which was a stepping stone toward Maikop and the oil fields. In the north a linkup with the Finns would have to be achieved during the winter. Manpower requirements would have to be met by combing out the Zone of Interior and all German-occupied territories. No divisions stationed in France were to be disbanded for the time being.

Hitler's Directive No. 39 (8 December 1941)

On 8 December Hitler issued a directive to the three services in which he acknowledged that the surprisingly early start of severe winter weather and the supply difficulties caused thereby called for immediate cessation of all major offensive operations and a switch to the defensive. The conduct of the defense would depend on the strategic and military-economic value of each specific area that would come under Russian attack. Another important consideration was the availability of rest and rehabilitation facilities, the use of which would enable the Germans to resume major offensive operations in 1942.

i The specific points of this directive made it even more obvious that tlitler did not consider making any major withdrawal. They read essentially as follows:

a. Army.

1. Most of the Army units in Russia were to switch to the defensive to save manpower. Once the front was consolidated, the armored and motorized infantry divisions would be withdrawn for rehabilitation.
2. Prior to any withdrawal not caused by enemy pressure a rear position would have to be prepared, offering better billeting and defense facilities than the hitherto occupied position. Lateral lines of communications would have to be held open for troop transfers.
3. Army Group South was to seize Sevastopol as soon as possible so that Eleventh Army would become available for another, not yet formulated mission. An advance leading to the seizure of the lower Don-Donets line would facilitate the spring offensive into the Caucasus.
4. Army Group North was to shorten its lines north of Lake Ilmen so that, after the arrival of reinforcements, the situation south of Lake Ladoga could be resolved. This maneuver alone could assure the isolation of Leningrad and permit the establishment of contact with the Finns in Karelia.

b. Luftwaffe.

The Air Force was to disrupt the rehabilitation of the Soviet armed forces by bombing such centers as Leningrad, Moscow, Gorki, Stalingrad, etc. The disruption of the Soviet lines of communications was particularly important. In addition, routine fighter protection and air reconnaissance missions were to be flown by the Air Force.

c. Navy.

Naval vessels were to secure supply and commercial shipping in the Gulf of Finland. The number of supply vessels to be constructed in Germany as well as in allied and occupied countries would have to be increased.

d. Personnel.

Sufficient replacements would have to be provided in 1942 to take care of any emergency. All armed forces agencies would have to be combed for young men who might in certain cases be replaced by older soldiers, presently serving at the front. Combat-ready divisions stationed in western Europe were to be exchanged against particularly worn-out divisions from the Russian theater. Contrary to previous orders, a temporary weakening of the forces in France would have to be taken into account. The Atlantic coast of western Europe, however, would have to be safeguarded in any event.

Young men in essential jobs who had been deferred from the draft were to be gradually replaced by prisoners of war and Russian civilians.

In the last paragraph of the directive the three services were requested to inform the Fuehrer of the measures taken toward its implementation.

The attack on Pearl Harbor, which had taken place the day before Directive No. 39 was issued, was not reflected in its contents. The Japanese move apparently took the Germans by surprise; they had not prepared any joint plans or military agreements. In fact, they had no clear concept of what Japan's entry into war really meant. Characteristic of this German unpreparedness was Jodl's request for a staff study on the question of whether the United States would give priority to the European or Far Eastern theater which was made only after Hitler had declared war on 11 December 1941.

At that time most German military men felt that the Axis had gained more strength than its opponents. Few, if any, Germans were able to visualize the extraordinary proportions the military conflict had suddenly assumed or the preponderance that the United States would eventually achieve. It was also believed that Japan's entry would greatly relieve the pressure borne by the Germans in different theaters of war, particularly in Russia. Even if Japan remained neutral, strong Soviet forces would be tied down in the Far East. Siberian troops then pouring in opposite Army Group Center, would no longer be moved to Europe. On the contrary, Soviet reinforcements from central Russia would probably be diverted from Europe to the Far East.

In addition, the Germans began to make careful attempts to influence the Japanese policy toward the Soviet Union. Although the divergence of Germany's and Japan's military objectives soon became obvious, the Germans continued to exert diplomatic pressure on the Japanese. But even the fact that the Soviets had withdrawn practically all their forces from the Far East failed to induce the Japanese to abandon their neutrality. The only Japanese effort that eventually was to have an indirect influence on German operations in the Russian theater was the promised intervention of Japanese submarines against the Allied supply lines leading through the Persian Gulf.

The Army High Command Order of 8 December 1941

The Operations Division of the Army High Command implemented Directive No. 39 on the day it was issued by disseminating an order pertaining to the mission of the German troops in Russia during the winter of 1941-42. Though more subdued in tone than preceding orders, these instructions must have struck the field commanders in front of Moscow as being singularly unrealistic. The introductory paragraph stated that with increasing cold and snow the operations of 1941 had generally come to an end; a few maneuvers that had not yet been concluded would be terminated as soon as possible. After the great victories of September and October the troops had reached the objectives designated at the beginning of the campaign against an opponent who had tremendous superiority in numbers and equipment. Moreover, the Russians had been deprived of vital economic resources and armament production centers. On the whole, German troops had destroyed the bulk of the Red Army before it could withdraw, and losses in men and materiel had decisively weakened the Soviet capacity to resist. The mission of completely eliminating Russian military power still remained to be accomplished after the winter.

Intelligence Estimate

The combat efficiency of the Soviet units was low, and they were insufficiently equipped with heavy weapons and guns. (This statement was in flagrant contradiction with the intelligence summary of the Eastern Intelligence Branch.) The Soviet tactical air force still had approximately 900 serviceable planes; in view of the production facilities remaining in Soviet hands, a steady increase in the number of planes was to be expected.

The ski training given to all Russian troops would enable the latter to carry out attacks during the winter months. The partisans and sabotage units could be expected to resume their activities with great vigor. The total strength of the Red Army was estimated as follows:

Red Army Strength (1 December 1941)

	Divisions		Armored Brigades
	Rifle	Cavalry	
Totals [a]	263	41½	51
Facing the Germans	[b] 200	35	40
In the Caucasus	17	2	3
In Finland	23	--------	1
In Asia	5	3½	2
In the Far East	18	1	5

[a] Additional units, including the Polish Legion, were being activated in the Urals, Siberia, etc.
[b] Including rifle, naval, and NKVD brigades.

Plans

The Army High Command intended to safeguard German territorial gains achieved during the 1941 campaign along the most favorable defensive lines, behind which the ground forces were to be reinforced, rehabilitated, and reorganized. In establishing such lines the following factors were to be considered:

1. Retention of the industrial and communications facilities which the Russians had lost since the beginning of the campaign;
2. Safeguarding of supply and communications lines, including the lateral ones needed for shifting units behind the front;
3. Conservation of strength; and
4. Bringing of German units up to strength and giving them some rest.

The Mission of the Army Groups

The army group headquarters were to direct their subordinate units in accordance with the following instructions:

1. Army Group South was to prevent Russian attempts to break through between the Sea of Azov and the Donets. Kharkov was to be held and the rail line Belgorod-Kursk secured with the assistance of Army Group Center. Special attention would have to be devoted to safeguarding the Crimea, even after Sevastopol had been captured. If possible, Army Group South was to prepare the seizure of the Maikop oil fields by the capture of Rostov and the Donets basin northeast of that city.

2. Army Group Center was to bring the Moscow offensive to its conclusion and then establish a defensive front against enemy counterattacks in the direction of the capital. Mobile divisions were to be rehabilitated behind the southern army group wing; they would have to be ready to intervene in the event of a Soviet thrust from the Voronezh area.

3. Army Group North was to continue its current operation south of Lake Ladoga, establish contact with the Finns, and thus cut off Leningrad from all sides. This objective had to be attained to avoid any waste of manpower and materiel in establishing a defensive front.

Conduct of Operations

It was realized that German strength had dropped to a new low. To keep the initiative and to deceive the Russians as to the true German intentions, the conduct of operations would have to remain as mobile as possible. The forces employed directly up front would have to be spread thinly so that troops could be rotated and reserves formed. Mobile reserve forces would have to be kept on the alert to intervene whenever necessary.

Desirable as a development in depth would be, it could not be effected because of the insufficiency of forces. The front line defenses would therefore have to be improved, strong points and obstacles constructed, etc. Rear area installations and billets would have to be prepared for all-around defense against enemy raids. Because of the weakness of the rear area security units, divisions withdrawn from the line for rehabilitation would have to form emergency combat groups to secure lines of communications, important terrain features, and boundary areas near the front. Effective air reconnaissance would be desirable to permit early recognition of enemy attack preparations and timely counteraction.

Organization

Replacements. Current losses would be compensated for by convalescents returned to duty. No decision had so far been made regarding the number of units that would have to be deactivated to obtain essential replacements for the remaining divisions. The army group headquarters would have to channel replacements to those divisions whose rehabilitation would produce the best results.

Equipment. Drastic measures would have to be imposed to remedy the shortage of motor vehicles and POL. Some of the infantry divisions and GHQ troops would have to be stripped of their motor vehicles, and all motorized supply units would have to be put under centralized control. Since future operations would largely depend upon the combat readiness of the armored divisions, the latter would have to be withdrawn from the front as soon as possible. Because of difficulties in transportation, their rehabilitation would have to take place in the theater of operations. The army group headquarters would have to find suitable locations for billeting, maintenance, and repair installations, etc.

The subsequent paragraphs of the order dealt with training and morale as well as supply for current operations during the winter, stressing particularly the importance of living off the land. Tactical air support was to be severely curtailed during the winter months. According to the instruction pertaining to signal communications, wire lines were to be improved, whereas radio traffic was to be reduced to a minimum. Intercept units were to keep partisan and enemy agent radio traffic under observation.

A survey of the transportation capacity indicated that no major troop movements could be executed, the rail lines being capable of supporting only very minor unit transfers involving the shipment of materiel and immobilized vehicles exclusively. Leave trains could be dispatched only at the expense of supply shipments.

This order did not take into account that the Russians would attack relentlessly at different points all along the front, defying cold and snow. No major German unit could be pulled out for rehabilitation during the winter months. And with the Russians holding the initiative, most of the German withdrawals took place under such heavy pressure that the field commanders had little latitude in selecting suitable defense lines.

The Red Army Seizes the Initiative

Beginning with the recapture of Rostov in November 1941 the Russians gradually seized the initiative, first opposite Army Group Center, then along the entire front. The moment was well chosen: the critical situation of the German forces was only too obvious. Standing deep in the heartland of Russia without sizeable reserves, the German Army was deployed in linear defense along an overextended front. Defective lines of communications to the rear caused continuous disruption in the flow of supplies. Lacking suitable winter clothing, the German troops were exhausted and disheartened. To make matters worse, the most severe winter imaginable suddenly set in with temperatures as low as -50 F. The fate that overtook Napoleon's army in 1812 obsessed the German leaders whose troops stood near the gates of Moscow.

By contrast, the Russians held all the trumps. Their lines of communications had grown progressively shorter, and they had remained in possession of Moscow, their supply and transportation center. They were accustomed to the Russian winter weather and were prepared for it. They had a vast reservoir of manpower which — though poorly trained — could be thrown into battle. Russian morale was bolstered by the almost miraculous turning of the tide that had taken place at the time of greatest stress and by the conviction that the Germans would meet the same fate which through the centuries had been the lot of those who dared to invade the vast reaches of European Russia.

The Red Army initially concentrated on pushing back the Germans before Moscow by a series of local attacks launched at all suitable points. Since this process was-continuous, it became more and more likely that the cumulative effect of Russian local penetrations would assume strategic proportions. By the same token the wider scope of the Russian operations seemed to indicate that Army Group Center was in danger of being crushed in a huge pincers whose northern jaw would swing via Ostashkov toward Vitebsk, and the southern one via Orel and Bryansk toward Smolensk. If this plan succeeded, the Russians would be free to strike at the rear of the other army groups. The German armies in Russia were thus faced by a very dangerous situation.

To meet this threat, two courses appeared to be open:

1. To execute a major withdrawal and to try and consolidate the crumbling Army Group Center front. Such a maneuver would shorten and strengthen the front and obviate the danger of a double envelopment; or

2. To hold in place, fight for every inch of ground, disregard local enemy penetrations, and hope to master the situation by sheer staying power.

Hitler decided to hold fast. For reasons of prestige alone he considered that any major withdrawal would be out of the question. He also feared that mobile warfare under winter conditions would have disastrous consequences because the troops had little mobility, their winter equipment was deficient, and no defensive positions existed in the rear.

The Fuehrer therefore ordered Army Group South to stay in place and assemble reserves behind the contiguous wings of Seventeenth and Sixth Armies. Army Group Center was to move up all its reserves to close the gaps north of Livny and west of Tula. The Fourth Army was not to retreat one inch. If they had no other choice, Third and Fourth Panzer Armies could gradually withdraw to a shorter line along the Rusa River-Volokolamsk-Staritsa, and Ninth Army would link up with the Third Panzer Army.

Army Group North was permitted to withdraw its armored units behind the Volkhov, but any other withdrawal movements could be executed only in the face of acute danger to the entire front. A definite line along which this army group was to hold would be determined in due course. Reinforcements totaling 131/2 divisions were to be transferred from western Europe and Germany. Every effort was to be made to improve the transportation system of occupied Russia.

This order was disseminated by the Armed Forces Operations Staff on 15 December. During the following weeks the Russians kept the Germans off balance and held the initiative. Having committed their fresh troops for the relief of Moscow, they found it more expedient to push back the Germans through local attacks at many different points instead of concentrating their forces on all-out efforts directed at breaking the siege of Leningrad, recapturing Smolensk, or liberating the Donets Basin.

The Russian successes west of Moscow had been achieved against German local air superiority over the Army Group Center area as shown by the following comparison of strength made on 12 December:

Army Groups	Number of Airplanes	
	German	Russian
Totals	1,050	1,060
South	310	600
Center	490	210
North	250	250

Analysis of radio intercepts had given the Germans a clear picture of the Russian order of battle. The entire theater was divided into eight "fronts," which corresponded approximately to German army group headquarters. Reading from south to north these were the *Caucasus, South, Southwest, West, Kalinin, Northwest, Volkhov,* and *Leningrad Fronts.* A number of armies were subordinate to each front. Corps-type headquarters were used exclusively to command mechanized units. Armored divisions were equivalent to German brigades, and in German reports and estimates they were therefore designated armored brigades for statistical purposes.

Developments to 25 December 1941

By 25 December the Russians had eliminated the threat to Moscow. Their counterattacks had pushed Army Group Center to the line from which it had launched its offensive on 15 November. The continuity of the German front was threatened when the Russians opened a gap between Second Panzer Army and Fourth Army to the north and south of Kaluga. A critical situation began to develop in this area, because the Germans, whose movements were restricted to major roads, were unable to seal off the Russian penetration.

The Army Group South area remained quiet. Local Russian attacks seemed to be of a probing nature. In mid-December Eleventh Army began its assault on Sevastopol.

In the Army Group North area the Russians were able to avert the threat posed by the German advance toward Lake Ladoga and to press the Germans back to the Volkhov. This was a bitter disappointment to the Finns who had been induced to believe in a swift victory and now saw themselves faced with a long war.

In the Finnish theater proper, no decisive result had been attained anywhere. Murmansk had not been taken and the Murmansk railroad had not been cut. The attempt at linking up with Army Group North had not been successful. Instead, the bulk of the Finnish forces were tied down in wasteful position warfare.

In his Directive No. 39 and the subsequent order of 15 December Hitler had allowed the army commanders a certain freedom of action within the framework of their overall mission of holding fast. A few local withdrawals executed in mid-December led to such losses of heavy weapons and equipment that Hitler decided to change his methods. On 18 December he ordered that no further large-scale withdrawal movements would be tolerated because of recent prohibitive losses. If the tide was to be stemmed, every inch of ground would have to be contested. The Fuehrer held the field commanders personally responsible for leading their troops in such a manner that they would offer fanatic resistance and hold their positions, even if Soviet forces should break through and attack from all sides. Only thus could sufficient time be gained to move up the reinforcements transferred from the West. After the reserves had arrived and taken up positions in the rear, the troops defending exposed salients might consider withdrawing to shorter lines.

Army Group South was to hold its positions and shift forces to Sixth Army so that they would be available south of Kursk for commitment near the boundary of Second Army.

Army Group Center was to receive the maximum number of reinforcements by all available means of transportation, including airlift. The most urgent need was for infantry replacements to reinforce some of the very weak divisions.

As an additional measure to strengthen Army Group Center, the Fuehrer had approved the transfer of five divisions which were scheduled to arrive at Vitebsk in January 1942. On 18 December the first airlifted replacements were flown in from East Prussia via Orsha to Staraya Russa. These replacements were transferred so hastily that they apparently arrived without weapons or winter clothing. When it turned out that no more German rifles were available and all captured ones had been issued, Hitler authorized an increase in rifle production. There were other shortages; the officer personnel, for instance, had been so decimated that all reserves were exhausted, with no replacements scheduled to become available before April 1942. The total casualties suffered by the German Army in Russia from 22 June to 31 December 1941 were 830,903, including 26,755 officers.

On 19 December Field Marshal von Brauchitsch resigned for reasons of health. Since 7 December his position had become more and more untenable until he was nothing more than a messenger. His departure was followed by that of Field Marshal von Bock; on 20 December Field Marshal von Kluge replaced the latter as commander in chief of Army Group Center. The two other army group commanders were also replaced within the next month. [See *chart 3.*] When Guderian withdrew his Second Panzer Army to the Oka-Shusa line without informing army group headquarters, Kluge requested Guderian's dismissal which Hitler approved immediately as of 25 December. Two weeks later Generaloberst (Gen.) Erich Hoepner, the commander of Fourth Panzer Army, was dismissed under ignominious circumstances.

In summary, during the first three weeks of the counteroffensive the Russians had achieved important tactical victories. The divisions of Army Group Center had suffered very heavy casualties, particularly from frostbite, and their effective strength was declining steadily. The supply situation was critical. At the front, German apprehension was general because, Russian aggressiveness showed no signs of diminishing. In the Zone of Interior signs of discouragement among the people were mostly to be attributed to the discrepancy between the official propaganda releases and the letters that soldiers sent from the front. Some of the military leaders felt that it would have been preferable to tell the truth. A dramatic Nazi appeal to the public, launched a few days before Christmas in which the people were urged to donate furs and winter clothing for the soldiers at the Russian front, contributed to the general lassitude.

The German Crisis in Mid-January 1942

The three weeks following Christmas of 1941 led to a major German crisis, the first one in World War II.

In the Army Group Center area the gap between Second Panzer Army and Fourth Army had been widened by a Russian breakthrough in depth, which extended far beyond Sukhinichi. [See *map 13*.] Farther to the north, the front was ripped open northwest of Maloyaroslavet. The Russians achieved a second major breakthrough at the boundary between Army Groups Center and North, where they drove via Ostashkov toward Toropets. These two thrusts seemed to indicate that the Russians intended to attempt a double envelopment of Army Group Center with the objective of squeezing the army group forces into the Vyazma area. At the same time the Rzhev-Sychevka railroad — the only supply line of the Third Panzer and Ninth Armies — was cut off by partisans.

Chart 3. German Order of Battle—Russian Theater (January 1942)

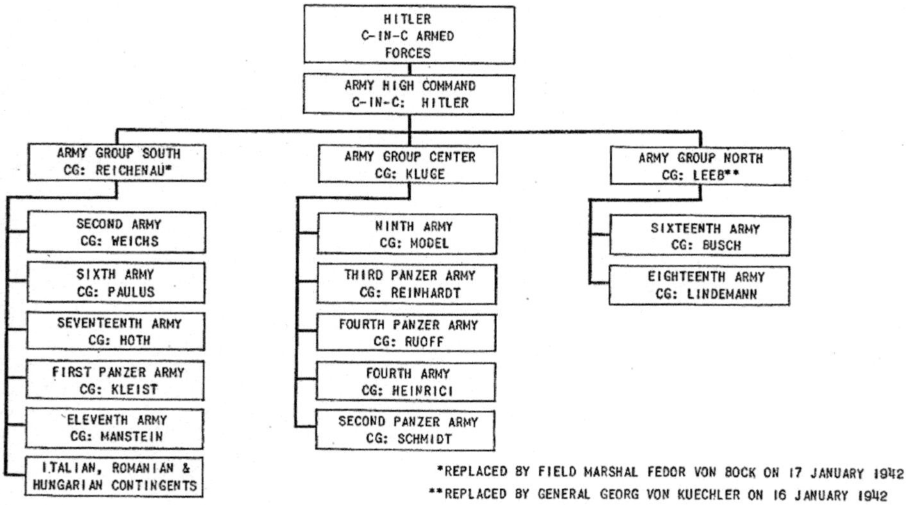

Russian attacks directly south of Lake Ilmen indicated that the Soviets also intended to open a wide gap in the Army Group North area. By attacking along the Volkhov the Russians attempted to crack the Army Group North front at the same time as they pursued their offensive against Army Group Center. The Russians were also building a railroad on the ice of Lake Ladoga. Luftwaffe reports indicated that the Ladoga ice road and railroad had better flak protection than London or any other British city.

The Army Group South area was the only one in which the Russian intentions were not yet apparent. Local counterattacks, however, continued without letup. In the Crimea the Russians recaptured the Kerch Peninsula, forcing the Germans to abandon the siege of Sevastopol.

The overall situation had definitely taken a turn for the worse. The unpreparedness of the German Army was manifest. During the evacuation of positions, for instance, many wounded froze to death because of a shortage of blankets. The care for the wounded was improved on 13 January, when 133 medical officers and 290 enlisted men were airlifted into the Army Group Center area. In the Zone of Interior the number of hospital beds proved insufficient, and schools had to be used as emergency hospitals.

An all-out effort was necessary to avert disaster. The Army High Command introduced all sorts of expedients that would strengthen the front of Army Group Center. Rear echelon troops were thrown into battle, improvised units were brought from Germany by air or priority rail transportation. Winter clothing began to arrive. All these measures only served to aggravate the transportation problem. In every respect the crisis approached its climax. Whether this situation could be overcome preoccupied every headquarters, and the tension was extreme. In the Zone of Interior special military police measures were enforced against deserters and men who were absent without leave.

Hitler discussed every aspect of the military situation in endless conferences and staff meetings, but refused to make a decision. Halder observed in his diary on 14 January that this type of leadership would result in the destruction of the Army.

As usual, the critical situation at the front found its expression in some changes in the command positions. On 16 January Leeb requested to be relieved from the command of Army Group North and was replaced by Generaloberst (Gen.) Georg von Kuechler. On the following day Field Marshal von Reichenau, the recently appointed commander of Army Group South, had a stroke and was replaced by Field Marshal Fedor von Bock whose retirement had lasted less than one month. General Strauss, who had commanded Ninth Army since the beginning of the campaign, was unable to continue in his duties and had to be relieved by General der Panzer (Lt. Gen.) Walter Model. By making this appointment Hitler disregarded all seniority rules and introduced new criteria into the personnel policy of the Army. [See *Appendio A.*]

On 15 January Hitler issued his first order of a large-scale withdrawal in World War II. He expected that his men would execute the movement "in a dignified manner" and inflict maximum damage on the Russians. He continued by stating that since the gaps north of Medyn and west of Rzhev could not be closed, he authorized the commander of Army Group Center to withdraw to a line extending from east of Yukhnov-east of Gzhatsk-northeast of Rzhev. The road connecting these localities would have to remain in German hands. The Russian advance was to be definitely stopped along this line. The order then defined the methods to be used in closing the two gaps.

During the withdrawal movements the following points were to be observed: POL supplies would have to be made available during the movement and upon arrival in the new line of resistance; no gun was to fall into Russian hands intact; no wounded were to be left behind; all railroad tracks, bridges, etc., were to be demolished; and all inhabited localities were to be burned down and the chimneys blown up.

A document that was very typical of the atmosphere then prevailing at the Army High Command headquarters was a memorandum General Halder addressed to all chiefs of staff in the Russian theater. The purpose of the memorandum was to counteract the "paralyzing effect that the tremendous number of enemy units identified opposite certain sectors had occasionally produced on certain field commanders." This kind of panic was contrary to the feeling of superiority typical for German soldiers. Halder pointed out that in many instances the immediate reaction of hopelessness caused by numerical inferiority was found to have been unjustified when the low combat efficiency of the Russian forces became manifest.

He continued by stating that field commanders ought not to succumb to a psychosis of numbers, "by reporting the tremendous number of enemy divisions and emphasizing the weakness of German units, which was only too well known to everyone from Hitler on down." In writing their estimates, intelligence specialists in the field would have to analyze all factors objectively. If that were properly done, ". .. the *élan* and morale of the German troops could [not] repeatedly give the lie to the figures submitted by worry-ridden statisticians."

The Crisis Reaches Its Climax (Beginning of February 1942)

Toward the end of January 1942 another critical situation developed in the Army Group South area, where the Russians attacked on a wide front on both sides of Izyum, broke through the German lines, and advanced practically unopposed. The gateway to Poltava and Dnepropetrovsk stood open, exposing the entire flank of Sixth Army and nearby bridges, across which ran the life lines of First Panzer and Seventeenth Armies. However, since the Russians did not exploit their advantage, Army Group South had time to strengthen the shoulders of the penetration in a makeshift manner. Army Group Center had succeeded in narrowing the gap near Sukhinichi by a series of local counterattacks, so that the danger at this point subsided. The cold weather hampered operations, since temperatures were still around -20° F.

In contrast to these fairly favorable developments, the situation of the German forces at the boundary of Army Group Center and North had deteriorated considerably. A gap of almost 120 miles yawned between Bely ard Kholm, giving the *Kalinin Front* free access to the Vitebsk-Velikiye Luki area. Once in possession of the latter area, the *Kalinin Front* might pivot south toward Smolensk or north toward Pskov. Whether the Russian forces would be sufficiently strong for either maneuver was still a matter for conjecture at the end of January; by then Russian forces pouring through the gap veered sharply southeastward into the rear of Third Panzer and Ninth Armies. In conjunction with these ground operations the Russians began to airdrop supplies and reinforcements in the rear of Fourth Army. Despite the improvement near Sukhinichi, the overall position of Army Group Center became almost untenable. Thus began a life-and-death struggle.

Directly southeast of Lake Ilmen the situation also grew more and more critical. There, two corps, whose front formed a salient protruding to the east near Demyansk, could either stay in place at the risk of being encircled or they could withdraw to a shorter line at the base of the salient. Hitler decided to leave them in place, advancing for the first time the idea of tying down Russian forces by holding salients. In the specific case of Demyansk he was probably right because the Russian forces tied down by the two corps would otherwise have poured through the wide gap farther south. In general, however, only a salient that constituted a potential threat served a useful purpose. Whenever the Russians did not feel threatened by a salient, they merely kept it under observation and the Germans tied down their own forces without achieving what they had intended.

Farther to the north the Russians had also advanced across the Volkhov with the objective of gradually breaking the ring around Leningrad.

In this exceedingly tense situation the Germans sought consolation in the hope that the Russians would overreach themselves in pursuing so many objectives at different points and would not be able to achieve any decisive success. This expectation, namely that the Soviets would dissipate their offensive strength, was not in vain. But before the German command was given respite, it was subjected to 10 more days of tension during which the situation grew even worse..

In the rear and on the exposed left flank of Army Group Center the situation had further deteriorated. The Russians landed some airborne reinforcements in the Vyazma area. Two Russian armies stood behind Ninth Army in the area west of Sychevka. Soviet spearheads had appeared in the vicinity of Velizh and Velikiye Luki. In the Army Group North area the encirclement of the German forces around Demyansk was imminent, and additional Russian units were crossing the Volkhov and advancing toward the northwest. On the positive side, Army Group South had been able to build a loosely knit front around the penetration in the Izyum sector and Army Group Center had eliminated the threat at Sukhinichi, thus warding off the danger of a double envelopment. German countermeasures were slow to get under way, mainly because low temperatures hampered essential movements. Thousands of tanks and motor vehicles were lost because of insufficient winterization.

The Russian Offensive Is Halted (20 February 1942)

By 20 February the crisis seemed to have passed its peak. Step by step the Germans stemmed the Russian offensive, bringing one danger area after another under control.

Army Group South had made the greatest progress. In the Izyum area, where Soviet aggressiveness seemed to have been exhausted, the Germans began to implement their plan to cut off the Russian salient and turn it into a pocket.

In the Army Group Center area the Russian penetration around Sukhinichi was under control and the situation in the rear of Fourth and Ninth Armies was sufficiently stabilized to present no immediate threat. The penetration into the Toropets region had not yet been checked, but since the Russians were not moving up reinforcements, the Germans hoped that this salient would eventually be contained.

In the Army Group North area the so-called Fortress Demyansk was encircled by the Russians. West of Demyansk, however, the Germans had formed a new front near Staraya Russa, from which relief of the encircled forces seemed possible. Along the Volkhov River the German forces had been able to prevent a widening of the Russian breach, and here too an operation to cut the salient at its base was under consideration. All Russian attempts to pierce the German front south of Lake Ladoga had failed.

In Finland the Russians started to seize the initiative at the beginning of 1942. They attacked along the Svir River in an attempt to clear the main line of the Murmansk railroad between Lakes Onega and Ladoga, and at the same time sought to drive back the German forces threatening the railroad from points in central and northern Finland. [See *map 4*.] Although these counterattacks remained fruitless, the problem of disrupting the Murmansk railroad traffic became a matter of increasing concern to both the Germans and the Finns. Large quantities of lend-lease materiel were reaching the Russians via this line. The Finns were unable to mount an operation against the railroad because the commitment of their forces on static fronts had left them without strategic reserves. They did, however, agree to carry out an operation against Belomorsk, the main junction of the Murmansk railroad on the White Sea, provided that the Germans first captured Leningrad. The Finns claimed that the forces needed to carry out and screen the Belomorsk operation would not be available until after Leningrad's fall. The strategic interdependence between the operations in southern Finland and those of Army Group North was greater than ever.

Critique

Generally speaking, the Russian counteroffensive had bogged down by the end of February 1942. In its course the Russians had seized the initiative on the entire front and had achieved major territorial gains, inflicting heavy casualties on the Germans whose combat effectiveness had been considerably reduced. Any immediate threat to the continued existence of the Soviet Government had been thwarted. But the Russians had failed to achieve a decisive reversal of the strategic situation. They had not annihilated entire German armies, let alone army groups. Though crumbling at many points and threatened at the rear and in the flanks, the German front had held. German losses had been heavy; the number of casualties had increased by 175,000 during January and February 1942 and had passed the million mark after eight months of fighting.

At the end of the winter the German position in the Russian theater might have been far stronger, if the Germans had been able to use an elastic, manpower-conserving defense system, instead of the rigid defense imposed by Hitler. As it happened, German effective strength dwindled and at the same time a number of divisions were forced to fight under conditions that contravened sound tactical doctrine. Piecemeal commitment of forces deprived the army group commanders of units which they urgently needed to cope with the critical situations that had developed at different points along the entire front.

Finally, Army Group Center stopped the Russian counteroffensive approximately along the line to which Field Marshal von Bock wanted to withdraw voluntarily in the first place. If he had been given the customary latitude within the framework of his mission, the withdrawal movement would have terminated along a line more favorable for stopping the Russian attacks, thus conserving manpower while still presenting a potential threat to Moscow. Instead, the center of the German front in Russia remained an open sore that did not heal for many months.

The fact that rigid defense methods did prove successful during the first winter, when the Russians committed a series of blunders, had a fatal influence on Hitler's conduct of operations during the following years. In any given situation the Fuehrer would justify his insistence on holding a position by referring to the fighting west of Moscow and to the so-called Fortress Demyansk, although prevailing conditions were in no way comparable to those of the winter of 1941-42.

Chapter 8 Preliminary Planning for a German Offensive in the Caucasus, 1942

Exploratory Steps (July 1940-September 1941)

To Hitler, the oil of the Caucasus had always been one of the foremost attractions of Russia. He had mentioned the necessity of seizing the Baku oil fields as early as 31 July 1940, during one of the initial discussions of his plan to invade the Soviet Union. In the spring of 1941 the Armed Forces High Command activated the so-called Oil Detachment Caucasus for the purpose of taking over the oil fields. At that time the Germans expected that their advance into the Caucasus would be so rapid that the Russians would not be able to severely damage the oil wells, and the tables of organization and equipment of the oil detachment were established accordingly.

The next step in this direction was the preparation of Directive No. 32, circulated by the Armed Forces High Command among the three services on 11 June 1941 — 11 days before the start of Operation BARBAROSSA. This directive envisaged a drive from the Caucasus across Iran as a part of the plan for the continuation of operations against the British Empire following the defeat of the Soviets. At that time German expeditionary forces were to be activated in the Caucasus and sent across Turkey and Syria to Palestine and across Iraq to Basra. The same directive also visualized the use of the Arab liberation movement against the British in the Middle East, and Special Staff F was designated to initiate and coordinate the corresponding military and subversive activities.

A few days later, on 16 June 1941, German counterintelligence submitted to the Armed Forces High Command a plan for securing the Caucasus oil fields as soon as the internal disintegration of the Soviet Union would become manifest. A nucleus of 100 Georgians, trained by German counterintelligence agents in sabotage and revolt tactics, was in existence in Romania. These Georgians would have to be brought to the oil fields by sea or air transport as soon as the German ground forces approached the Caucasus region. In a somewhat optimistic vein the plan foresaw the employment of the Georgians in two to three weeks after D Day.

On 24 July 1941 the Army Operations Division wrote a memorandum on the conduct of operations after the conclusion of Operation BARBAROSSA. With regard to the Caucasus it was anticipated that the British would seize and block this area as soon as the Germans approached the Sea of Azov. The first British troop concentrations were believed to be taking place along the northern and eastern border of Iraq. Because of terrain difficulties a German offensive from the southern slopes of the Caucasus across Iran into Iraq could not be executed before the spring of 1942. Meanwhile, data regarding the Caucasus were to be collected; a list of German tourists, who had climbed the Caucasus Mountains during recent years and knew the terrain and weather conditions, was drawn up, and books dealing with the same subjects were carefully scrutinized.

At the beginning of August the German Naval Operations Staff submitted an estimate of the probable reaction of the Soviet Black Sea fleet in the event of a German penetration into the Caucasus. It was believed that the fleet could seriously hamper operations by keeping the coastal road and railroad between Tuapse and Sukhumi under fire. Among the Soviet ships suitable for such operations were 1 battleship, 6 cruisers, and 15 modern plus 5 outdated destroyers. In the Black Sea area the German Navy had no units capable of stopping or disturbing the movements of the Soviet fleet. Coastal batteries would be of limited use; even if they did drive the Soviet ships farther off shore, the latter would still remain within reach of the coast. Air force protection was the only effective means of safeguarding coastal traffic.

In late September reports from agents and radio intercepts indicated that the Russians had from five to six divisions in the Caucasus and three in Iran. It was estimated that British troops entering the Soviet Union would take three weeks to get from Iran to the Caucasus and four weeks to the Crimea.

The First Plan for a Caucasus Operation (October 1941)

In October 1941 the Operations Division of the Army High Command drew up the first detailed plan for a Caucasus operation. The scope of the offensive was limited to seizing the oil resources of the Caucasus and to reaching the Iranian and Iraqi border passes for a possible farther advance toward Baghdad. [See *map 14*]. The operation was to be executed in six separate phases, extending from November 1941 to September 1942. These phases were outlined as follows:

1. Seizure of the approaches to the northern Caucasus, starting in November 1941;
2. A series of preliminary attacks leading to the seizure of favorable jumpoff areas by May 1942;
3. Launching the offensive across the Caucasus Mountains in two different stages in June 1942;

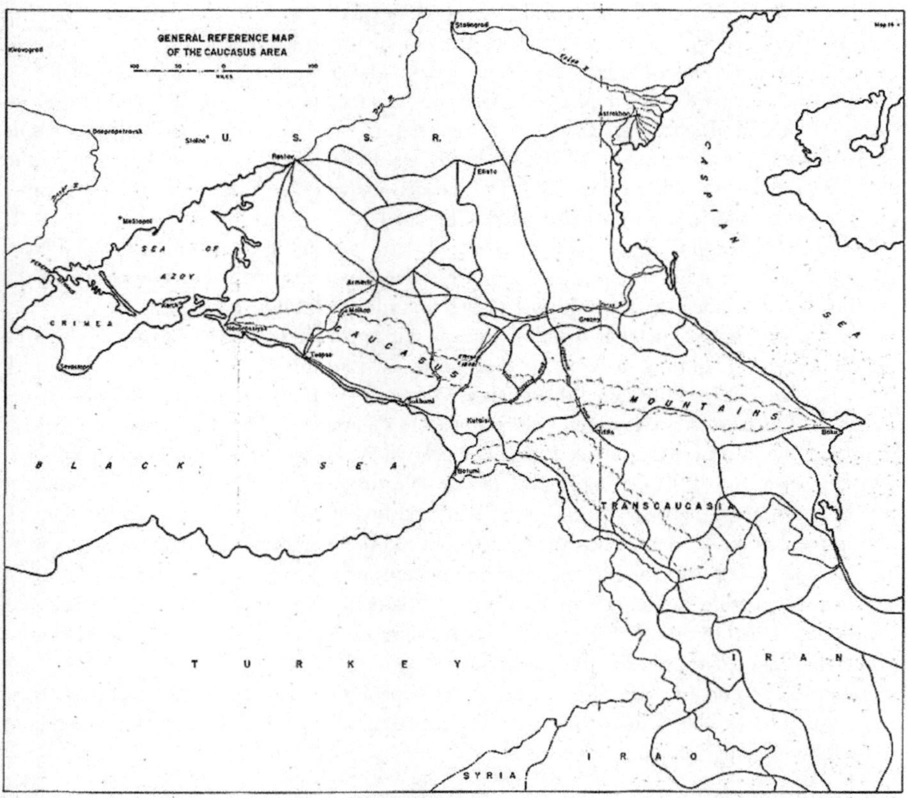

Map 14. General reference map of the Caucasus area.

4. The advance across Transcaucasia toward the Turkish and Iranian borders;
5. Seizure of favorable jumpoff areas within Iran; and
6. Capture of the border passes leading into Iraq. The last three phases were to take place in the period July-early September 1942. The feasibility of the entire offensive would depend on the course taken by current operations in the Russian theater. The second and third phases could be executed only if German troops reached the lower Volga during the winter of 1941-42. The scope of the preliminary attacks to be launched during the second phase would depend on the overall plan adopted for the offensive across the Caucasus. The latter could be launched via the two roads following the Black and Caspian Sea coasts respectively and over the mountain

road leading to Tiflis. The interior roads crossed the mountains over passes more than 10,000 feet in altitude. These roads could be negotiated only by mountain divisions. The movement along the Caspian coastal road would be easier because only a few outdated Russian destroyers were liable to interfere.

During the first stage of the offensive proper, two motorized and two mountain corps were to be employed, driving toward Sukhumi and Kutaisi in the west, Tiflis in the center, and Baku in the east, respectively. As soon as any one of these forces had achieved a breakthrough, one additional motorized corps that was being held in reserve was to move up and launch the pursuit. The commitment of this reserve force would determine where the point of main effort was to be placed during the second stage of the offensive. The employment of two corps in the west during the first stage would be necessary because of the vulnerability of the lines of communications along the Black Sea. Moreover, in the west was the only opening for launching an enveloping drive, since unfavorable terrain conditions prevented any such maneuver elsewhere. During the second stage of the offensive the penetration into the mountains would have to be exploited by the reserve corps which could thrust either via the Black Sea coastal road to Batumi and from there via Tiflis to Baku; or across the mountains to Tiflis and from there either to Batumi or Baku; or along the Caspian shore to Baku and from there, if necessary to Tiflis.

While the offensive was in progress, German naval contingents would have to protect Novorossiysk and Tuapse by taking over captured coastal batteries. In addition, some submarines would have to keep the Russian Black Sea fleet under control, and the Navy would also have to make available the shipping space needed for carrying supplies from Novorossiysk to Batumi once the Russian fleet had been eliminated.

The Luftwaffe would have to protect and support the ground forces; combat the Red Navy and its ports; commit airborne troops to capture the major cities; use dive bombers against the pass fortifications; and prepare transport planes to airdrop supplies.

This plan met with general approval at an exploratory conference held at Army High Command headquarters upon request of the Operations Division on 24 October 1941. An attack across the Caucasus was considered the quickest solution to Germany's MiddleEastern problems. The effect of such an offensive would induce Turkey to join the Axis Powers. In addition, British forces that would otherwise oppose Rommel in North Africa would be tied down in Iran.

An offensive launched in the spring of 1942 would first lead to the seizure of the Caucasus oil fields, then open the passes from Iran to Iraq, and finally permit the capture of the Iraqi oil fields in the autumn of 1942, when the weather favored the commitment of large ground forces. The essential prerequisite for such far-reaching operations was the seizure of the west bank of the lower Volga from Stalingrad to Astrakhan. This realization implied that if, for instance, the Germans failed to capture Stalingrad, a complete re-evaluation of the plans for an offensive against the Caucasus would become necessary.

Among the essential preparations for a Caucasus operation discussed at this conference were the production of military maps and tropical clothing as well as the activation and equipment of special mountain troops.

Caucasus Planning in November 1941

In a conversation with Field Marshal von Brauchitsch on 7 November Hitler mentioned that the seizure of the oil fields would have to be delayed until the following year. This delay had actually been anticipated by the Operations Division of the Army High Command. However, a new point was brought up by the Fuehrer when he added that he had no intention of going beyond the Russian border. The scope of the offensive was thus limited to the Caucasus; this change in plans was probably due to the slowdown in the 1941 advance caused by the, muddy season.

According to all available intelligence the Red Army intended to put up stiff resistance in the Caucasus. By 9 November German intercept units had identified 5 army headquarters in that area. If exact, this information would imply the presence of at least 15 divisions, whereas prior to that time the presence of only 5 had been assumed. It seemed improbable that the Russians would move sizeable forces across their border into Iran. And it seemed even more unlikely that the British would send strong forces northward into the Caucasus. For the time being the situation in the Caucasus remained obscure.

In a conversation with General Halder on 19 November, Hitler stated that the first objective for 1942 would be the Caucasus. An offensive lauched for this purpose in March-April 1942 would bring the German forces to the Soviet border with Iran. Depending on the situation at the end of 1941, offensives in the center could subsequently be launched beyond Moscow toward Vologda or Gorki by the end of May 1942. Other objectives for 1942 could not yet be designated. Their scope would depend mainly on the capacity of the railroads. The question of whether a defensive wall separating Asiatic from European Russia was subsequently to be constructed remained open.

Hitler thus revealed a number of interesting facts. Even as late as 19 November he seemed convinced that the Germans would be able to capture Moscow before the end of 1941. Furthermore, he seemed to believe that the Caucasus offensive across difficult mountain terrain could be successfully executed within a few weeks in April and May, as a kind of southern interlude prior to another offensive farther north. Three days later, on 22 November 1941, Halder ordered a light infantry division organized for the Caucasus operation and mountain personnel withdrawn from combat. As late as 16 days before the turning of the tide in front of Moscow the atmosphere at Army High Command headquarters appeared definitely optimistic.

Effects of the Moscow Setback (January 1942)

An order dated 10 January 1942, originating from the Armed Forces Economics Office and the Organization Branch of the Armed Forces Operations Staff and signed by Hitler brought out the newly imposed material limitations — if not the change in scope — of the 1942 operations.

In the introductory paragraph Hitler stated that the long-range strategic plans remained unchanged; the Navy and the Luftwaffe were to be expanded for the showdown with the Anglo-Saxon powers. Until further notice, however, the operations scheduled for 1942 would not permit a reduction in armaments destined for the Army. On the contrary, the Army would have to be given even more than its ordinary share of manpower and armaments so that it could accomplish its mission for 1942.

In effect, the Army was to have top priority on armament production. Wherever shortages of raw materials developed, the Navy and Luftwaffe would have to take the cuts. Greater standardization, the introduction of more substitutes, and the increased use of captured munitions were recommended as means to overcoming production bottlenecks,

The ground forces were to be ready for offensive commitment by 1 May 1942; supplies for at least four months of continuous operations would have to be accumulated by that time. The units taking part in the offensive would have to be amply provided with supply and service troops as well as motor vehicles, while those committed along the Atlantic Coast would not need many trucks. Ammunition supplies for all weapons used in the Russian theater would have to be built up to one month's expenditure in addition to the basic load.

The Navy was to concentrate on submarine construction and maintenance. The Luftwaffe was to continue its current programs, except for a temporary curtailment of its ammunition and bomb production schedules.

Among the military-economic programs, oil had first priority. The railroad transportation, signal, and other programs were to be carried on along the same lines as before, whereas the motor vehicle output was to be increased. Military manpower requirements were to be coordinated with the industrial ones.

Perhaps the most striking note in this order was its pessimistic undertone. Written at a time when the Germans were desperately trying to stem the Russian tide west of Moscow, the order showed the many weaknesses in the German war machine which had become manifest after less than seven months of fighting in Russia. During the following weeks further planning for the summer offensive came to a standstill, probably because of the life-and-death struggle that raged along the Army Group Center front.

The First Preparatory Orders (February 1942)

With the acute danger past at the front, the military planners were able to pursue more actively the preparations for a summer offensive. On 12 February 1942 the Operations Division of the Army High Command issued a directive for the conduct of operations after the end of the winter. An introductory statement anticipated that the Russian winter offensive would not succeed in destroying the German troops and their equipment. During the coming weeks the Germans would have to consolidate their lines, eliminate Russian forces that had penetrated into their rear areas, and generally attempt to seize the initiative. At the same time they would have to prepare themselves for the muddy period following the spring thaw.

The directive then went into great detail in describing the different aspects of the muddy season and the countermeasures to be taken. The Army High Command intended to use this probable lull in operations to rehabilitate and regroup its forces.

Army Group South was to hold its positions and make preparations for the planned offensive. First, the Russian penetration west of Izyum would have to be eliminated, then the Kerch Peninsula recaptured and Sevastopol seized, so that the forces stationed in the Crimea would become available for employment elsewhere.

Army Group Center was to seize Ostashkov and shorten its front line by eliminating various dents and penetrations.

Army Group North was to hold its lines near Kholm, Staraya Russa, and north of Lake Ilmen.

After the end of the muddy season all three army groups were to improve their front lines and establish continuous defensive positions, if possible. Because of the precarious supply situation, it seemed doubtful whether more than isolated strong points could be held along certain sectors of the front. Armored and motorized reserves would have to be assembled in accessible areas.

Units withdrawn from the frontline for rehabilitation would have to train their recently arrived replacements on the basis of past experience in combat. Because of a shortage of equipment, only a certain number of divisions could be fully rehabilitated. The ones selected for this purpose were the armored and motorized divisions as well as the army and corps troops of Army Group South, and three armored and three motorized infantry divisions as well as some of the army and corps troops of Army Groups Center and North. In the process of rehabilitation, each armored division was to have three tank battalions, and each motorized infantry division one. The armored divisions of Army Groups Center and North that were not to be rehabilitated would have to transfer some of their cadres to the south. Three armored and six infantry divisions of Army Group Center were to be moved to western Europe without their equipment. There they were to be completely rehabilitated and reequipped. The armored and motorized infantry divisions remaining with Army Group Center and North would have to be rehabilitated in the line without being issued any new equipment. The armored divisions in this category would probably have only one tank battalion. Approximately 500,000 replacements were supposed to arrive in the theater by the end of April 1942.

A special rehabilitation area for Army Group South was to be established near Dnepropetrovsk, while for Army Group Center similar areas could be set up near Orsha, Minsk, Gomel, and Bryansk. Those few units of Army Group North which were to be rehabilitated would probably be transferred to the Zone of Interior. Rehabilitation was to begin in mid-March at the latest. After the muddy season the fully rehabilitated units of Army Group Center were to be transferred to Army Group South.

The exigencies of the last few months had led to the commitment of a great number of technical specialists as infantrymen. The overall persomlel situation and the shortage of technically trained men made it imperative either to return all specialists to their proper assignment or to use them as cadres for newly activated units. The future combat efficiency of the Army would depend upon the effective enforcement of this policy.

The high rate of materiel attrition and the limited capacity of the armament industry were compelling reasons for keeping weapons and equipment losses at a minimum.

In the implementing order to the army groups and armies, the Organization Division of the Army High Command directed on 18 February that those mobile divisions that were to be fully rehabilitated would be issued 50-60 percent of their prescribed motor vehicle allowance and infantry divisions up to 50 percent. Every infantry company was to be issued 4 automatic rifles and 4 carbines with telescopic sights; armor-piercing rifle grenades were to be introduced. Bimonthly reports on manpower and equipment shortages as well as on current training and rehabilitation of units were to be submitted by all headquarters concerned.

The element of surprise was essential to the success of the summer offensive. On 12 February Keitel therefore issued the first directive for deceiving the Russians about future German intentions. The following information was to be played into Soviet intelligence hands by German counterintelligence agents:

> *At the end of the muddy season the German military leaders intended to launch a new offensive against Moscow. For this purpose they wanted to concentrate strong forces by moving newly activated divisions to the Russian theater and exchanging battle-weary ones in the East for fresh ones from the West. After the capture of Moscow the Germans planned to advance to the middle Volga and seize the industrial installations in that region.*
>
> *The assembly of forces was to take place in secret. For this purpose the capacity of the railroads was to be raised before the divisions were transferred from the West. German and allied forces would meanwhile launch a major deceptive attack in the direction of Rostov.*
>
> *As to Leningrad, the prevailing opinion was that this city would perish by itself as soon as the ice on Lake Ladoga had melted. Then the Russians would have to dismount the railroad and the inhabitants would again be isolated. To attack in this area appeared unnecessary.*

In addition, those German troops that were earmarked for the Russian theater and presently stationed in the West were to be deceived by the issuance of military maps and geographic data pertaining to the Moscow area. The units that were already in the theater were not to be given any deceptive information until the current defensive battles had been concluded. The same directive also requested the Army and Luftwaffe to submit suggestions for other deceptive measures. The maintenance of secrecy was strongly emphasized.

The Navy's Role (February 1942)

The German Navy's principal concern in the Black Sea area was the transportation of supplies for the Army. The difficulties were caused by the shortage of shipping space and the absence of escort and combat vessels. Measures taken to improve the German position in the Black Sea included transfer of PT boats, Italian antisubmarine vessels, small submarines, and landing craft; mine fields were also being laid. Orders had been issued to speed up these measures and support the Army by bringing up supplies. Russian naval forces in the Black Sea would have to be attacked and destroyed. The degree of success obtained would determine the outcome of the war in the Black Sea area. Attention was called to the fact that eventually it would become necessary to occupy all Russian Black Sea bases and ports.

On the other hand, the remainder of the Russian Baltic fleet stationed in and around Leningrad had neither strategic nor tactical value. Ammunition and fuel supplies were exceedingly low. About 12 of the high speed mine sweepers had been sunk so far, so that only 4 or 5 were left. About 65 out of 100 submarines had been sunk by the Germans.

Intelligence Estimate (20 February 1942)

In a summary dated 20 February 1942 the Eastern Intelligence Division of the Army High Command stated that the Russians were anticipating a German offensive directed against the Caucasus and the oil wells in that area. As a countermeasure the Red Army would have the choice between a spoiling offensive and a strategic withdrawal. Assuming the Russians would attack, it was estimated that their offensive would take place in the south. There they could interfere with German attack preparations, reoccupy economically valuable areas, and land far to the rear of the German lines along the Black Sea coast. If they were sufficiently strong, the Soviets would also attempt to tie down German forces by a series of local attacks in the Moscow and Leningrad sectors.

Numerous reports from German agents in Soviet-held territory indicated that the Red Army had been planning the recapture of the Ukraine for some time. At the earliest the Russian attack could take place immediately after the muddy season, i. e. at the beginning of May.

The Russian forces identified opposite Army Group South consisted of 83 infantry divisions and 12 infantry brigades as well as 20 cavalry divisions and 19 armored brigades, plus an unknown number of newly organized units.

Interference from British forces seemed unlikely. The latter would move into the Caucasus area only if their supply lines could be properly secured, a time-consuming process that had not even been initiated. On the other hand, lend-lease materiel was arriving in considerable quantities; the first U. S. fighter planes had been encountered along the German Sixth Army front.

Hitler's Preoccupations in Early March 1942

On 5 March an order signed by Keitel summarized the various instructions issued by Hitler to the services during recent weeks. In the general part of this order, the Army and Luftwaffe were reminded that premature attacks conducted without concentrating sufficient forces had failed on several occasions. Efforts to stop Russian penetrations all along the front had led to piecemeal commitment and dissipation of ground forces. The Russians would have to be stopped wherever they threatened vital communications. In the event of a Soviet breakthrough full-strength units were to be assembled along the shoulders of the salient and the gap was to be closed after the bulk of the Russian forces had passed through.

Minor rectifications of the defense lines were permissible so long as no important installations were thereby abandoned. No local attacks, the results of which were out of proportion with the losses, were to be launched. Luftwaffe support was to be requested only for essential operations, such as destroying concentrations of Soviet armor prior to an attack. Many a Russian attack could be delayed or altogether weakened beyond repair by disrupting Soviet lines of communications. To achieve greater effect, the heaviest bombs available were to be used for all-out air attacks. Since there was a shortage of artillery along many stretches of the front, effective air support for offensive operations was essential. Because of the current emergency, air transport was so scarce that no additional airlift operations could be carried out during the muddy period.

In the second part of the order the mission of each army group for the immediate future was set forth as follows:

a. *Army Group South.*

> (1) If the Crimea was to be seized with a minimum of delay, the Kerch Peninsula would have to be captured before starting the siege of Sevastopol. The Russian ports and Black Sea fleet would have to be neutralized from the air before ground operations were started in the Crimea.
>
> (2) The next step was to eliminate the Izyum salient by first letting the Soviets exhaust their offensive power in that area and then cutting off the salient by thrusts directed from the shoulders. The armored divisions of the First Panzer Army were to carry out these thrusts and were therefore given top priority on tank and motor vehicle deliveries.

b. *Army Group Center.* All forces available in the Army Group Center area were to be assembled for a Ninth Army thrust in the direction of Ostashkov. This drive was to take place before the spring muddy period. The lines of communications that had been frequently disrupted would have to be secured.

c. *Army Group North.* The airlift operations that had been initiated to bring the situation under control were to be stepped up. More reinforcements were to be moved up to permit the consolidation of the situation at Demyansk and prevent an encirclement along the Volkhov. Eventually, Sixteenth Army was to attack from the Staraya Russa area in a movement that was to be coordinated with the Ninth Army drive toward Ostashkov. The VIII Air Corps was to support this operation as well as the Volkhov maneuver.

Another directive, signed by Hitler on 14 March, dealt with the problem of Allied assistance to the Soviet Union. It stated that British and American efforts to bolster Russia's power of resistance during the decisive months of 1942 would have to be curbed. For this purpose the Germans would have to strengthen their coastal defenses in Norway to prevent Allied landings along the Arctic coast, particularly in the Petsamo nickel mine area in northern Finland. Moreover, the Navy would have to intensify submarine operations against convoys crossing the Arctic Ocean. The Luftwaffe was to strengthen its long-range reconnaissance and bomber units in the far north and transfer the bulk of its torpedo planes to that area. The flying units were to keep the Russian ports along the Murmansk coast under constant attack, increase their reconnaissance activities, and intercept convoys. Close interservice cooperation was essential.

The Situation at the End of March 1942

The overall situation remained static during the month of March. The Russians showed signs of exhaustion, while the Germans were incapable of launching any major counterattack. Like two groggy boxers, the opponents warily eyed each other, neither of them strong enough to land a knockout blow. The weakness of the Russians became manifest through a number of incidents. In the area around Velizh, for instance, the Germans captured rifles, the butts of which were unfinished, indicating that the weapons had been issued before they were ready. The shortage of infantry weapons, though nothing new, seemed more acute than ever. Russian prisoners stated that wooden rifles were being used for training recruits in the Zone of Interior. In another instance, the Russian cavalry divisions opposite Army Group South were so short of horses — their strength had dropped to approximately 60 horses per regiment — that the men had to be employed as infantry.

The true condition of the German forces could be gathered from a status report of 30 March 1942. Out of a total of 162 combat divisions in the Russian theater, only 8 were immediately available for any mission, 3 were capable of offensive missions after a rest period, 47 were available for limited offensive missions, 73 were fully suited for defensive missions, 29 were only capable of limited defensive missions, and 2 were not suited for immediate commitment. The 16 armored divisions in the theater had a total of 140 serviceable tanks, that is to say less than the normal complement of one division. Because of the shortage of motor vehicles and prime movers, few divisions were more than 20 percent mobile. The few available tanks and self-propelled guns were distributed among various armored and infantry divisions.

Under these conditions the arrival of the muddy season at the end of March, which practically enforced a truce in the fighting, was a relief for both protagonists. Although the mud was less severe than during the preceding autumn, it did not hamper operations for some time.

During March Army Group South was not engaged in any largescale fighting, and Bock, who had assumed command of the army group after Reichenau's sudden death on 17 January 1942, used this lull to reinforce the wall around the Russian breach near Izyum.

In the Army Group Center area the heavy fighting in the rear of Fourth and Ninth Armies continued. The Russians did everything in their power to supply their forces behind the German front, and they exerted constant pressure on Army Group Center's only supply line, the Smolensk-Vyazma-Rzhev railroad. German efforts to keep this route open were handicapped by a shortage of troops. Also, in the Vitebsk-Velikye Luki area there was a latent threat which the Germans were unable to eliminate. But they were fortunate that the Russians in this region had dispersed their forces over a wide area instead of concentrating them for a southward drive.

South of Lake Ilmen Army Group North had assembled a relief force to establish contact with the Demyansk pocket. The situation along the Volkhov front had deteriorated because a strong attack launched by the Russians northeast of Lyuban resulted in a deep breach, which — in conjunction with the Volkhov penetration — threatened to develop into a double envelopment of the German forces in that area.

Chapter 9 Preparations for the German Summer Offensive

Directive No. 41 (5 April 1942)

There can be no doubt that Hitler himself conceived the plan for the German summer offensive. In addition to designating the principal objectives, he plotted most of the details and even went so far as to dictate the text. His self-confidence as military leader had greatly risen since he had overcome the winter crisis without abandoning a major part of Germany's territorial gains in Russia. In his recently acquired position of commander in chief of the Army he seemed less than ever disposed to listen to his advisers. Whereas the plans for Operation BARBAROSSA had been prepared according to German General Staff procedures, those for Operation SIEGFRIED — the summer offensive of 1942 — were drafted by General Halder and his immediate assistants according to detailed instructions received from Hitler who dictated the final version. In so doing, the Fuehrer completely rewrote Directive No. 41, adding very important parts pertaining to the conduct of operations in particular. At the same time the code designation SIEGFRIED was changed to BLAU, and Hitler specified that the services be given separate instructions regarding the maintenance of secrecy and the scope of strategic propaganda directed at the Caucasus area.

Hitler's directive was issued on 5 April 1942. It read essentially as follows:

a. Introduction. The winter battles in Russia were approaching their end and the Germans had won a "defensive success of unequalled magnitude." The Russians had suffered extremely heavy losses and used up the reserves they had earmarked for subsequent operations.

As soon as weather and terrain conditions permitted, the Germans would regain the initiative so that they could eradicate the remaining Russian military potential and deprive the Soviets of the resources on which their economy was still based. All available forces of Germany and its allies were to be employed for this purpose, taking into account that the occupied territories in northern and western Europe, and especially their coast lines, had to be safeguarded.

b. Overall Plan for the Russian Theater. While Army Group North was to seize Leningrad and establish contact with the Finns, Army Group Center was to hold. In the south, German attack forces were to penetrate into the Caucasus. To attain the latter objective, the Army would have to proceed by phase lines. In planning the conduct of this offensive factors to be considered were the course of the front lines along which the winter fighting would be brought to a conclusion and the availability of manpower, equipment, and transportation.

All available forces would have to be concentrated for the principal operation in the south in order to first destroy the enemy forces in the Don bend, then seize the oil resources of the Caucasus, and finally cross the Caucasus mountain ranges. The Leningrad operation was to be made contingent upon developments in the overall situation.

c. Conduct of Operations. As a first step toward accomplishing these missions, the Army was to consolidate its position along the entire Russian front. That would require a number of limited-objective attacks which would have to be conducted with maximum power to assure local superiority and rapid success, and to strengthen the German troops' self-confidence.

Once this consolidation had been achieved, the Kerch Peninsula would have to be cleared and Sevastopol captured. During these preliminary operations the Luftwaffe and Navy were to disrupt Russian communications in the Black Sea. Moreover, the Russian forces that had dented the German lines at Izyum would have to be cut off along the Donets and destroyed.

After these preliminary operations the Army was to launch the Caucasus offensive proper. During the initial phases the Russian forces south of Voronezh and west and north of the Don would have to be destroyed. Since the divisions available for this operation could not detrain and assemble simultaneously, the offensive would have to be executed by consecutive phases that were to complement one another. The delivery of individual attacks in different parts of the theater would have to be so coordinated that maximum power could be developed at the right time at the decisive point.

Encirclements of Russian forces resulting from German breakthroughs and envelopments would have to be tight; the enveloping forces would have to avoid any delay that would offer the Soviets an opportunity to escape. While movements were underway, the armored and motorized infantry units were to avoid losing contact with the infantry divisions; whenever the latter were unable to make headway, motorized elements were to lend them support.

The offensive was to start with a breakthrough from the area south of Orel in the direction of Voronezh. Two enveloping forces were to seize Voronezh. During the second phase, while some of the infantry divisions established a strong defensive line from Orel to Voronezh, armored and motorized divisions were to continue their southeastward drive along the Don, performing another double envelopment in conjunction with forces thrusting eastward from the Kharkov area.

During the third phase of the offensive the forces following the course of the Don were to link up near Stalingrad with those advancing eastward from the Taganrog area. Every attempt was to be made to seize Stalingrad or at least bring the city within reach of German artillery so that the Soviets would be deprived of its production and transportation facilities. Subsequent operations would be greatly facilitated if the bridges at Rostov could be seized intact and bridgeheads could be established south of the Don.

The German attack force on the right advancing eastward from Taganrog was to be reinforced with armored and motorized divisions in order to prevent major Russian elements from escaping across the Don. Defensive positions would have to be built along the Don while the advance was in progress. These positions would have to be amply provided with antitank guns and so constructed that, if necessary, they could be of service during the winter. Allied forces, supported by German troops, would have to man these positions, and German divisions would have to serve as strategic reserves behind the Don front.

Because of the advanced season the movements across the Don toward the south would have to be so timed that the Caucasus could be reached without major stoppage.

d. The Luftwaffe. Apart from giving direct support to the ground forces, the Luftwaffe was to protect the concentration of forces in the Army Group South area by strengthening the antiaircraft defense, particularly those of the Dnepr railway bridges. In the event that reconnaissance information should indicate the assembly of Russian attack forces, the Luftwaffe would have to disrupt Soviet lines of communications and above all destroy the railroad bridges across the Don

e. The Navy. In the Black Sea the Navy's main function was to carry out naval transports Since the Russian Black Sea fleet had so far not been affected by military events, German naval vessels transferred to these waters would have to be prepared for combat without delay. The Russian Baltic fleet was to be neutralized in the Gulf of Finland.

Special security precautions were to be taken, which — together with strategic propaganda — were the subject of instructions issued simultaneously. The number of persons initiated in the plan for the summer offensive was to be held to a minimum; conversations about possible operations were strictly forbidden; no long-distance calls discussing preparations were to be made beyond army group, air force, and VIII Air Corps headquarters. All orders and messages were to be forwarded by courier in writing, and differences of opinion were to be cleared up in personal conferences or through an exchange of coded messages. Germany's allies were to be informed of only the most essential facts.

Strategic propaganda was to be directed at the Caucasian tribes to whom full independence was to be promised. Liaison officers were to be attached to allied propaganda agencies to guarantee adherence to German policies.

This directive leaves no doubt that Hitler's principal objective for the summer offensive of 1942 was the possession of the Caucasus and its oil resources. The shortage of combat troops and the precariousness of the transportation network made it necessary to place great emphasis on the preliminary operations, whereas the main drive toward the Caucasus was outlined only in its initial phase — the seizure of bridgeheads across the Don. More specific orders for a Caucasus operation were not issued until 23 July 1942, when the operation was in full swing and Hitler signed Directive No. 45. At the time Directive No. 41 was written, no basic conflict between the eastward thrust toward Stalingrad and the southward drive into the Caucasus was anticipated. Like Voronezh, for instance, Stalingrad was to be a stepping stone along the approach road toward the Caucasus. In the Fuehrer's mind, however, the desire to conquer the city on the Volga by house-to-house fighting gradually became a fixation. This was all the more difficult to understand because in 1941 he had rejected any direct attack on Leningrad and Moscow. The diversion of more and more forces toward Stalingrad was made to the detriment of the principal drive into the Caucasus, and eventually both efforts were to bog down for lack of strength.

Estimates, Delays, and Disappointments in April 1942

Intelligence Estimate

Despite the bitter experiences of the winter 1941-42, the Germans continued to underestimate their Russian opponent. According to an estimate submitted by the Eastern Intelligence Division on 10 April 1942, the Red Army had been greatly affected by the winter fighting. Newly activated units showed deficiencies in training, weapons, and equipment. Not only was there a shortage of manpower, but the limitations imposed by the loss of armament production capacity would hamper the further activation of armored units.

In 1942 the Russians would limit themselves to defensive operations, possibly interrupted by intermittent limited-objective offensives to harass the Germans. Being aware of the German plans for an offensive in the southeast, the Russians could be expected to use every means at their disposal to maintain their lines of communications with the Caucasus. As yet there was no indication that the Russians intended to launch a spoiling attack in the south. In the center they would try to consolidate the defense system around Moscow, whereas in the north the relief of Leningrad would probably be given top priority.

Few Russian units appeared to be at full combat efficiency. While the activation of new rifle divisions was feasible, that of armored divisions seemed no longer possible. Steel production was the bottleneck. No major Russian offensive was to be expected in the foreseeable future. The bulk of the Soviet forces would probably be massed in the south.

Making these ideas his own, Halder reported to Hitler that the great number of Russian divisions identified since November 1941 seemed to indicate that the Red Army had mobilized all its manpower resources and had used up a major part offensive.

Delay in the Preliminary Operations

On 16 April Generaloberst (Gen.) Fritz Erich von Manstein, commander of Eleventh Army in the Crimea, suggested to Hitler that the attack on the Kerch Peninsula be delayed until 5 May because he was still short some essential items of supply. Hitler approved Manstein's request, adding that the Luftwaffe would have to give strong support to the ground forces. As soon as Kerch was cleared, Army Group South was to pinch off and eliminate the Izyum salient, after which the siege of Sevastopol was to be begun. The timing of these three preliminary operations was to be made contingent upon the availability of essential air support. Because of the delay in the start of the first attack, the Sevastopol operation would not begin before mid-June at the earliest.

The Situation at Army Group Center

As a result of the shifting of forces to the West, to Army Group South, and to rehabilitation centers, Army Group Center was forced to abandon the attacks on Ostashkov and Toropez. Despite its reduction in strength, however, the army group was ordered to eliminate the partisan forces in its rear, consolidate its front line, reorganize its remaining units, and set aside reserves. After these missions had been accomplished, the army group was to undertake a series of limited-objective attacks.

Chain of Command

The first phase of the summer offensive was to be conducted by Army Group South, composed of Second and Sixth Armies, Fourth Panzer Army, and the Hungarian First Army. During the second phase First Panzer Army, the Italian Eighth Army, and probably also Eleventh Army were to intervene. The newly activated Army Group A was to assume control of the movements foreseen for the following phases, while Army Group South would become responsible for securing flank protection along the Don front.

Transportation

The divisions that were to participate in the German offensive were to be moved up in three echelons. The 41 divisions — 21 of which were allied — that were to reinforce the units stationed in the south were none too many for an offensive of such dimensions. Since the Russians had the better railnet for their assembly, they might be able to jump off before the Germans. Much would depend upon the quantities of lend-lease equipment they would receive via Murmansk by June 1942.

Divisions to be Moved Up for the Summer Offensive

Echelon	Divisions				
	Total	German	Italian	Hungarian	Romanian
Totals	41	20	6	10	5
First	20	15		3	2
Second	12	5	3	4	
Third	9		3	3	3

The delays in the start of the preliminary attacks would necessarily affect the time of the offensive proper, all the more so because as late as April the Russians were still holding the initiative.

Turkey Remains Neutral

Hitler, who believed that Turkey would sooner or later join the Axis Powers, ordered the German Ambassador in Ankara to offer the Turks 150 million marks worth of military equipment at a time when he could hardly spare a rifle. However, the deal was not consummated because Turkey refused the passage of German submarines and PT-boats through the Dardanelles into the Black Sea. In his search for another solution Hitler ordered the boats disassembled, transported cross country, and reassembled in Black Sea ports. This order was carried out, but it produced no significant results.

Logistical Preparations

Timing

During the first phase — the drive on Voronezh — the offensive forces were to be supplied from the supply depots of the Kursk district. After the seizure of Voronezh, the railroad connecting that city with Kursk would become the principal feeder line for the Don front. Nonorganic truck transportation columns were to carry the supplies for the spearhead divisions.

The Kharkov supply district was to support the attack forces participating in the second phase. An advance base was to be set up at Valuiki as soon as the Voronezh forces linked up with those coming from Kharkov.

During the third phase additional advance bases would have to be set up along the railroad leading from the Stalino supply district to Stalingrad and east of Valuiki along the Don. Supply points would also have to be established south of the lower Don as soon as German troops crossed the river for the drive into the Caucasus.

To carry out these different missions, a large number of truck transportation columns would have to be held in readiness. Special supply reconnaissance teams were to follow the spearheads during each movement.

Chain of Command

Until Army Group A assumed control in the southern part of the Army Group South area, the supply preparations for Operation BLAU were to be the responsibility of the newly formed Command Staff South.

Supplies

Aside from the initial issue carried by the troops, the following quantities of supplies were to be stored in depots:

Supply District	Short Tons		
	Ammunition	POL	Rations
Totals	68, 000	39, 600	55, 000
Kharkov	18, 000	11, 000	15, 400
Kursk	15, 000	8, 300	14, 900
Stalino	35, 000	20, 300	24, 700

Detailed preparations could be made only for the first two phases for which the necessary data were available. Depots in the Kharkov and Kursk districts were to break down supplies according to the estimated requirements of the forces that were to be assembled in these areas, whereas at Stalino supplies were to be stored in bulk.

Motor Vehicles

By the start of Operation BLAU it was hoped that most of the participating units would be adequately equipped with motor vehicles. Prime movers were still scarce. The preliminary operations as well as the long distances some of the motorized units would have to cover to reach the assembly areas might cause further attrition in organic motor vehicles before the start of the offensive proper. Despite intensive maintenance and repair efforts the spearhead divisions would probably have only 60 percent or less of their organic motor vehicles by the time the offensive was launched. Truck transportation columns with a total capacity of 11,000 short tons would be available by 20 June 1942 to compensate for the shortage of organic vehicles.

Rail Transportation

During the initial phases of the operation the attack forces could rely on three major rail lines with detraining points in the Iursk, Kharkov, and Donets Basin areas. During the third phase the left arm of the pincers directed at Stalingrad would lack rail support as it extended southeastward along the Don. The right arm would be dependent upon the single railroad connecting Stalino with Stalingrad.. This was the only railroad by which the attack forces could be supplied once they were approaching the Volga.

Summary

The supply situation during the first phase appeared satisfactory with sufficient ammunition and rations apparently available for the second phase. But POL reserves would be consumed by 15 July, and the continuation of the offensive would have to be assured from current shipments.

Organizational Problems

Rehabilitation of Units

The predominant problem facing the Organization Division of the Army High Command was the rehabilitation of units. Altogether 3 armored and 5 infantry divisions committed in the Russian theater were selected to be exchanged for 1 armored and 9 infantry divisions stationed in the West. The troops to be withdrawn from the Russian theater were to be deloused twice: first before entraining and then again after detraining.

Some of the army and corps troops as well as the divisions that were to be rehabilitated within the theater could not even be pulled out of the front. They were to be rehabilitated in place, a very unsatisfactory procedure not propitious to raising the combat efficiency of the respective units. Leaves were to be granted to all those men who had served uninterruptedly in the theater since the start of the campaign. Two leave trains per week were scheduled for each army group.

Shortage of Technicians

The armored divisions complained about the continued shortage of technicians and the weakness of their cadres. Tank and truck drivers were at a premium. Several orders were issued requesting field commanders to return technicians and specialists to the assignments for which they were trained. To relieve the manpower shortage within the theater, native units were to be activated from the prisoners of Tatar, Caucasian, Georgian, Armenian, and Cossack nationality who would probably be captured during the summer offensive. These units were to assume some of the routine duties heretofore carried out by German troops, thus permitting a more judicious employment of the latter.

Construction of Fortifications

On 26 April General Halder issued an order calling for the establishment of a defense system. In view of the general weakness of the front lines, enemy breakthroughs could be prevented only by constructing fortifications, establishing switch positions, and building specific fortified areas.

The front lines were to be fortified in depth. Switch positions were to protect the Bryansk-Kharkov line. Since there was not sufficient manpower to construct continuous lines in the rear, it would be necessary to establish fortified areas that could be held for prolonged periods by weak forces against superior enemy pressure. These fortified areas were to secure important supply and communications centers, such as Melitopol, Dnepropetrovsk, Poltava, Bryansk, Roslavl, Smolensk, Nevel, Luga, Gatchina and Pskov.

By securing the most important road and rail junctions, river crossings, etc., situated between the front line and the fortified areas in the rear, the Germans could create a defense system capable of successfully withstanding any Soviet armored elements that might break through the front.

Engineer staffs were to be responsible for the construction of the fortifications. Only indigenous labor was to be used because of the shortage of German manpower. The material needed for the construction program would also have to be procured from local resources.

Oil Brigade Caucasus

The Oil Detachment Caucasus, formed in the spring of 1941, was expanded because of recent experiences with the Russian scorched-earth policy. Since the oil fields would be more severely damaged than originally presumed, the detachment was brought to a strength of 10,794 men and redesignated Oil Brigade Caucasus. The brigade was issued 1,142 vehicles and 6 planes and ordered to stand by, ready to move into the Caucasus oil fields immediately behind the combat troops.

Casualties and Replacements

At the end of the winter fighting, on 30 April 1942, total German casualties, excluding sick, numbered 1,167,835 officers and men. A number of measures to save personnel had been introduced, such as lowering the T/O strength of the infantry divisions. Nevertheless, by 31 October 1942 the estimated shortage of replacements in the Russian theater would amount to 280,000 men, even if all operations proceeded according to plan. The Organization Division believed that it would be impossible to provide sufficient replacements for all three army groups. The three solutions therefore taken under consideration at the end of April were as follows:

1. To give Army Group south its full complement of replacements, in which case the situation at Army Groups Center and North would not be relieved until July 1942;
2. To fulfill only 80 per cent of the Army Group South requirements, as a result of which the position of the other two army groups would improve quite considerably by July 1942; or
3. To give Army Group South its full complement and accelerate the arrival of additional replacements by transferring during May and June to each of the two other army groups 100,000 men with only two months of training.

General Halder chose the third solution, fully cognizant of the disadvantage incurred by committing replacements with only two months of training. Actually, he had little choice in the matter. The monthly report on the rehabilitation of units in the Army Group Center area during April 1942 indicated that the unabated intensity of the defensive fighting as well as the withdrawal of divisions for transfer to the West had almost completely obstructed the reorganization and rehabilitation of the units that stayed in place. In general, the divisions which were to be rehabilitated in place would have only limited mobility and reduced combat efficiency, the shortage of motor vehicles and horses being their greatest handicap.

The Participation of Germany's Allies

During the summer of 1942 Germany's allies were to play a much more significant part in the Russian theater than heretofore. In an effort to intensify their participation in the struggle against the Soviet Union, Keitel had visited Hungary and Romania during the preceding winter and Hitler had made a personal appeal to Mussolini. The Armed Forces High Command was to provide all the weapons and equipment it could spare for the allied contingents. The political differences were to be partly overcome by interspersing Italian corps or armies between Hungarian and Romanian ones. In compliance with requests received from Germany's allies, Hitler on 15 April ordered national units to fight under the command of their own army or at least corps headquarters. This decision was to cost the Germans dearly when their allies collapsed along the Don front under the blows of the Russian counteroffensive.

To ascertain smooth cooperation at different levels of command, the German Army organized a number of liaison staffs to be attached to allied division, corps, and army headquarters. Hitler showed his continued anxiety over the morale of the allied troops a few weeks later, when he stated that Italian and other allied military achievements should be given proper credit in German news releases. Fanatical loyalty on the part of the Germans would in turn inspire their allies with similar feelings.

The Germans counted on the assistance of the following allied forces:

Allied Divisions Available for the Russian Theater (Summer 1942)

Nationality	Divisions					
	Total	Inf.	Mtz Inf.	Armored	Cavalry	Security
Totals	52	38	4	2	3	5
Romanian	27	22	--------	1	3	1
Hungarian	13	9	--------	1	--------	3
Italian	9	6	3	--------	--------	--------
Slovak	2	------	1	--------	--------	1
Spanish	1	1	--------	--------	--------	--------

On the other hand, Hitler was unable to satisfy the requests of Generaloberst (Gen.) Erwin Rommel after his meeting with Mussolini at the beginning of April 1942. No motorized army artillery and engineer units could be made available for the North African theater before the successful conclusion of the Caucasus offensive in the autumn of 1942. By June, however, Rommel's advance into Egypt seemed so promising that Hitler suddenly decided to divert to North Africa a number of tanks, trucks, and weapons which had been reserved for the rehabilitation of two Russian-theater divisions.

Aside from Germany's allies, a number of European states, even some of the recently vanquished ones, offered contingents of volunteers who desired to participate in the campaign against the Soviet Union — which for a time tended to assume the characteristics of a crusade against Bolshevism. But Hitler, distrusting his former enemies, reluctantly permitted only a limited number of Frenchmen to serve in national units up to regimental strength. Party political considerations induced him to transfer the responsibility for organizing foreign military volunteer units from Army to National Socialist Party (Waffen-SS) control.

Rear Area Security

Anxious to secure the lines of communications of the combat forces, General Halder decided that three German security divisions plus Hungarian and Romanian troops were to follow behind the advance. Each security division was to be composed of one infantry and one security regiment, one motorized military police, one artillery, and one signal battalion, as well as one Cossack troop. Military administrative headquarters and prisoner of war processing units were to be formed in addition.

Army Group South's Defense Line

One of the problems that constantly preoccupied Hitler during the preparatory period was the exposed flank that would extend from Voronezh to the area northeast of Kursk. The Fuehrer ordered this defense line amply provided with antitank guns. A total of 350-400 self-propelled 75-mm antitank guns — more than half of them captured French weapons — and some 150 captured Russian 76-mm guns were to be distributed along this front to repel Soviet medium and heavy tanks. Tractors and captured prime movers were to be employed to give a certain degree of mobility to those guns which were not self-propelled.

The Role of Army Group A

The new Army Group A was to be formed under the command of Field Marshal Wilhelm List. To prevent premature discovery of the German intentions by the Russians, the arrival of all higher headquarters in the assembly areas was to be delayed to the last possible moment. The Army High Command was to control the movements of all Army Group A and Fourth Panzer Army units as well as those of the army and corps troops.

The cover names given to each of the Army Group A units were to convey the impression that they were engaged in fortification work. List himself was not to arrive in the theater until shortly before the start of operations. The forward echelon of his headquarters was transferred to Poltava on 12 May, the remaining elements were to arrive at Stalino later in May. By approximately 15 June, when the first phase of Operation BLAU was to be launched, Army Group A headquarters was to be ready to secretly assume command over the Eleventh and Seventeenth Armies, and possibly over the First Panzer Army. The overt assumption of command was to take place shortly afterward.

Feint and Counerfeint

At the beginning of May 1942 Molotov flew to Great Britain and the United States, where he was promised that a second front would be opened before the end of the year. On 2 May a news agency report from Moscow indicated that the Russians were expecting a German spring offensive launched from the Bryansk-Orel-Kursk area. The probable objective was Voronezh, after which the German troops would advance down the Don to seize Stalingrad, while other German forces thrusting from the Kharkov region would advance eastward.

This news report must have produced a certain effect, since only five days later the Chief of the Armed Forces Operations Staff issued a new directive concerning deception. Referring to the previous directive on the same subject dated 12 February 1942, Jodl divided the period before the start of Operation BLAU into two phases.

During the first phase, which was to last up to 25 May, the existing uncertainty with regard to the true German intentions was to be increased, and the preparations and movements for Operation BLAU were to be dissimulated by showing no point of main effort. Since some of the troops needed for the preliminary operations around the Izyum salient were to assemble behind Army Group Center, the Russians would have difficulty in recognizing the objective of the next major offensive. To German units the troop movements were to be explained as a series of simple exchanges of battle-weary divisions from the Russian theater for fresh divisions from the West. The rehabilitation of numerous divisions had long been overdue. As soon as the preliminary operations got under way, maps of the Moscow area up to the middle Volga were to be distributed to the Luftwaffe units.

The second phase was to start after 25 May. By that time the Russians would be at least partly aware of the German distribution of forces. If their attention was drawn away from Army Group South toward Army Group Center, it might be possible to deceive them with regard to the real German main effort and objective. This deception was to be achieved by replacing German units with allied ones at the front, thus simulating a weakening at a point where in reality strength was being built up. An attack on Moscow was to be simulated by assembling some of the attack forces at the boundary between Army Groups South and Center. By intensifying reconnaissance activities along sectors of the Army Groups Center and North fronts one might simulate offensive intentions. Other means suggested were deceptive radio traffic and supply activities; the formation of fictitious staffs; night march movements of rear elements of security divisions; the erection of dummy planes on airfields in the Army Group Center area; rumors spread by military attaches assigned to neutral countries; the planting of articles in military magazines published in neutral countries, in which special emphasis was placed on Moscow's significance as the center of Russian resistance, as the traffic hub, and the key to armament production, indicating that after the loss of Moscow the Red Army would be unable to offer active resistance west of the Volga.

To judge by the results, the net effect of these deceptive measures was disappointing, since on 16 June another news agency report from Moscow contained details concerning the German intentions and came very close to the real plans.

Warning Notes (May 1942)

Some hesitancy regarding the success of the German summer offensive was expressed by Jodl on 10 May when he stated to one of his associates that Operation BLAU was very risky because of the weakness of Army Groups Center and North. The Russians might try a stab at Smolensk even though it was doubtful that they could muster sufficient manpower and daring for such a venture. A little later Hitler agreed with Jodl that, once the German offensive in the south got under way, all available Russian forces would automatically be diverted to the south.

The Army felt much stronger on the same subject. In a report, submitted on 12 May in reply to a request for a survey of its potential strength in 1942, Halder struck some warning notes. The contents of this report are so revealing that it is presented here in an only slightly edited version.

The Armed Forces Potential in the Spring of 1942

1. Introduction

In the summer of 1942 the organization and potential of the German military establishment were to be geared to war against the Anglo-Saxon powers. This reorientation, based on a decision made in July 1941, gave the Luftwaffe and Navy priority over the Army.

By the late autumn of 1941 developments in the Russian theater made it obvious that, as a requisite for concentrating all efforts against the British, the USSR would first have to be decisively beaten in 1942. For this purpose the entire German war machine had to be reversed and redirected toward rehabilitating and strengthening the Army.

The effects of this reorientation in the armament effort would not, however, make themselves felt to the Army during 1942. Other factors that were also detrimental to the effectiveness of the ground forces were as follows:

a. The long duration of the winter battles with the resulting high attrition of materiel.

b. The unusual cold which affected production and communications.

c. The increasing shortage of raw materials and manpower. The combined effects of these factors would have to be taken into account in assessing the true strength of the German forces in the spring of 194'.

2. Overall Numerical Strength

Date	Number of divisions					
	Total	Inf.*	Mtz Inf.**	Armored	Security	Replacement***
1 Sep 41	210	148	15	21	26	31
1 May 42	225	158	16	25	26	31

*Including light, mountain, and fortress divisions.
**Including a transformed horse cavalry division and several SS divisions.
***In the Zone of Interior and occupied territories.

The purely numerical increase in the number of divisions during the eight months from 1 September 1941 to 1 May 1942 was therefore 15 divisions plus an insignificant number of army and corps troops. A considerable part of these forces had been diverted to Norway and North Africa during the winter of 1941-42.

3. Manpower

Although 1,100,000 replacements —excluding hospitalized personnel returned to duty within the theater —were transferred to the Russian theater from 22 June 1941 to 1 May 1942, the infantry divisions of Army Group South were at approximately 50 percent of their prescribed strength, those of the other two army groups at 35 percent. By the beginning of the offensive the infantry divisions in the south were to be at full strength, while those of the other army groups were to be brought to 55 percent by August 1942.

Other factors to be considered were that experienced commissioned and noncommissioned officers who became casualties could not be adequately replaced for the time being; that the combat efficiency of the armored and motorized divisions was reduced because of the shortage of trained technicians and specialists; that differences in age, training, and experience both within and among units led to an overall reduction in combat efficiency compared to the preinvasion ground forces; and that the mental strain caused by the exertions of the past winter was bound to show its effect. On the other hand, there were also a few positive factors, such as the availability of a cadre of experienced officers and men for training replacements and the existence of a relatively efficient supply system. Everything would depend upon how much time the Russians allowed the German troops for rehabilitation and rest.

4. Firepower

a. Artillery. Because of the high rate of attrition in the Russian theater, the demands of all three army groups could not be fully satisfied in addition to fitting out newly formed units and rehabilitating wornout ones. The divisions of Army Group South would be brought up to their T/E allowances by the start of the offensive, but the other two army groups would have only three guns per artillery battery.

b. Tanks. In accordance with previous plans each armored division of Army Group South would have three tank battalions and each motorized infantry division one. The panzer divisions of the two other army groups, however, would have only one tank battalion each. At the start of the summer offensive the Germans would have 3,300 tanks in the Russian theater against 3,350 on 22 June 1941. The 1942 tanks were better armed than the ones with which Germany invaded the Soviet Union the previous year.

c. Antitank weapons. A considerable number of 37- and 50-mm antitank guns had been lost during the winter fighting, but these losses would be compensated for by the use of heavier caliber captured French and Russian guns. By introducing better guns, hollow-charge and antitank rifle grenades, etc., the defense against tanks would gradually be strengthened. Mines were available in sufficient quantities.

d. Antiaircraft Units. Only the spearhead divisions would have organic antiaircraft units. In general, however, the commitment of numerous corps and army flak battalions had improved overall antiaircraft protection. With operations extending over wide areas, the antiaircraft units would have to be spread very thinly.

e. Ammunition. The retrenchment on ammunition production imposed during the summer of 1941 and the high rate of expenditure of the following winter had led to a shortage of heavy-weapons, howitzer, and antitank ammunition, which was expected to continue through the autumn of 1942. By August 1942 shortages might affect operations. In this estimate the possibility of an increased expenditure before the outset of the offensive had not been taken into account. Expedients, such as imposing expenditure quotas and arranging for ammunition transfers from the West, had already been introduced.

5. Transportation

The heavy attrition of motor vehicles suffered during the winter battles — 75,000 vehicles lost against the arrival of only 7,500 vehicle replacements for the period 1 November 1941-15 March 1942 — complicated the effort of restoring full mobility to the ground forces by the start of the summer offensive. Current production was insufficient for both replacing past losses and equipping new units. Only the spearhead divisions would receive new vehicles. At the same time, most of the infantry divisions would be deprived of their motor vehicles and the motorized units in other sectors would be faced with a reduction in their organic vehicle allowance. Since spare parts production and repair installations would be incapable of fully satisfying the demands made by far-reaching offensive operations, whatever stocks and facilities were available would have to be diverted to the spearhead units.

To make matters even worse, there was an acute shortage of horses. During the winter 180,000 horses had died from hunger and exposure as well as enemy action, with only 20,000 replacements arriving in the theater. Although 109,000 horses had been shipped from the Zone of interior by 1 May and another 118,000 had been requisitioned from occupied countries, the number of horses available by the start of the offensive would still be insufficient.

In summarizing the transportation picture, the Army estimated that the spearhead divisions in the south would have 85 per cent of their organic motor vehicle allowance by the time the offensive got under way. The infantry divisions would be restricted in their movements because of an almost complete lack of motor vehicles. Major operations in the other army group areas could be effected only along rail lines having adequate capacity. In any event, the logistical support that could be given to Army Groups Center and North during the summer would not be sufficient for conducting extensive operations.

6. Reserves

No further reserves would be available in the Zone of Interior. The unavailability of trained manpower and up-to-date equipment would prevent the activation of new divisions. Any replacements, weapons, and equipment that would become available during the course of the summer offensive would be needed to make up current losses. No further increase in the number of divisions was possible since the 18-year olds had already been inducted. Additional motorized and armored divisions could be activated only by disbanding existing infantry units.

7. Summary

A full rehabilitation of the German forces in the Russian theater before the start of the 1942 offensive would not be feasible. Personnel and materiel shortages hampered every effort to obtain greater mobility and raise combat efficiency. These shortages as well as the wear and tear on man, beast, and vehicle caused by the winter fighting seemed to have reduced the stamina of the German Army.

Halder's report revealed that the German ground forces that were to launch the summer offensive of 1942 could not compare with the troops that had invaded Russia a year earlier. The spearhead divisions would be almost up to strength, but the followup infantry was weak and slow, and no reserves were available. No wonder the Army High Command felt apprehensive about executing Hitler's overambitious plans. An equally somber note was struck by the Organization Division of the Army High Command in its memorandum to the Chief of the Armed Forces Operations Staff, dated 27 May 1942.

In reporting on the composition and condition of the Army Group South units by the beginning of the summer offensive, the Organization Division repeated that only part of the personnel and materiel losses suffered during the winter could be replaced. For this reason, all available replacements had been channeled to the spearhead divisions and the T/O & E's of numerous units had been modified to redistribute manpower and equipment. Two types of units had been created: highly effective attack forces and units having little punch or mobility.

Of the 65-67 German divisions that were to participate in the offensive in the south, only 21-23 were either being newly activated or fully rehabilitated behind the front, whereas the remaining 44 divisions were to be rehabilitated while committed at the front. Each of the fully rehabilitated infantry divisions would receive 1,000 replacements with only two months of training. The mobility of these divisions would be limited because they were short of horses and lacked most of their organic motor vehicles. The reconnaissance battalions were now equipped with bicycles. Contrary to previous reports, the spearhead divisions would have only about 80 percent of their organic motor vehicles.

In revising the distribution of forces greater consideration would have to be given to the unequal strength and mobility of the different divisions. Since no reserves of manpower or equipment were available, the rehabilitation of units would have to be accomplished with insufficiently trained men and untested equipment coming directly from the assembly lines. The possibility of forming strategic reserves before or during the course of the initial operations appeared unlikely.

The report further stated that German desertions had dropped sharply with the beginning of spring weather after having reached an alarming rate during the winter fighting.

The Preliminary Operations (May-June 1942)

Three preliminary operations were to take place before the launching of Operation BLAU. The first one, the seizure of the Kerch Peninsula, started on 8 May. Under Manstein's brilliant leadership, Eleventh Army forces soon began to clear the peninsula against strong resistance. The second operation, directed against the Izyum salient, was given the code designation FRIDERICUS. According to the German plan, the ground forces needed for the elimination of the Russian salient were to be assembled by 17 May. Five days earlier, however, the Red Army launched a strong spoiling attack south and east of Kharkov against the right of Sixth Army. This Russian drive threatened the entire logistical buildup for Operation BLAU because it was directed at the extensive depot and repair facilities in the Kharkov area, which were vital to the German supply system. The Russian maneuver also disrupted the rehabilitation of the spearhead units, since the threat to Kharkov led to a change in priorities and a diversion of tanks and self-propelled antitank guns to the danger area.

As soon as the fighting in the Kerch Peninsula had taken a favorable course, Hitler withdrew some of the air support units from this area and committed them for the defense of Kharkov. By 13 May the situation around that city had grown so serious that the Fuehrer ordered the transfer of additional Luftwaffe contingents from the Crimea. He also decided to advance the date of the attack on the Izyum salient, originally scheduled for 18 May. In Hitler's opinion this counterthrust would be the most effective and fastest method of assisting Sixth Army in the defense of Kharkov. One of the most disquieting facts about the Russian attack was that, for the first time since the start of the campaign, the Red Army committed its armor in mass formation, thus copying the hitherto successful German tactics.

On 17 May — a day earlier than scheduled — two corps of Seventeenth Army forming the southern arm of the Izyum pincers jumped off, while the forces that were to compose the northern arm were still being assembled. During the first three days the German counter-move did little to relieve the defenders of Kharkov. It was not until 20 May that the acute danger at Kharkov seemed to have passed. The effect of the Russian spoiling attack was to be felt throughout the remaining weeks before the start of Operation BLAU, mainly because of the changes in schedule that became necessary.

Russian resistance on the Kerch Peninsula collapsed by 19 May. Five days later Hitler decided that the siege of Sevastopol, scheduled as the third and last preliminary operation, was to start on 7 June and the first phase of Operation BLAU eight days later. Under these circumstances the air support units would have to be withdrawn from the Izyum area by 6 June to assist the attack forces in the Crimea. After only three days in that part of the theater, the Luftwaffe contingents would have to be redeployed to the assembly area for Operation BLAU, where they had to arrive by 10 June at the latest. Considerations of wear and tear on planes and crews apparently did not enter the calculations on which this tight schedule was based.

On 28 May Jalder suggested a change in the timing and execution of the preliminary attacks. He wanted to continue the successful German counterattack northeast of Kharkov in the Volchansk area first, leaving the Izyum salient to be eliminated next. By applying this procedure, the Russian forces would be systematically destroyed and the preliminary operations would be more directly related to the offensive proper. Hitler approved Halder's ideas in principle but decided to investigate the situation on the spot.

On 1 June the Fuehrer and a small staff flew to Army Group South headquarters at Poltava. Field Marshal von Bock and the field commanders whose troops had been directly involved in the battle for Kharkov reported on the situation, whereupon Hitler explained his ideas on the continuation of operations. Advantage would have to be taken of the extremely favorable developments around Kharkov by destroying the Russian forces near Volchansk and Izyum as quickly as possible. The principle to be applied was that "whatever forces could be annihilated now, would not be there to interfere with Operation BLAU," even if the practical application of this idea implied some change in plans.

On the basis of additional information provided by Bock, the Fuehrer decided that the preliminary operations would be executed according to a revised schedule, even if Operation BLAU had to be delayed. The new schedule was as follows:

a. The attack on the Volchansk area was to take place on 7 June.

b. The assault on Sevastopol was to begin on the same day.

c. The attack on the Izyum salient was to be launched on or after 12 June.

d. Operation BLAU on or before 20 June.

As it turned out the Volchansk operation had to be delayed because of bad weather. The assaults on Sevastopol started on time, but made little progress despite intensive preparatory fire and air force bombardments lasting five days. Because of the strong resistance encountered at Sevastopol, Hitler reversed his previous decision and did not withdraw the air support units after only three days. By 19 June some of the outer defenses of the fortress had been breached.

The Izyum operation had meanwhile taken a very favorable course, and by 25 June the First Panzer Army reached the Oskol River, thus cutting off the salient from Kupyansk to a point near Izyum, at the confluence of Oskol and Donets. The operation had been brought to a successful conclusion, and the pocket was being mopped up.

The Russians were meanwhile transporting reinforcements to Sevastopol by submarine. The fortress was still holding out, and its capture before the end of June seemed unlikely. As soon as Sevastopol did fall, a number of Eleventh Army divisions and all the heavy siege batteries would become available for another mission which Hitler considered as the second major objective of 1942: the seizure of Leningrad, permitting a link up with the Finns.

While these preliminary operations took place in the Army Group South area, Army Group Center units were engaged in a see-saw struggle in the rear areas of Fourth and Ninth Armies, which lasted throughout the spring. During the second half of June, Fourth Army finally got the upper hand and succeeded in wiping out a number of partisan and regular troop units in its rear. Around Velikiye Luki, however, the situation remained serious.

Army Group North had reduced and mopped up most of the Volkhov pocket, thus disposing of this threat near Leningrad. The German forces in the Demyansk pocket had been relieved by the end of April, but the Ostashkov breach remained an open sore along the army group boundary.

During May 1942 Army Group Center had suffered fewer casualties than Army Group South in the Kerch and Kharkov fighting or Army Group North along the Volkhov and near Demyansk. The replacements transferred from the Zone of Interior during June were distributed as follows:

Total	**130,000**
Army Group North	**25,000**
Army Group Center	**45,000**
Army Group South	**60,000**

This left 7,000 replacements at the disposal of the Army High Command.

Last-Minute Incidents and Impressions (June 1942)

Approximately 10 days before the intended start of the summer offensive — 19 June — the operations officer of the 23d Panzer Division, which was to participate in the crucial breakthrough west of Voronezh, flew to the front, taking with him a number of highly classified documents in violation of existing security regulations. He crash-landed in Russian-held territory, and the documents, which included a corps order outlining the entire attack plan for the first phase, had disappeared when a German patrol recovered his body three days later. Hitler relieved of command a number of officers whom he held responsible for this incident.

With this plan in Russian hands, the element of surprise was bound to have been lost during the crucial initial phase. Since a change in plans was no longer feasible because of the advanced season, the operation either had to be executed according to the plan or cancelled. Hitler decided to go ahead as planned.

This decision may have been partly motivated by his low opinion of the Red Army in 1942. During the daily situation conference on 25 June he stated that approximately 80 Soviet divisions had been destroyed during the preliminary operations. Russian resistance was much weaker than during the preceding year. The various phases of Operation BLAU would therefore be executed faster and easier than hitherto assumed by the Army planners. It might not even be necessary to commit all the armor earmarked for the second phase of the operation, and two of the armored divisions could perhaps be diverted to cut off the Sukhinichi salient in the Army Group Center area.

While the Fuehrer anticipated developments in Russia with so much optimism, he seemed worried about the possibility of Allied landing attempts in the West. The German defensive forces were too weak to interdict mass landings of parachute and glider troops. Hitler felt that some of the armored divisions, which were to return to the Russian theater after rehabilitation in the West, would have to stay on to reinforce the Atlantic defense system. He seemed to believe that he could defeat the Red Army without them.

The Army judged the situation more soberly: on 26 June Halder reported that the Russians were withdrawing troops along the entire front to form reserves. Moreover, they were suddenly launching massed air attacks against German troops moving into assembly areas near Kursk.

Chapter 10 Initial Operations and New Plans (July 1942)

The First Phase (28 June-6 July 1942)

By 27 June those German forces that were to participate in the first phase of the summer offensive had moved into their assembly areas according to schedule. On the next day Fourth Panzer Army and Second Army jumped off with forces consisting of three armored, three motorized, and nine infantry divisions. Four Hungarian divisions covered the southern flank; in addition two German and six Hungarian divisions, constituting the reserves, were still enroute.

The mission of the spearhead divisions was to break through to Voronezh, [See *map 15.*] The infantry divisions were then to build up strong flank protection along a line extending from Livny to Voronezh, while the motorized forces were to thrust southeastward along the Don River. The forces available for this operation were none too strong. The protection of the Livny — Voronezh sector — about 100 miles wide-would divert most of the German infantry divisions, with the Hungarians taking over the defense of the Don south of Voronezh.

From the very first day of the offensive the Russians launched counterattacks, committing numerous armored brigades whose presence had not been discovered by German intelligence.' Sizeable Russian forces were detraining in the Yelets area.

By 2 July the German spearheads were at the outskirts of Voronezh. The city fell after four days of furious fighting, during which the divisions of Fourth Panzer Army became more heavily engaged than Hitler had thought necessary. The first phase of the offensive was completed on that day, with flank protection being secured between Livny and Voronezh.

The Second Phase (30 June -7 July 1942)

During the second phase the Sixth Army forces, consisting of 2 armored, 1 motorized, and 16 infantry divisions, jumped off from the area northeast of Kharkov, crossed the Oskol River, and linked up with the armored spearheads of Fourth Panzer Army on the upper course of the Valuy River. The maneuver was completed by 7 July. To gain sufficient time for establishing defensive positions along the Don, the Russians had fought a series of delaying actions west of the river. In isolated instances, such as east of Kupyansk and opposite the first German bridgeheads across the Oskol, they seemed determined to make a temporary stand. Although some Soviet forces had been enveloped during the course of the German advance, few prisoners and little booty had fallen into German hands. In general, the offensive had thus far proceeded according to expectation.

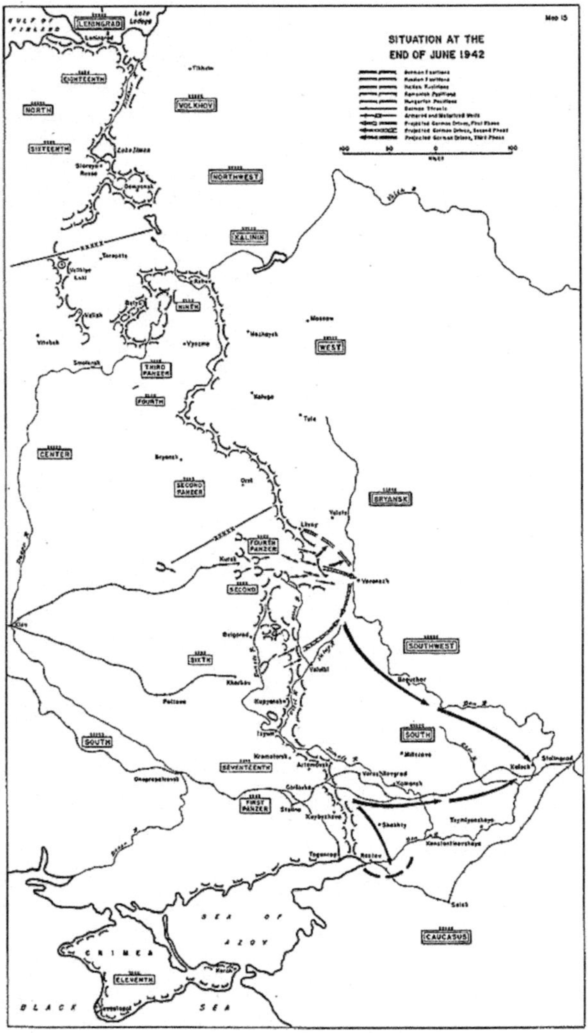

Map 15. Situation at the end of June 1942.

The German personnel shortage induced Halder to send a memorandum to Army Group South on 2 July, requesting the latter to provide a new type of information. He first explained that current operations of Army Group South were conducted almost without reserves echeloned in depth. Because of the long distances to be covered to reach the objectives, this shortage of forces could have grave consequences unless the Army High Command knew at all times the strength, condition, and casualties of all units, particularly the armored ones. Only with this on hand could the Army High Command properly accomplish its functions.

Changes in the German Order of Battle (July 1942)

The first two phases of the offensive had been directed by Field Marshal von Bock, whose command, Army Group South, was redesignated Army Group B on 9 July. [See *chart 4.]* Four days later Bock was replaced by Generaloberst (Gen.) Maximilian von Weichs, the former commander of Second Army, ostensibly because of Hitler's dissatisfaction with Bock's conduct of the Voronezh operation. In reality Hitler wanted to tighten his control over the conduct of the German summer offensive.

The first group of officers appointed to the staff of Army Group A arrived in Poltava at the end of May. When the new headquarters assumed control at the beginning of July, a forward echelon moved to Stalino, where the future headquarters of the army group was to be established. From the outset the command net broke down repeatedly because the signal troops were insufficiently trained.

The Army Group A Offensive

The Operation Plan

Army Group A was to intervene during the third phase. Its forces were to jump off from the Taganrog-Artemovsk area, break through the Russian lines, and drive eastward across the Donets River as far as the Don bend, where they were to link up with the Sixth Army and Fourth Panzer Army spearheads driving down the Don. By this maneuver the Russians were to be trapped in the Don bend. Some allied forces were to provide flank protection — the Italians on both sides of Boguchar, the Romanians along the sector adjacent to the east. Other army group elements were to thrust southward, envelop Rostov, and establish bridgeheads south of the Don.

Chart 4. German Order of Battle—Russian Theater of War (Beginning of July 1942).

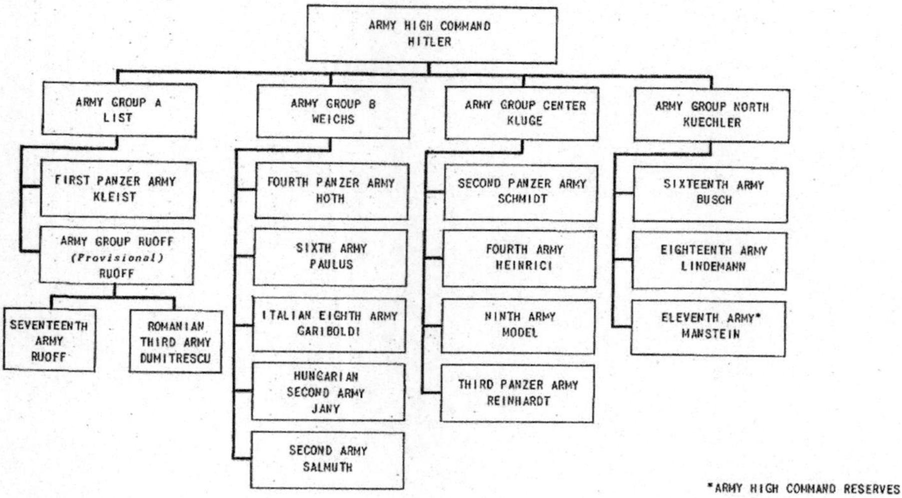

The Russian *Southwest, South* and *Caucasus Fronts* were commanded by Marshal Timoshenko, whose headquarters was in Stalingrad. Intelligence reports indicated that the defeats and losses suffered during the spring of 1942 seemed to have had little effect on the performance of the Russians. To explain the Russian soldier's attitude one had to understand his way of thinking in terms of tangible evidence. Since he ate better rations, saw more and more comrades joining him in combat, and noticed the relative stability of his sector, he probably felt that a definite change for the better had taken place since the last year's disastrous defeats.

Total German casualties for June had been slightly lower than those suffered in May, but higher by 10,000 than expected by the Army High Command. Approximately 157,000 reinforcements had arrived in the Russian theater, exceeding the number of losses by about 31,000 men.

In calculating future manpower distribution quotas for August, it was estimated that 70,000 replacements would be available in August 1942. Of this total 4,000 men would be needed in northern Finland, 10,000 for activating a special desert unit and as replacements for Rommel's casualties in North Africa, and 9,000 to make up for the July deficits of First Panzer and Seventeenth Armies. Of the remaining 47,000 men, 15,000 would go to Army Group A, 10,000 to Army Group B, 14,000 to Army Group Center, and 8,000 to Army Group North. In view of the scope of the summer offensive the Army Groups A and B quotas were not too reassuring.

On 1 July 1942 the total strength of the German Army field forces, including civilians with assimilated ranks, was 3,948,200; the number of officers included in this figure was 150,100.

The Army Group A Attack

On 7 July Field Marshal List assumed command of Army Group A, composed of the First Panzer, Eleventh, and Seventeenth Armies. Two days later his newly formed army group launched its attack with First Panzer Army thrusting toward Voroshilovgrad. The advance proceeded according to schedule. On 11 July an order signed by Timoshenko was captured. In it Timoshenko instructed his unit commanders to halt the German offensive by using delaying tactics. Since the Germans considered the Russian lower command echelon incapable of executing such a complicated mission, Army Group A issued orders to hit the Russians wherever they bogged down during the retreat and to seize as much of their materiel as possible.

By 13 July Army Group A had made such good progress that Hitler wanted to initiate the southward thrust toward the Caucasus. He therefore instructed List to advance southward in the direction of Konstantinovskaya, seize the Don-crossing facilities in that city and at Tsymlyanskaya, envelop the Russian forces west of the Donets and south of the Don by thrusting westward to Rostov, and cut off the Salsk-Stalingrad rail line. To carry out these missions Fourth Panzer Army and one infantry corps were transferred from Army Group B to Army Group A. The infantry divisions of Army Group A were to move up in forced marches so that they could assist the armored spearheads in preventing a Russian withdrawal.

Army Group B was to provide flank and rear protection for this maneuver by moving the Italian Eighth Army via Millerovo to the middle Don and covering the Chir River. On 15 July air reconnaissance information indicated that the Russians were speeding up the evacuation of the Donets Basin and were withdrawing south and southeastward.

German and Russian Weaknesses

Even before mid-July a shortage of POL began to hamper the movements of the spearhead divisions of Army Group B. Airlift operations were under consideration when, on 15 July, Fourth Panzer Army reported that its further progress would be assured by the capture of sizeable quantities of gasoline. Soon afterward, however, the Germans discovered that the dump they had seized intact contained only about 200 tons of fuel, not even enough to fill the tanks of one weak armored division.

By contrast, the First Panzer Army still had sufficient gasoline to continue its advance as scheduled. The Russian units opposing this army were disorganized; recently captured prisoners originated from as many as 30 different divisions and brigades. A tendency toward mass desertion became manifest at various points, such as at Millerovo, where 1 officer deserted with 500 enlisted men. Prisoner interrogation reports conveyed the impression that the Russian command had lost control in certain areas and that the confusion in the enemy ranks was spreading.

The Russian retreat was directed southward behind the Don with men and equipment crossing the river by ferries and across emergency bridges. At the same time trains out of Stalingrad were moving fresh troops westward. To counteract this maneuver Fourth Panzer Army was ordered to drive straight toward Konstantinovskaya. The army was to protect its flank in the Millerovo area and east of the lower Donets.

Directive No. 43

On 11 July Hitler issued Directive No. 43 which dealt with the German flank attack from the Crimea across the Kerch Strait into the Caucasus. After mopping up the Kerch Peninsula and Sevastopol — the latter had fallen on 1 July after a surprise landing of German assault detachments north of the fortress — Eleventh Army was to make preparations for crossing the Kerch Strait by early August.

Strong units were to land in the rear of the enemy's coastal fortifications and capture the ports of Anapa and Novorossiysk, thus depriving the Russians of these two naval bases. Most of the Eleventh Army forces were then to advance along the northern slopes of the Caucasus and seize the Maikop oil fields. A secondary thrust along the coastal highway via Tuapse was to be envisaged.

The Navy was to prepare crossing facilities, support the landing forces, and — together with the Luftwaffe — protect the operations from interference by the Russian Black Sea fleet. As part of the preparatory measures the Luftwaffe was to neutralize the Russian harbor installations and naval forces in the Black Sea. During the operation the Air Force was to give direct support to the landing forces. The possibility of employing airborne troops was to be taken into consideration.

An attempt to deceive the Russians was to be made by pretending that strong Eleventh Army forces were being shifted into the area north of the Sea of Azov. Counterintelligence agents were to parachute into the Maikop area to protect the oil fields, execute sabotage missions against the railroad lines leading to the Taman Peninsula, and destroy harbor and coastal installations.

Five days after issuing this directive Hitler moved to his newly established headquarters in the Ukraine, situated in a small triangular woods 10 miles northeast of Vinnitsa along the highway to Zhitomir. Hitler, his intimates, and his military staff — the field echelon of the Armed Forces Operations Staff — were billeted in log cabins and prefabricated barracks. The Army High Command set up its field headquarters in Vinnitsa proper.

The Continuation of Operations

On 16 July a conference of Army Group A commanders, their chiefs of staff, and the chief of staff of Fourth Air Force took place at Gorlovka. In his introductory remarks List stated that the advance had proceeded much faster than anticipated, since the army group forces had already reached the Don.

He also revealed that First Panzer Army, which had jumped off with 40 percent of its prescribed strength, now had only approximately 30 percent. There was no overall reduction in tank strength, because current losses were being replaced from new production. Each division of First Panzer Army had one tank battalion. Whereas the German divisions of Seventeenth Army were considered good, the Italian ones — with the exception of one classified as "quite good" — had not yet been involved in any fighting. This army had no nonorganic artillery units and was particularly anxious to receive some self-propelled assault guns. Four of the Fourth Panzer Army divisions were considered good, two very good. Their automotive equipment was very poor, and it was solely by expedients that the army kept rolling.

List then outlined his plan for future operations: the spearhead divisions of First Panzer Army were to cross the Donets near Kamensk and turn southward to Shakhty; some of the infantry units were to follow the course of the Donets and advance in a southeastward direction to protect the flank of the Fourth Panzer Army. The latter was to cross the Don near Konstantinovskaya and pivot west or southwestward according to the situation prevailing at that time. Infantry divisions were to follow with a minimum of delay to protect the army flank north of the Don, their deployment depending on developments in the Stalingrad area. On 18 July the Seventeenth Army was to launch an eastward or southeastward attack from the Kuybyshevo area. The double purpose of this attack was to tie down the Russians and close in on Rostov as soon as possible.

By 19 July the Russians were withdrawing the bulk of their forces toward Rostov. They covered their retreat by leaving strong rear guards, particularly opposite the right of Seventeenth Army. List intended to throw an ever-tightening ring around Rostov while Fourth Panzer Army forces were to send two armored corps across the Don and form bridgeheads as soon as possible. Their task was complicated by the fact that, when they finally reached the Don at the confluence of the Donets, the bridges had been blown and the Russians were entrenched on the south bank of the river. According to an intelligence estimate dated 18 July the Russians had been able to withdraw two-thirds of their infantry strength across the Don. No figures regarding the armored brigades were available. By that date the total number of prisoners taken by Army Group A was 54,000. Because of the disorganization and loss of materiel caused by the withdrawal, the combat strength of the Russian units had dropped considerably.

The Situation of the Other Army Groups by 20 July 1942

By 20 July only the infantry divisions of Sixth Army and the units of one panzer corps of Army Group B continued to advance in the direction of Stalingrad. The bulk of the German forces in the south were engaged in the Rostov operation under the control of Army Group A. [See *map 16*.] Flank protection along the Don up to the area east of Boguchar had been established. The Hungarian Second Army had taken over its designated sector south of Voronezh, while the Italian Eighth Army was marching northeastward from the Voroshilovgrad area in order to relieve the German forces in the Boguchar sector. The German Second Army front between Voronezh and Livny had defied a series of savage armored assaults in the vicinity of Voronezh.

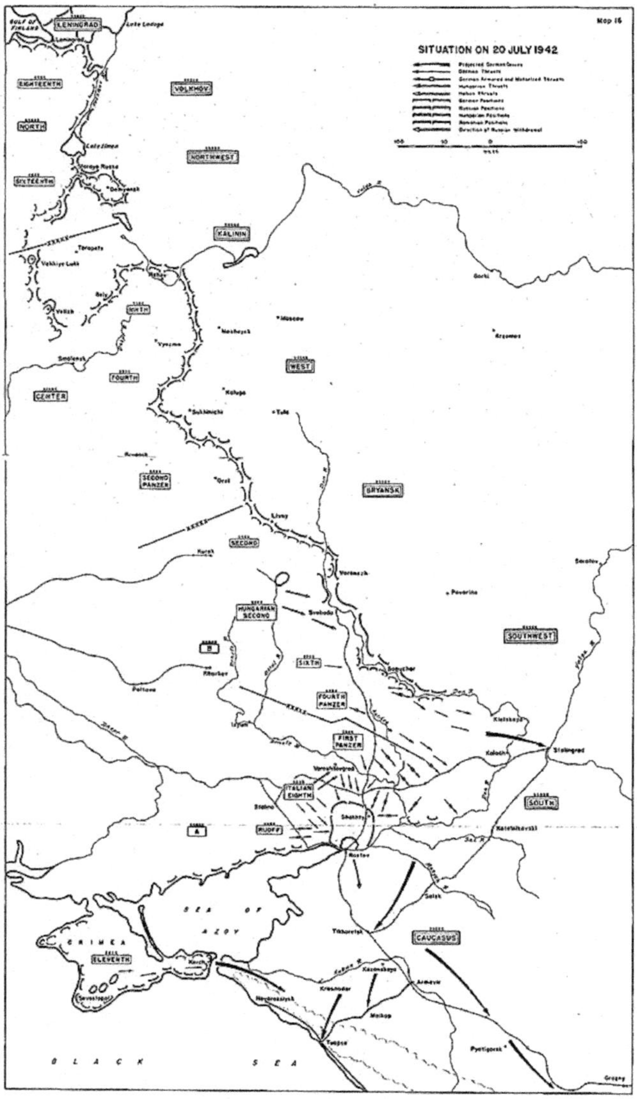

Map 16. Situation on July 1942.

Army Group Center had cleared the rear area of Fourth Army of partisan forces. The immediate threat deep in the flank of Ninth Army had also been eliminated. In the Toropets area the front had been strengthened, but here the grave potential danger persisted. Moreover, the Russians maintained continuous pressure along the entire front, particularly in the Second Panzer Army sector. Their local attacks seemed to be intended to relieve the Soviet forces in the south. However, by 20 July no critical situation had developed.

On the other hand the scope of the partisan operations behind the German front had changed noticeably. Whereas in the past the Russian command had used partisan units to soften up sectors that were subsequently to be attacked by regular troops from the front, guerrilla operations were now extending far into the German rear areas. Instead of employing large partisan units as in the past, the Russians committed more and more small raiding detachments and sabotage teams to cut off the German lines of communications and inflict losses on reinforcements moving to the front.

In addition three air forces had been formed out of flying units previously attached to individual armies. It was estimated that approximately 800 serviceable planes supported the Russian ground operations against Army Group Center.

Army Group North had to contend with local attacks, mainly at Staraya Russa and along the Volkhov, which had been repelled without too much difficulty. German preparations for an all-out assault on Leningrad progressed very slowly.

A mid-July report on the rehabilitation of the Army Groups Center and North units indicated that their personnel and materiel situation had improved considerably. Most of the infantry divisions had been reduced to six infantry battalions each and the artillery batteries to three guns each. Their mobility had improved with the arrival of horses and the introduction of more effective automotive repair procedures. The motor vehicle situation nevertheless remained very serious. Motorized elements averaged only half their authorized allowances; the majority of the divisions were capable only of limited-objective attacks.

Developments along the fronts of Army Group Center and North had no adverse effect on the German offensive in the south, and Hitler was able to concentrate on his attack plans without fear of diversion.

Directive No. 44 (21 July 1942)

Directive No. 44 pertained to warfare in northern Finland. The rapid progress of the operations in the south gave rise to the hope that the Soviet Union would soon be cut off from the Caucasus. As a result the Soviets would lose their oil resources, and the vital supply route for lend-lease shipments via Iran would be blocked. This blow, together with the loss of the entire Donets Basin, would be fatal to the Soviet military position.

In Hitler's opinion the next step would be to cut off the northern supply route by which the Allies kept the Soviet Union in the war. This had to be achieved by cutting the Murmansk railroad, which carried the bulk of lend-lease supplies during the winter months. [See *map 4*.] The importance of this route would increase when unfavorable weather prevented effective interception of the convoys in the Arctic Ocean.

The Twentieth Mountain Army, together with the Fifth Air Force, was therefore to seize the Murmansk railroad near Kandalaksha during the autumn of 1942. To facilitate this drive, Leningrad was to be captured in September at the latest, thus releasing Finnish forces, and one German mountain division was to be transferred to Finland.

A Finnish attack against Belomorsk was to be coordinated with the Twentieth Mountain Army offensive. In general, the most important task of the German forces in Finland remained the protection of the Petsamo mines, since Germany would probably have to cease the production of high-alloy steel for airplane and submarine engines without nickel shipments from Finland.

Oddly enough, the Finnish theater was the only one in which the Russians did not enjoy numerical superiority, since about 500,000 Finns and Germans faced approximately 300,000 Russians. However, contrary to the hopes expressed in Directive No. 44, this superiority could not be brought to bear because the prerequisite to any major operation — the capture of Leningrad-had not materialized; Army Group North had not proved sufficiently strong to seize the city. The German forces stationed in Finland did not influence the struggle for victory in the south, since no decisive action took place in the Finnish theater during 1942.

Directive No. 45 (23 July 1942)

On 21 July a recently captured Russian General Staff officer stated during his interrogation that the Russians intended to defend Rostov to the bitter end. At Army Group A headquarters, however, the impression prevailed that Russian resistance in the city would soon collapse because the garrison had lost much of its equipment and morale seemed to be low. This opinion was soon justified: Rostov fell on 23 July except for a few isolated nests of resistance in the western part of the city.

At this decisive moment Hitler began to show increasing interest in Stalingrad, the Volga city that was still approximately 100 miles from the German spearheads. The old Russian dictum that the motherland could not be defeated unless the invader got across the Volga seemed to have gained new significance in Hitler's mind. Several of his requests to divert two panzer divisions from the Rostov operation had previously been ignored in the heat of battle. Now he issued a direct order transferring ole panzer corps composed of two armored divisions from Fourth Panzer to Sixth Army and thus from the Caucasus to the Stalingrad operation. The concept of an orderly advance by consecutive phase lines, which had been followed since the beginning of the summer offensive, gave way to two simultaneous drives in divergent directions, one toward the oil lands, the other toward Stalingrad.

Directive No. 45, dealing with the continuation of the summer offensive, was issued on 23 July. In the preamble Hitler stated that during an offensive of little more than three weeks' duration, the long-range objectives set for the southern attack forces had been attained for all intents and purposes. Only a few small contingents of Timoshenko's armies had been able to escape and reach the other bank of the Don, where they would probably be reinforced from the Caucasus area. Another Russian force was being assembled in the Stalingrad area, where the Soviet command apparently intended to offer strong resistance.

As its next objective Army Group A was to encircle and annihilate those enemy forces south and southeast of Rostov which had escaped across the Don. Strong motorized units were to advance southwestward and cut the rail line connecting Tikhoretsk with Stalingrad.

In addition to losing the panzer corps transferred to Army Group B for the continuation of the drive toward Stalingrad, Army Group A was to release the Motorized Infantry Division Grossdeutschland which was to stop its advance as soon as it reached the Manych River and prepare its units for transfer to the West.

After accomplishing the mission of destroying the Russians south of the Don, Army Group A was to seize the Black Sea coast and thus paralyze the Russian Black Sea fleet. As soon as the movement of the main army group forces had progressed sufficiently, elements of Eleventh Army were to cross the Kerch Strait and advance along the Black Sea coastal road.

Another force, consisting of mountain and light divisions, was to cross the Kuban River and seize the elevated ground near Maikop and Armavir. The mountain divisions were to cross the western Caucasus passes and operate in conjunction with the forces advancing along the Black Sea coast. At the same time an attack force consisting of motorized elements was to move into the Grozny area, block the passes of the Ossetin and Georgian military roads leading across the central Caucasus, and then thrust along the Caspian toward Baku.

In addition to building up a defense' line along the Don, Army Group B was to advance toward Stalingrad, destroy the Russian forces assembling in that area, and block the corridor between the Don and the Volga. Motorized units were then to drive down the lower Volga toward Astrakhan and there block the principal branch of the river.

The Luftwaffe was to support the ground forces crossing the Don and advancing toward Tikhoretsk, and concentrate on destroying Timoshenko's forces and the city of Stalingrad. Occasional raids were to be conducted on Astrakhan, and shipping on the lower Volga was to be disrupted by the sowing of mines. During the further course of the operation the Air Force was to operate in conjunction with the ground forces advancing toward the Black Sea ports and protect them from Russian naval interference. Other Luftwaffe units were to support the thrust via Grozny to Baku.

Because of the crucial importance of Caucasus oil to the future German war effort, air attacks against oil wells or oil tanks were to be made only in case of absolute necessity. The Russians, however, were to be deprived of Caucasus oil deliveries by German air attacks that were to disrupt the rail and pipe lines and destroy the port installations.

The Navy was to lend its support during the crossing of the Kerch Strait and prevent the Russian Black Sea fleet from interfering, Moreover, the Navy was to organize light forces for disrupting Russian communications across the Caspian Sea.

The local operations previously planned for Army Groups Center and North were to be executed with a minimum of delay in order to produce the greatest possible effect on the opposing forces. Army Group North was to seize Leningrad by the beginning of September. For this purpose five divisions as well as the nonorganic medium and heavy artillery units of Eleventh Army were to be transferred from the Crimea to the north. Two German and two Romanian divisions were to be left in the Crimea temporarily.

Special attention was called to maintaining the secrecy of this directive.

Directive No. 45 resulted in the diversion of one motorized infantry division of Army Group A and five divisions of Eleventh Army from the Caucasus operation. Hitler's absolute confidence in victory induced him to leave in the Caucasus only sufficient forces to carry out a pursuit. The breach in the Russian front seemed so enormous that the shifting of a few divisions from Army Group A to Army Group B could not possibly affect the Caucasus drive. At the same time Hitler felt that such a move would guarantee a speedy advance to the lower Volga. The Russian forces assembling in the Stalingrad area would be overrun by the German spearhead divisions. After reaching the city the latter would immediately turn southeastward and continue their drive toward Astrakhan and the Caspian Sea.

Thus in a way Hitler reverted to the original concept on which the Operations Division of the Army High Command in October 1941 had based its plan for the Caucasus operation. According to this plan an offensive across the Caucasus Mountains could be envisaged only after the German flank along the lower Volga had been secured. The instructions issued in Directive No. 45 constituted a belated attempt to secure the flank along the Volga while relatively weak forces simultaneously advanced into the Caucasus.

German Shortages

Tanks

On 25 July the number of tanks in serviceable condition in the Army Group A area totaled 435 for 8 spearhead divisions or an average of 54 tanks per division. The best equipped panzer division had 109 tanks, the poorest 24.

Gasoline

The First Panzer Army's shortage of gasoline was so great that all motorized elements of the XLIV Infantry Corps were immobilized and the infantry units were unable to move because of the breakdown of the supply system.

By 25 July the gasoline situation had grown more critical than ever. When General Halder inquired at Army Group A headquarters why gasoline supplies were so unsatisfactory, he was told that the shortage was caused by bad weather, the long distances covered during the offensive, and the priority given to the Sixth Army for its assault on Stalingrad. Airlifted supplies had temporarily alleviated shortages, but the bulk of the essential POL requirements could not be moved by this mode of transportation. Since the available truck transportation had proved insufficient, an improvement could be expected only after the Stalino-Shakhty railroad had been repaired. Both panzer armies were temporarily immobilized by lack of gasoline.

Stalingrad Takes Priority Over the Caucasus (End of July 1942)

On 29 July the last rail line connecting the Caucasus with central Russia was blown up at several points by German armored elements. The Caucasus was isolated and Hitler seemed to believe that it was his for the taking. On the next day Army Group A was warned that the heavy fighting near Stalingrad would force the Army High Command to transfer one additional German corps and two Romanian ones with a number of divisions to Army Group B in order to assist Sixth Army in its struggle. The Fourth Panzer Army headquarters mightalso be pulled out to take charge of this support thrust, in which case only one of its corps would continue to participate in the drive toward Maikop under First Panzer Army control. The definite decision would depend on developments in the Stalingrad situation.

That same evening List told Hialder that the transfer of three corps, which apparently was under consideration, would endanger the eastern flank of the southward thrust into the Caucasus. Halder replied that the transfer would take place after the corps had reached the south bank of the Don and that their diversion in the direction of Stalingrad would actually constitute an alternative flank protection. List thereupon insisted that at least the Grossdeutschland Division remain with Army Group A to protect its flank against a Russian surprise thrust. Halder reassured him that the division would not be transferred to the West before mid-August. On the other hand, he had little hope of any further delay since Hitler had recently asked him: "What is the use of victories in Russia, if I lose western Europe?"

Halder continued by saying that Hitler did not believe the Army Group A flank would be in danger. List did not share this opinion. He wanted at least the Grossdeutschland Division in reserve. The army group commander then reminded Halder that the success of the Caucasus operation would depend primarily on the ready availability of POL. Hitler's plan struck him as a great gamble, since driving into the Caucasus with relatively weak forces, whose flank was not sufficiently protected, meant taking extraordinary risks.

While these conversations were taking place Russian troops were retreating into the Caucasus, with no sign of a new front being built up farther to the south. Stalin's order, that every officer and enlisted man would have to fight to the end without giving way, showed that the Russian command was aware of the seriousness of the situation.

On 31 July Halder sent an order to Army Groups A and B in which he confirmed the transfer of Fourth Panzer Army. In the introductory remarks he stated that with the severing of the rail communications between the Caucasus and Stalingrad the Russian front south of the Don was split wide open. The Russians in front of Army Group A would attempt to stop the German advance into the Caucasus, but it seemed doubtful whether they would have the necessary forces to do so. At Stalingrad they would throw all their resources into the battle to maintain control over their life line, the Volga.

Army Group A's immediate mission was to seize the Black Sea coast and thus paralyze the Russian fleet, which in turn would guarantee the security of the German lines of communications across that body of water.

On 1 August the Fourth Panzer Army with two German and one Romanian corps, a total of eight divisions plus corps and army troops, would be transferred from the Caucasus to the Stalingrad operation. Army Group A was to assemble its remaining motorized units under First Panzer Army for a drive in the direction of Maikop. From there some army elements were to cut off the withdrawing Russian forces, while others were to drive via Tuapse toward Batum. Some motorized units would have to protect the eastern flank of the army. Mountain divisions were to be employed for the thrusts across the passes in the Caucasus. The much contested Grossdeutschland Division would be available for eight days more, after which it was to prepare to entrain on 12 August at Stalino.

The mission of Army Group B was to remain unchanged.

Chapter 11 The Period of Stagnation (August-October 1942)

Developments to Mid-August 1942

German hopes that Army Group A would be able to encircle the enemy forces in the region immediately south of the lower Don were unfulfilled. The Russians evaded destruction by withdrawing to the Caucasus, whereupon the Germans seized Krasnodar and Maikop against light resistance. Their divisions followed the retreating Russians closely and penetrated into the western Caucasus up to the mountain passes. Fully realizing the danger which threatened them the Russians successfully blocked the only road leading over the mountains to Tuapse.

In the Crimea elements of Eleventh Army prepared the crossing of the Kerch Strait, while the bulk of the army forces entrained for Leningrad. In the central Caucasus area First Panzer Army moved in the direction of the Grozny oil fields, but very slowly being greatly handicapped by a shortage of gasoline at the very time when Russian resistance was stiffening.

The operations of Army Group A thus gave the impression of a dispersed effort with 20 divisions advancing along a front of more than 500 miles. The army group's two points of main effort — northeast of Tuapse and at Pyatigorsk — were 200 miles apart. Most of the air support units had been shifted to the Stalingrad area after the army group had crossed the Don. The supply situation was very unsatisfactory. Because of the shortage of rolling stock, the only rail line leading from the Rostov area into the Caucasus could not satisfy more than the most elementary requirements, and insignificant shipments across the Sea of Azov failed to alleviate the shortages.

The situation of Army Group B was equally disappointing. The Russians in the Don Bend took advantage of the slowness of the Sixth Army advance — caused by the 10-day lack of gasoline and a momentary shortage of ammunition — and suddenly offered strong resistance. Although this maneuver led to the encirclement of some Russian forces, it also helped the Soviet command to gain time for the strengthening of the defenses of Stalingrad. In any event, by 18 August the Germans had cleared the Don bend and prepared for the final reduction of the city. After some confusion, caused by an almost 1800 turn of its forces, Fourth Panzer Army had moved into the area north of Kotelnikovski and was ready to push toward Stalingrad from the south. Flank protection along the Don was provided by the Italian Eighth and Hungarian Second Armies, which — supported by a few German divisions-occupied wide sectors. [See *chart 5*.] The Romanian Third Army, scheduled to take over the sector on both sides of Kletskaya, was unable to take its place because of rail transportation difficulties. For the time being Sixth Army had to assign German divisions to this sector which in turn reduced the striking power of the assault forces at Stalingrad. During the preparatory attacks the Luftwaffe gave close support and simultaneously carried out some strategic bombing missions against the lines of communications connecting Stalingrad with Moscow.

The German supply situation was alarmingly bad. The assault forces were dependent on a single, low-capacity railroad which ran eastward from the Donets Basin. Available truck transportation was insufficient to bridge the long distances between the supply bases and the spearhead units.

Hitler had ordered Army Group Center to launch a pincers attack against the Russian salient around Sukhinichi. The two armored divisions of Fourth Panzer Army that had been transferred from Army Group B during the second half of July because of the shortage of POL in the south were to participate in this attack. Field Marshal von Kluge strongly protested against this mission, indicating that the consolidation of the Rzhev front was far more urgent. On 7 August a conference at Hitler's headquarters near Vinnitsa ended with Kluge's exclaiming that he would not disobey a direct order to launch the Sukhinichi attack, but that the responsibility would be Hitler's.

The attack failed despite all German efforts. Soon afterward Army Group Center became engaged in such heavy fighting that air and ground reinforcements had to be diverted from other parts of the theater. Finally, strong Russian attacks against Ninth Army at Rzhev were repelled in sharp local actions. Meanwhile Army Group North was continuing its preparations for the attack on Leningrad.

The distribution of Luftwaffe units corresponded to that of the ground forces. Of some 1,230 operational aircraft available in the Russian theater in mid-August 1942, approximately 720 supported Army Groups A and B.

Chart 5. German Order of Battle—Russian Theater of War (12 August 1942)

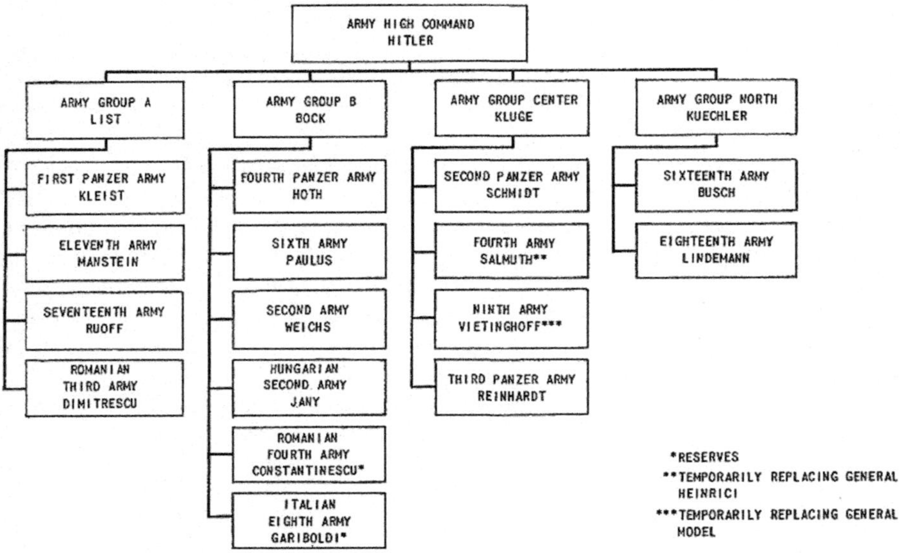

The Eastern Intelligence Division estimated overall Russian strength on 15 August as follows:

Units	Total*	Russian western front*	Reserves*	Other fronts*
Infantry Divisions	287	134	73	80
Infantry Brigades	142	47	66	29
Cavalry Divisions	33	7	20	6
Armored Brigades	131	34	86	11

*Equivalent of full-strength units.

Personnel and Other Problems (16-18 August 1942)

In a letter to Marshal Keitel, General Halder again drew the attention of the Armed Forces High Command to the seriousness of the Army's personnel situation. According to recent estimates the Russian theater would be short of at least 120,000 replacements by 1 November 1942. The 400,000 men who would be inducted and trained in the interim period might compensate for current losses, but would not reduce this deficit, and the requirements of other theaters had not been taken into account. In any event, the estimated shortage of more than 700,000 replacements would involve serious risks.

In addition to the vexing personnel shortages at the front, the partisan problem had assumed such importance that Hitler issued Directive No. 46 on 18 August in order to standardize German operating procedures against the enemy in the rear areas. In this directive the Fuehrer ordered every German in partisan-infested areas to participate in the antiguerrilla struggle. However, though the new policy was well intended, its enforcement suffered from a chronic shortage of personnel and equipment which permitted great numbers of partisans to escape from one well-set trap after another.

This same personnel shortage created another problem. Germany's allies, who had had to bear such heavy burdens during the summer offensive in order to supplement the Wehrmacht's strength, now stood along greatly exposed sectors of the Don front. In this connection Hitler was apprehensive lest Stalin repeat his classic maneuver of 1920: an attack across the Don near Serafimovich in the direction of Rostov, similar to the one the Bolsheviks had launched against Wrangel's White Russian Army with such devastating results. The Fuehrer felt that the Italian Eighth Army which was responsible for the security of this Don sector would be incapable of stopping such an attack. He therefore urged repeatedly that the 22d Panzer Division be withdrawn from Stalingrad and rehabilitated behind the Italian Eighth Army sector.

The Romanians who were providing the largest contingent among Germany's allies were the subject of a memorandum Halder sent to Army Groups A and B on 18 August. Those Romanian units assigned to Army Group A — with the exception of the four mountain divisions committed in the Crimea and Caucasus — were to secure the area west and southwest of Astrakhan after the Russian Black Sea coast had been cleared and the fleet eliminated. The plans, however, would be subject to approval by Marshal Antonescu who was to assume command of a newly activated Romanian army group composed of the Romanian Third and Fourth and German Sixth Armies. The army group would secure the German flank along the lower Volga after the fall of Stalingrad.

The Dieppe raid, 18-19 August 1942, came as a complete surprise and somewhat of a shock to the Germans. Hitler's immediate reaction was to strengthen his defenses in the West, an objective that could be attained only at the expense of the Russian theater. The personnel and equipment diverted to North Africa, which was more than justified by Rommel's brilliant exploits, also constituted a drain on Germany's limited resources. A few weeks later Hitler directed the diversion of more troops to reinforce the Crete garrison. He believed that a large-scale Allied invasion of the Mediterranean island fortress was imminent and ordered the crack 22d Infantry Division transferred from the Crimea to Crete.

The Situation in the Caucasus (Second Half of August 1942)

On 19 August Army Group A headquarters estimated the situation in the Caucasus as follows: Russian resistance in the northwestern parts of the Caucasus Mountains was extremely stubborn. Approximately 20 Russian reserve divisions known to be in the Caucasus had not yet been committed for the defense of this area, perhaps because they were insufficiently trained and equipped. The fact that the Red Army considered Caucasian replacements as unreliable might have delayed their employment.

There was no indication of any assembly of Russian forces in the Astrakhan area. The Russians apparently did not intend to threaten the flank and rear of Army Groups A and B from that side. On the contrary, repeated air attacks on Elista — the German-held town in the gap between Army Groups A and B — semed to indicate that the Russians were worried about a German thrust toward Astrakhan.

In its conclusions the report stated that the Russians seemed to employ delaying tactics in the Caucasus. They were continuing the evacuation of industrial machinery and military forces. Because of the advanced season, however, it was not to be expected that they would completely evacuate the Transcaucasus. In carrying out their mission, the Army group forces would have to face a hard and time-consuming struggle along the entire Caucasus front even though sizeable Russian forces had been destroyed during the past weeks. The steadily growing lines of communications, the vast territory to be kept under control, the scarcity of motor fuel, and the increasing terrain obstacles were the principal factors that would slow down the advance.

Two days later a German propaganda release proudly announced that at 1100 on 21 August a detachment of mountain troops had raised the German flag on Mount Elbrus. But the conquest of the 18,481-foot peak of the Caucasus Mountains did not alleviate the oil shortage.

The acute shortage of gasoline was at this point the primary cause for the delay in the advance, because it prevented the heavy truck columns from moving up supplies from distant railheads. Instead, the Germans had to use short, undamaged or repaired sections of rail lines and establish truck shuttle services between detraining and entraining points. The delays incurred by transshipping bulky supplies were reflected in the unsatisfactory progress of the army group forces.

By 28 August the Russian forces opposite Army Group A had set up their defenses. The Red Army had regained control over its units, reorganized its forces, and moved up reinforcements from Transcaucasia, Iran, and also — via the Caspian — from central Russia. By the end of August strong Russian ground forces, having the advantage of local air superiority, blocked the access to Novorossiysk along well-built, deeply echeloned defense lines and launched occasional counterattacks. The Russians also were on the offensive along the Tuapse road, where German motorized units were restricted to the few existing mountain roads.

The advance of the German mountain corps was delayed by smaller, but equally well-entrenched forces. The Italian Alpine Corps that was to participate in the thrust across the Caucasus failed to arrive, apparently because the Italian Eighth Army refused to transfer the corps to the respective German army command. Along the Terek River bend the Russians had concentrated strong ground forces that had the advantage of local air superiority.

At the end of August the Russians were employing 10-12 divisions along the Black Sea coast, 1 or 2 in the mountains, and 8 divisions along the Terek front for a total of 19-22 divisions. Additional forces and replacements were arriving. The Soviets seemed to be determined to hold their Caucasus positions until the outbreak of winter. Nevertheless, they were continuing to evacuate industrial and agricultural supplies and machinery from the Caucasus area.

On 31 August Hitler, who was very dissatisfied with the situation at Army Group A, received Marshal List, its commander, at his headquarters. List explained that he intended to continue his thrusts into the western Caucasus at three points:

1. Near Anapa and Novorossiysk and, after the seizure of these two cities, along the coastal road;
2. On both sides of the mountain road to Tuapse; and

3. Along the Sukhumi road, where the mountain troops were to make their main effort.

In the central Caucasus, List suggested, the First Panzer Army should destroy the Russian forces in the Terek bend and seize the Grozny oil fields beyond that river. Hitler approved these plans.

General Warlimont visited Army Group A and a number of its subordinate headquarters during the last days of August and reported that morale was high. The responsible commanders apparently felt confident that they would be capable of accomplishing their missions.

The Opening of the Battle for Stalingrad (End of August 1942)

Early on 23 August one corps of General Paulus' Sixth Army crossed the Don in force and reached the Volga north of Stalingrad that same evening. On the following day heavy Russian counterattacks endangered the German toehold which, however, was strengthened by the arrival of additional units on the west bank of the Volga.

Fourth Panzer Army and Sixth Army had the mission of seizing Stalingrad and securing the lower Volga. The two armies totaled 25 divisions, some of which were greatly understrength. The Russian *Sixty-Second Army,* composed of some 8 divisions under General Chuikov, was responsible for the defense of Stalingrad. The Germans had local air superiority, being supported by some 1,000 aircraft of all types. During the last days of August, the Germans advanced with relative ease through the outer suburbs of Stalingrad.

While this advance was proceeding in a satisfactory manner, Hitler continued to be preoccupied with protecting both flanks of the forces driving across the Don toward Stalingrad. He ordered one of the few remaining motorized infantry divisions of Army Group A detached from the drive into the Caucasus and shifted to the Elista area west of Astrakhan to secure the growing gap between Army Groups A and B.

On the other flank the Russians attempted to gain another bridgehead against the Italian Eighth Army deployed along the Don. Although the Russians attacked cautiously and with only relatively small forces, the Italian right withdrew apparently without offering resistance. The Russians thereupon moved a. guard cavalry corps into the area of penetration and two days of heavy counterattacks were required before the situation was restored on 27 August. Two additional Russian bridgeheads existed opposite the Hungarian Second Army which held the Don sector adjacent to the Italian left. Farther to the north the Germans observed that the Russians were gradually transferring attack forces from the Voronezh to the Stalingrad area.

On 28 August Generaloberst (Gen.) Wolfram von Richthofen, Commander, VIII Air Corps, made a personal reconnaissance of the region, during which he consulted with the commanders of Fourth Panzer and Sixth Armies. The consensus was that no interference from strong enemy forces was to be expected in the Stalingrad area. Luftwaffe reconnaissance aircraft flying northward were unable to discover any Russian forces in a terrain that offered little cover or concealment. Richthofen's general impression was that the Russian command was disorganized in this area.

Halder, however, contested the accuracy of this information and Hitler thereupon decided to move the forward echelon of Army Group B headquarters far to the front and airlift infantry replacements to Sixth Army in order to speed up the conquest of Stalingrad.

The German Leadership Crisis (September 19421)

Throughout the summer of 1942 General Halder [Chief, Army General Staff] had noted in his diary that he was experiencing increasing difficulties in working with Hitler. The latter's chronic tendency of underrating Russian capabilities had gradually assumed grotesque proportions, finally developing into a positive danger. In fact, the situation had become more and more intolerable for the military. According to Halder, it was almost impossible to accomplish anything useful. Hitler's exercise of command was characterized by pathological reactions to impressions of the moment and by his complete lack of understanding of command procedures.

Under such circumstances the military men in top-level positions were bound to be the first victims of any unfavorable turn of events. As early as 30 August, for instance, while German progress was still quite satisfactory, Halder noted that the Army leaders had once again been the target of the Fuehrer's abuse. According to Hitler, they suffered from intellectual conceit, mental inflexibility, and a complete incapacity of grasping essentials.

During the first days of September the military events continued to be favorable for the Germans. On the first day of the month German troops succeeded in crossing the Kerch Strait and landing on the Taman Peninsula. After seizing Anapa, they joined in the drive along the Black Sea coast toward Novorossiysk. A few days later Marshal List [Commander, Army Group A] suggested that the bulk of IL Mountain Corps engaged in the central Caucasus be pulled out after leaving some blocking units near the passes. This mountain corps could be more advantageously employed in the Maikop area to achieve a breakthrough toward the coast. Since he did not share List's opinion, Hitler sent General Jodi [Chief, Armed Forces Operations Staff] to investigate on the spot and discuss the matter with List.

Upon his return Jodl reported that List's plan seemed sound and he advocated its implementation. In the subsequent argument Hitler accused List of not having followed orders and of having dispersed his forces over much too wide an area. In his reply Jodl tried to prove that List had followed to the letter all orders he had been given. The Fuehrer thereupon became extremely irritated and asked that his orders to List, including notes of verbal instructions, be submitted to him. In addition, he instructed that court stenographers be brought from Berlin to Vinnitsa to take down the minutes of all future military conversations and conferences.

On 9 September Hitler was informed by Halder that List intended to let the Russians attack the German bridgeheads across the Terek until their strength had been exhausted, and that he would then resume the offensive. Hitler considered this idea as fundamentally wrong since its execution would imperil the very existence of the German bridgeheads against which the Russians were moving a constant stream of reinforcements.

This last misunderstanding, coming after so many similar conflicts, led Hitler to consider a number of changes in top-level positions. List was asked to hand in his resignation, which he did on the evening of 9 September. For the time being Hitler decided to assume command of Army Group A in person, so that in addition to his civilian functions he now held the position of an army group commander in Russia, commander in chief of the German Army, and commander in chief of the German armed forces. Three top echelons of military command has thus been unified in a singular manner.

The chief of staff of Army Group A, General von Greiffenberg, remained at army group headquarters at Stalino as "head of the message center and transmitting agent for orders." Halder was notified on the same day that Hitler intended to relieve him because he "was no longer equal to the psychic demands of his position." General der Infanterie (Lt. Gen.) Kurt Zeitzler replaced Halder on 24 September.

The conflict between Hitler and Jodl — brought to the surface by Jodl taking List's side — was so deep that Hitler considered the dismissal of his closest military adviser. He was to be replaced by Paulus who a few months later was to play such a tragic role when he surrendered the remnants of the Sixth Army at Stalingraq. Keitel's position as Chief of Staff, Armed Forces High Command, was also jeopardized with Goering trying to replace him with one of his own protégés. General Warlimont, Jodl's immediate assistant, fell in disfavor and was sent on extended leave from which he did not return to duty until his superior — who had survived the turmoil — recalled him after the Allied landings in North Africa in November 1942.

In the opinion of an eyewitness who was at Hitler's headquarters at Vinnitsa during the period under review, the crisis which developed in September 1942 was far more than a conflict over the misinterpretation of orders and was by no means settled with the relief or temporary absence of a few military men. Hitler himself showed signs of such deep and lasting depression that the causes must have been less superficial than was generally assumed. For the first time the Fuehrer seemed to have realized that Germany could not win the Russian campaign and would therefore lose the entire war. It took him many weeks before he was able to restore his outward composure, and then he achieved it only by immersing himself in the innumerable military and political details of his daily work.

Faulty Intelligence and its Interpretation

On 9 September the Eastern Intelligence Division submitted an estimate according to which the Russians seemed to have no sizeable reserves along the entire front. On the contrary, in order to form points of main effort, they had to shift units over long distances. Because of insufficient training and a shortage of equipment the troops still available and the units presently in the process of activation would probably not be ready for commitment for some time. Halder accepted this estimate and concluded that the Russians lacked strategic reserves.

Such favorable information was always well received by Hitler who, on 13 September, ordered Army Group B to launch a pursuit in the event Russian resistance north of Stalingrad should collapse. At the same time the existing plans for a thrust toward Astrakhan were to be reexamined and data regarding their execution submitted. Hitler then instructed the army group commander to launch local attacks at the boundary of Sixth Army and the Italian Eighth Army, correct some dents in the German lines in the Don bend, and construct a switch position behind the German front west of Voronezh. Obviously, the Fuehrer took great interest in every tactical detail concerning the army group adjacent to his own.

The German Offensive Grinds to a Halt (26 September 1942)

None of the objectives of the summer offensive were attained by the Germans. Although Army Group A made local gains in the direction of Tuapse and Grozny, these minor successes were not decisive. The army group had exhausted its strength. The only major oil fields that had fallen into German hands — those at Maikop — were almost completely destroyed. In 1941 their output had amounted to 2.5 million tons or 8 per cent of the total USSR production. The oil wells and refineries were demolished. Only two storage tanks and a few stretches of pipeline were found intact.

Army Group B's assault on Stalingrad met with unexpected resistance. Beginning 14 September the Russian garrison received a steady flow of reinforcements, and on 16 September Sixth Army under General Paulus was given control of all German units that had entered the city, including some Fourth Panzer Army elements. As early as 20 September Halder noted that the attack forces were gradually succumbing to exhaustion. But for the next two months the battle raged within the city, marked by feats of magnificent heroism on both sides. The Russian toehold west of the Volga was split into four separate bridgeheads with a total frontage of some 15 miles running through the built-up downtown area. The main 5-mile bridgehead held by the Russians had a depth varying from 600-3,000 feet on the west bank of the river.

During these weeks of house-to-house fighting Stalingrad lost its initial significance as a flank protection anchor for the Caucasus offensive. Instead of a means to an end, Stalingrad had become an end in itself. More and more troops poured into the city from both sides. After the Romanian Third Army had finally arrived and taken up its positions along the Don between the Italian Eighth and the German Sixth Armies, Paulus was able to shift into the city those German divisions that had hitherto protected his flank.

The Romanians felt none too happy about the new assignment they had received. In an inquiry addressed to the Operations Division of the Army High Command on 24 September, they pointed out that the Romanian Third Army would have to defend a 105-mile sector with 69 battalions, or an average of 1.5 miles per battalion. Considering that the Romanians had no mobile forces for counterattacks and no self-propelled antitank guns, the Romanian line was very weak. If present plans were implemented, the situation of the Romanian Fourth Army would be even worse, since only 33 battalions would have to hold a frontage of 250 miles, an average of almost 8 miles per battalion. This army would be scarcely strong enough to keep its sector under observation.

The Germans did not attach too much importance to these alarming weaknesses; in their reply they pointed out to the Romanians that everything would depend on the outcome of the battle of Stalingrad. They also answered evasively the other Romanian inquiries regarding German armored support, the availability of motor transportation, etc.

The fighting in the sectors of Army Groups Center and North had resumed with new intensity. Strong Russian attacks against Second and Third Panzer Armies and Ninth and Eighteenth Armies were repelled only with considerable effort. The Russians were by no means at the end of their strength. On the contrary, despite the life-and-death struggle raging in the south, they were attempting to gradually regain the initiative in these parts of the theater. The German Eleventh Army forces earmarked for the attack on Leningrad had to be committed to wail off these Russian assaults, so that the all-out offensive on the city of Leningrad — the second major objective of the summer of 1942 — had to be abandoned.

The German offensive had bogged down everywhere and the imminence of the muddy period, quite apart from all other factors, made its resumption impractical. The personnel situation in the Russian theater, which had slightly improved until the end of July, had deteriorated considerably since then.

German Personnel Strength Variations in the Russian Theater (Summer 1942)

Month of 1942	Losses*	Reinforcements**	Strength	
			Increase	Decrease
May	134, 230	158, 900	24, 670	--------
June	126, 050	157, 500	31, 450	--------
July	156, 600	177, 800	21, 200	--------
August	256, 100	89, 750	--------	166, 350
September	185, 000	83, 750	--------	101, 250
October	130, 100	97, 200	--------	32, 900

* Including personnel transferred out of the theater.
** Including convalescents returned to duty.

German Estimates in October and Early November 1942

General Zeitzler, the new Army Chief of Staff, indicated at the daily situation conference on 9 October that the complete calm along wide stretches of the front could not yet be interpreted with complete certainty. Either the Russians had withdrawn a number of units to rehabilitate them or they were transferring them to some other points for a winter offensive. Under these circumstances it would be particularly important that the German army groups form reserves for such a contingency.

Army Group A

Intelligence agents informed their contacts in the Army Group A area that American and British materiel and technicians were arriving at Baku, Batum, and in the Transcaucasus. The disposition of the Russian forces in the Caucasus, as plotted from radio intercepts, was as follows:

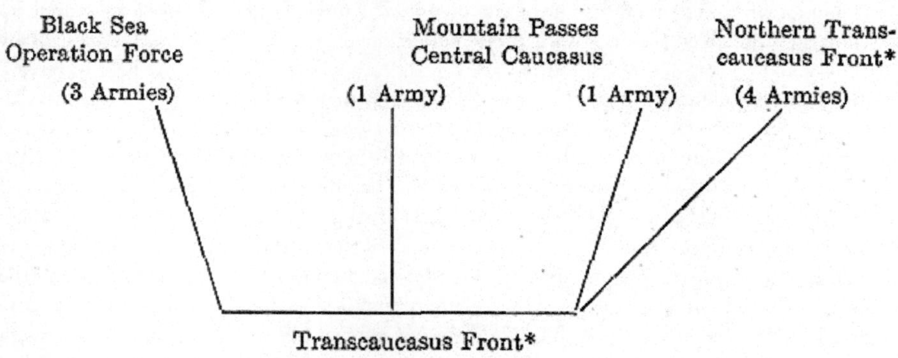

*Equivalent to an army group.

During the first half of November there was a notable increase in reinforcements arriving in the eastern Caucasus area. According to various reports 3 divisions had arrived in Baku, 4 were transferred from Baku to Tiflis, 1 to Makhachkala on the Caspian, and 18 additional troop transports were on the way to the latter.

Army Group B

By mid-October Army Group B received many reports of troop concentrations in the Saratov area, which seemed to confirm that the Russians were making initial preparations for an offensive near Stalingrad. Air reconnaissance had so far failed to confirm these reports, but this was by no means a proof of their inaccuracy, since Russian concentrations had often gone unnoticed from the air until practically completed. In any event, the Germans were then too deeply committed in Stalingrad to turn back from an operation which had become an obsession with Hitler.

Reports from the front indicated that traffic in the Serafimovich area increased nightly, but Army Group B interpreted these movements simply as supply traffic serving to replenish stocks consumed during recent combat actions. It was precisely from this point that the Russian counteroffensive was launched on 19 November.

On 26 October Sixth Army reported confidently that, even though strong Russian resistance might prevent the army from completing the seizure of Stalingrad before 10 November, the city would be completely in German hands by that date.

In his conversations with the men in his immediate entourage Hitler often revealed his concern over a major Russian offensive, perhaps a winter offensive, across one of the allied sectors along the Don in the direction of Rostov. Russian troop movements and the construction of bridges in the Italian and Romanian sectors were indications of the Soviet command's offensive intentions. Hitler ordered some newly organized Luftwaffe ground divisions moved up to strengthen the allied sectors. With these reinforcements on the line, a few German Army divisions could be transferred behind the allied positions, where they could be held in reserve during their rehabilitation. Meanwhile, he ordered the air force to bomb intensively Russian bridge sites and presumed staging areas in the forests along the northern bank of the Don.

The intelligence summary for the second half of October reported the arrival of Russian reinforcements in the Kletskaya-Serafimovich area. The cross-river traffic near Kletskaya had increased, and railroad traffic northwest of Stalingrad had grown heavier. So far none of these reinforcements had been committed in battle. Radio silence in the Saratov area was complete. Similar indications of troop concentrations were observed opposite the Italian Eighth and the Hungarian Second Armies along the Don, where several bridges had been constructed to consolidate Russian-held bridgeheads. The Germans did not yet know whether the forces arriving in the Saratov area were combat-ready units or new ones in the stage of activation or training. The mere presence of these units however, was significant if considered in connection with potential Russian offensive intentions.

By 3 November intelligence sources reported that the Russians were preparing an attack against the Romanian Third Army. Whether this offensive would be a diversion or an operation with a far-reaching objective was not known. During the following days the Russians seemed to carry out large-scale movements opposite the Romanian Third Army. On the night of 8-9; November some 2,000-2,500 vehicles had been observed in the area north of Kletskaya. The establishment of the headquarters of the *Southwest Front* northwest of nearby Serafimovich was considered as definite proof of offensive preparations in this area.

The Estimate of 6 November

This convincing evidence of an impending Russian attack in the Army Group B area was apparently not properly interpreted by the Eastern Intelligence Division. In an estimate dated 6 November this agency expressed the opinion that the Russians were concentrating their forces opposite Army Group Center. Whether they would be capable of conducting another major operation in the south seemed doubtful; in any event, indications for the launching of such an offensive in the south in the near future were lacking. That the Russians had altogether abandoned their previous intentions of thrusting across the Don could not be verified.

The following reasons were given for a major Russian offensive on the Army Group Center front:

1. There was a definite need for a rapid success that could be achieved more easily in the center than in the south. Moreover, such an offensive would definitely dispel the German threat to Moscow;
2. The favorable course of the Russian front opposite Army Group Center offered advantageous jump off positions for a Red Army offensive against Smolensk;
3. In the event of success the offensive could be pursued to the Baltic, thus cutting off the German forces in the Leningrad area; and
4. Any operation across the Don, directed against German-held Rostov, would present greater logistical and technical problems than the one in the center. Even if such an offensive in the south succeeded, it would destroy only the southern wing of the German forces without offering the strategic possibilities of the thrust in the center. This did not imply that the Russians would not launch a secondary offensive across the Don.

According to available information the Russian preparation for the offensive in the center had not sufficiently advanced to permit its start before the muddy season. The arrival of German reinforcements and German radio deception -were given as reasons for having delayed the attack. Although the Russian forces so far identified in assembly areas would appear relatively small for an operation against Smolensk, this factor had little significance since motorized units could be moved up within a short time. Moreover, some of the assembled forces might not have been identified. Also, the Russians had often shown a tendency of overextending themselves by reaching for objectives that were not properly related to their available strength.

During recent offensive operations the Russians had first launched infantry attacks to open gaps in the minefields and had then committed their tanks for penetrations in depth. They had shown remarkable skill in dissimulating their offensive plans by excellent deception which made it difficult to estimate the extent of their preparations. Whether the Russian offensive would be launched on 7 November, as stated by Russian prisoners, was doubtful. Actually, its start would depend both on Russian preparedness and weather conditions. Taking into account all known factors, the launching of the offensive on the Army Group Center front could be expected with the start of freezing temperatures.

This estimate, made only 13 days before the Russian counteroffensive was launched in the south, showed that the Russians had succeeded in deceiving the Germans as to their true intentions. The reasoning used to prove the theory of an offensive in the center rather than in the south was an interesting example of intelligense rationalization.

On 12 November — seven days before the Russians jumped off — the Eastern Intelligence Division correctly estimated the threat to the Romanian Third Army, but arrived at the conclusion that the scope of the offensive would be limited to cutting the railroad line that connected Stalingrad with the west. The purpose of such a Russian operation would be to force a German withdrawal from Stalingrad and to resume the Volga boat traffic.

The Oil of the Caucasus

German Efforts at Production

Late in September German counterintelligence personnel were still planning *a coup de main* in order to spare certain important installations in the Baku area from complete Soviet destruction. German agents were to infiltrate behind the Russian lines, contact reliable persons employed at the respective installations, and prepare so-called fake demolitions. The latter would be easily repaired once the Germans had seized the respective area.

By early November the unfavorable course of events forced German counterintelligence to switch from fake-demolition attempts to real acts of sabotage. The most successful sabotage act was perpetrated at Grozny, where parachute agents blew up a large Russian ammunition dump, causing great damage and heavy casualties.

The Oil Brigade Caucasus was meanwhile continuing its efforts against heavy odds. In a memorandum dated 29 October Oil Brigade Headquarters complained about the situation at Ilskaya, a town southwest of Krasnodar. There, the German outpost line went straight through the oil fields. Inspecting officers from Oil Brigade Headquarters had requested the responsible tactical commander to advance his defensive positions by 900 yards. This request had gone to the chief of staff of Seventeenth Army, who expressed his concern over any such action since German forces faced greatly superior Russian units in that sector. From the German point of view this refusal was all the more regrettable because the Russians had apparently left their drills intact and production could have started sooner there than elsewhere.

The Ilskaya wells produced no oil while under German control. Neither did most of the other wells at Maikop or elsewhere in the Caucasus. Reviewing the German effort to exploit the Caucasus oil resources in his economic survey of 1942, General Thomas stated that the staff of Oil Brigade Caucasus had taken the continuance of the German advance into the Caucasus for granted. Expecting that they would be able to exploit the rich Grozny oil fields, the Oil Brigade personnel had failed to concentrate their efforts on the Maikop and other fields, which had been in German hands for several months. The technical difficulties encountered by the Germans because of Russian demolition of oil wells and transportation facilities were far greater than anticipated. After inspecting the Maikop area the technical experts reported that it would be more effective to use the drilling equipment and personnel of the Oil Brigade in Romania or near Vienna than in the Caucasus.

This suggestion was not accepted. Instead, the Oil Brigade operated at Maikop and elsewhere under precarious circumstances, and the Armavir-Maikop railroad was not reconditioned until too late. When the brigade finally struck oil, its commander was ordered to evacuate and blow up the laboriously reconstructed installations; the small quantities of oil produced could not be taken along due to the lack of transport facilities.

Russian Supplies

In reviewing the Russian oil supply, General Thomas expressed the opinion that blocking the Volga at Stalingrad would not by itself suffice to reduce the Soviet Union's POL supplies to such a degree that it would impair the Russian conduct of operations in 1943. This could be achieved only if all supplies from Baku were cut off completely by the spring of 1943. In this case Russian stocks would be exhausted by the summer of 1943. The Soviet armed forces and civilian economy would be severely handicapped without oil from the Caucasus. Since approximately 70 percent of the total high-octane gasoline consumed in the Soviet Union was produced from Baku oil, the seizure of the Baku wells and not the occupation of the lower Volga from Stalingrad to Astrakhan would lead to extensive paralysis of the Russian Air Force.

This report, like so many others by which General Thomas tried to warn the men who were responsible for Germany's military planning, served only one practical purpose: to make its author even more unpopular in National Socialist circles.

Local Engagements (October-Mid-November 1942)

During October and early November the strength of Army Groups A and B was further dissipated in local engagements on the road to Tuapse, in the Pyatigorsk area, and particularly within Stalingrad. [See *map 17.*] During heavy fighting the Germans achieved some local gains and improved their positions, but in many instances they had to ward off Russian counterattacks. These local engagements, however, had no effect on the overall situation. The autumn muddy season, which started in mid-October, brought no relief to the weary troops.

The Romanian and Italian sectors were still far from strong. No German divisions were available to support the allied sectors in case of emergency, because the motorized divisions originally earmarked for this purpose were fully engaged in the battle for Stalingrad and could not be released by the Sixth Army. On the contrary, on 2 November the Fuehrer approved Zeitzler's suggestion to pull organic engineer battalions out of certain divisions in the south and commit them at Stalingrad. A request to stop the offensive for eight days to give the German troops a much-needed rest was disapproved by Hitler. The supply situation, particularly in ammunition and gasoline, remained extremely critical, railroad transportation being unequal to the task of moving basic requirements to the front.

The situation of Army Group Center had improved with the gradual consolidation of the front line; a continuous line had been established even around the Russian-held Toropets salient. The Russians launched attacks in different sectors, but with little practical effect. On 22 October Hitler discussed the new shock tactics used by the Russians in the Army Group Center area, which consisted of massing forces along a narrow stretch of the front in deeply echeloned formation. To counteract these tactics, the Fuehrer advocated the use of the same defensive methods which the French had employed during the major German attack at Reims in 1918. They had kept their artillery at great distance from their MLR, firing large quantities of ammunition to meet the onslaught. Hitler did not realize, however, that the Germans in 1942 could not expend as much ammunition as the French in 1918.

In the Army Group North sector, intermittent fighting around the German-held Demyansk salient did not lead to any major change in the front line. South of Lake Ladoga the situation became tense for the Germans who checked a Russian breakthrough toward Leningrad at the cost of heavy casualties. The strong artillery forces shifted from the Crimea — about 800 guns — were to be used to tighten the ring around Leningrad.

On 31 October and 1 November Hitler, his entourage, and the Armed Forces Operations Staff returned from Vinnitsa to their former headquarters in East Prussia.

Chapter 12 Critical Analysis of the German Summer Offensive in 1942

Different Concepts of Strategy

According to the postwar conclusions of Generals Halder, Heinrici, etc., the German summer offensive should never have been launched. The German Army had emerged greatly weakened from the ordeal of the winter 1941-42. It had no strategic reserves. To concentrate the essential forces for a large-scale offensive, wide sectors of the Russian front had to be stripped of all their local reserves. Even though the Russians were equally weak by spring 1942, they had manpower reserves and natural resources that were not available to the Axis Powers.

In Halder's opinion the appropriate German strategy for the summer of 1942 would have been to stabilize the front, eliminate the numerous Russian salients and dents in the German lines, and shorten the front line to save personnel. While using active defense tactics at the front, the German Army could have reorganized and refitted for an offensive to be launched at the first favorable opportunity.

Hitler, however, was adverse to any such delay in the continuation of the offensive. In his opinion the Russians had been hard hit during their winter onslaught, and if given time, would get back on their feet. He doubted whether the German Army would be in a more favorable position in 1943 than in 1942. Also, Germany would have to seek a decision in Russia that year, because the Allies might attempt an invasion of western Europe in 1943. While direct and indirect United States aid to Britain and Soviet Russia was steadily increasing, Italy's military and economic power was gradually deteriorating. The crushing blows suffered by the Italian armed forces in the African and Mediterranean theaters had affected the staying power of Germany's principal ally in Europe. Moreover, by adopting a defensive strategy, Germany would lose face with Japan and the neutral powers. Finally, Hitler believed that a dictatorship, to maintain itself, had to produce an incessant stream of successes. An offensive in 1942 would be all the more necessary because, with the military-economic situation steadily growing worse since the start of the Russian campaign, time was working against Germany.

Differences over the Choice of Objective

The original objective of the campaign against the Soviet Union was "to eradicate the remaining Russian military potential and deprive the Soviets of the resources on which their economy was still based." The experience of 1941 indicated that this objective could not be attained unless the Russians were prevented from withdrawing. Halder at the time asserted that this would be extremely difficult in the south, where the Russians could afford to trade space for time without suffering a decisive defeat.

The situation could have been different in the center, where the Russian capital was still within German reach. A deep enveloping sweep launched from the Voronezh-Orel region to points east and northeast of Moscow would have had a telling effect. There was little doubt that the Russians would again have summoned all their strength to defend their capital as they had done during the preceding winter. An offensive in this area would therefore have given the Germans a far better chance to deal the Soviets a knockout blow than an operation in the south.

The German offensive in 1942 was, however, launched in the south because Hitler felt that a decisive victory could be won in southern Russia. Germany's growing shortage of strategic materials influenced the Fuehrer's thinking so much that he became convinced the Soviets were suffering from similar handicaps after having lost so many rich provinces to the Germans. He argued that if their vital oil supply from the Caucasus was threatened, they would use all their remaining manpower and materiel for its defense. Another factor was that possession of this oil would be of greater importance to the German war effort than anything Moscow had to offer.

According to the postwar writings of General Halder and his associates, Hitler's decision to launch an offensive in the summer of 1942 in the southern part of the Russian theater was at best a doubtful gamble. His objective could have been obtained only if the Russians had committed the bulk of the Red Army in the Don bend and if the Germans had succeeded in cutting off and destroying these Soviet forces.

Mistakes in the Execution of the German Offensive

In addition to being handicapped by Hitler's basic mistake of choosing the wrong time and place for his second attempt to defeat the Soviet Union, the German summer offensive was affected by the following factors:

a. Strength vs. Objectives. The relationship between the objectives of the summer offensive and the forces available for attaining them was not sound. The objectives — conquest of the Caucasus and linkup with the Finns via Leningrad — were too distant and difficult to attain with the forces that could be mustered. The solution to proceed by phases in southern Russia was a useful expedient, so long as the objective in each case was reached before the next phase was tackled. The first two phases were executed according to plan, but by the end of the third phase — 23 July 1942 — the objective of cutting off and destroying the Russian forces in the Don bend as a preliminary step to the invasion of the Caucasus had not been achieved. The proper action would have been to stop and consider every facet of the existing situation. Instead, Hitler issued Directive No. 45 which committed his exhausted forces to two simultaneous drives into the Caucasus and toward the Volga.

b. Faulty Intelligence Estimates. Even though the Germans had built up an efficient system of collecting information, their evaluation and interpretation often was colored by wishful thinking. The desire to avoid unpleasant incidents with the Fuehrer frequently seems to have overshadowed the realities of the situation. Hitler had underestimated the Russians from the beginning of the campaign. Ever since June 1941 he had been convinced that the Red Army was on the verge of defeat and the Soviet regime ready to collapse. He repeatedly asserted that if the German Army could deliver only a few more blows in the summer of 1942, the entire house of cards would tumble. If anyone objected to his arguments, Hitler would ask him, "Are you insinuating that the Russians could outperform us?"

c. Logistical Difficulties. The various supply reports and statistics distributed before the start of the summer offensive reflected a certain overconfidence and self-assurance that were not fully justified. Even though stocks in depots and dumps seemed ample, transportation of supplies to the rapidly advancing troops was bound to create numerous problems unless the few existing rail lines could be complemented by a tremendous truck and airlift effort. But it was no secret that the German armed forces had neither the necessary trucks and cargo planes nor the gasoline, not to mention the persistent inadequacy of maintenance and repair facilities, and the shortage of qualified technicians, spare parts, etc. From the outset there was actually not the slightest hope that the supply services would be capable of keeping up with an advance to the Volga and beyond the Caucasus.

d. Mistakes in Occupation Policy. Hitler's attitude toward the Russians found its expression in the occupation policies applied by the National Socialist Party functionaries. Overriding the repeated protests of the commanders in the field, Hitler's henchmen perpetrated such ruthless acts of suppression that they destroyed all chances for gaining the support of the population of the occupied territories.

e. Inflexible Luftwaffe Tactics. Throughout the summer offensive of 1942 the Luftwaffe had continued its rigid adherence to the tactics that had proved so successful in earlier campaigns but had failed in Russia in late 1941. The method of concentrating practically its entire strength on close support of the armored spearheads was ineffective because of the depth and width of the theater. The striking forces of the Luftwaffe, drawn far away from their bases and beset by maintenance difficulties, were exposed to Russian attacks on their lines of communications.

In the autumn of 1942 these developments led to a revision of policy by which Luftwaffe tactics and organization were adapted to the needs of the Russian theater. Balanced air forces, better equipped with defensive aircraft, were to assist the ground forces in repelling any possible Russian counteroffensive, but they were "too little and too late."

f. Hitler's Intuition. It is remarkable how early Hitler realized at which point the major Russian counteroffensive would hit the German and allied lines. But he was incapable of drawing the proper conclusions from his realization. When the Russians launched their attack and succeeded in trapping the Sixth Army within a few days, Hitler was unable to make the right decision. For this reason the German summer offensive of 1942 ended in a heavy defeat that could not be recouped, especially since it was soon to be followed'by a second catastrophe, the capitulation of the German and Italian armies in Tunisia. The battle of Stalingrad — the climax and aftermaths of which will be described in a later volume dealing' with the period 1943 — 45 — initiated the series of defeats that brought about Germany's collapse and ruined Hitler's recently acquired reputation as a *Feldherr* (Great Captain).

Appendixes

Appendix A List of German Military Leaders July 1940 - November 1942)

BOCK, Fedor von
Grade: Field Marshal—19 Jul 40.
Assignments: CG, Army Group B—Oct 39–31 Mar 41.
CG, Army Group Center—1 Apr–18 Dec 41.
CG, Army Group South—17 Jan–13 Jul 42.

BRAUCHITSCH, Walther von
Grade: Field Marshal—19 Jul 40.
Assignment: CinC of the Army—4 Feb 38–19 Dec 41.

FROMM, Friedrich
Grade: Generaloberst (General)—19 Jul 40.
Assignment: CG, Replacement Trining Army—End of 39–21 Jul 44.

GOERING, Hermann
Grade: Reich Marshal—19 Jul 40.
Assignment: CinC of the Luftwaffe—1 Mar 35–23 Apr 45.

GREIFFENBERG, Hans von
Grades: Colonel—3 Oct 38.
Generalmajor (Brigadier General)—1 Aug 40.
Generalleutnant (Major General)—1 Apr 42.
Assignments: Chief, Operations Division, Army High Command—26 Aug 39–24 Oct 40.
Officers Reserve Pool—25 Oct 40–15 Jan 41.
CofS, Twelfth Army—15 Jan–10 May 41.
CofS, Army Group Center—10 May 41–5 May 42.
C of S, Army Group A—5 May 42–1 Aug 43.

GUDERIAN, Heinz
Grade: Generaloberst (General)—19 Jul 40.
Assignments: CG, Second Panzer Group—May–5 Oct 41.
CG, Second Panzer Army—5 Oct–22 Dec 41.

HALDER, Franz
Grade: Generaloberst (General)—19 Jul 40.
Assignment: Chief, Army General Staff—1 Nov 38—24 Sep 42.

HITLER, Adolf
Assignments: CinC of the Armed Forces—2 Aug 34–30 Apr 45.
CinC of the Army—19 Dec 41–30 Apr 45.
CG, Army Group A—9 Sep–22 Nov 42.

HOTH, Hermann
Grade: Generaloberst (General)—19 Jul 40.
Assignments: CG, Third Panzer Group—16 Nov 41–5 Oct 41.
CG, Seventeenth Army—5 Oct 41–25 Apr 42.
CG, Fourth Panzer Army—1 Jun 42–15 Nov 43.

JODL, Alfred
Grades: Generalleutnant (Major General) } 19 Jul 40.
General der Artillerie (Lieutenant General) } 19 Jul 40.
Assignment: Chief, Armed Forces Operations, Staff (Office)—26 Aug 39–8 May 45.

KEITEL, Wilhelm

Grade: Field Marshal—19 Jul 40.

Assignment: CofS, Armed Forces High Command—4 Feb 38-8 May 45.

KINZEL, Eberhard

Grades: Lieutenant Colonel—1 Mar 39.
Colonel—1 Feb 41.

Assignments: Chief, Eastern Intelligence Division—26 Aug 39-1 May 42.
Officers Reserve Pool—1-23 May 42.
CofS, XXIX Corps—23 May-12 Nov. 42.

KLEIST, Ewald von

Grade: Generaloberst (General)—19 Jul 40.

Assignments: CG, First Panzer Group—Jun-5 Oct 41.
CG, First Panzer Army—5 Oct 41-21 Nov 42.

KLUGE, Guenther von

Grade: Field Marshal—19 Jul 40.

Assignments: CG, Fourth Army—1 Sep 39-26 Dec 41.
CG, Army Group Center—18 Dec. 41-12 Oct 43.

KUECHLER, Georg von

Grades: Generaloberst (General)—19 Jul 40.
Field Marshal—30 Jun 42.

Assignments: CG, Eighteenth Army—5 Nov 39-15 Jan 42.
CG, Army Group North—16 Jan 42-31 Jan 44.

LEEB, Wilhelm von

Grade: Field Marshal—19 Jul 40.

Assignments: CG, Army Group C—Jul 40-Mar 41.
CG, Army Group North—1 Apr 41-16 Jan 42.

LIST, Wilhelm

Grade: Field Marshal—19 Jul 40.

Assignments: CG, Twelfth Army—1 Sep 39-Oct 41.
CG, Army Group A—26 Jun-10 Sep 42.

MANSTEIN, Fritz Erich von

Grades: General der Infanterie (Lieutenant General)—1 Jun 40.
Generaloberst (General)—1 Jan 42.
Field Marshal—1 Jul 42.

Assignment: CG, Eleventh Army—18 Sep 41-21 Nov 42.

MARCKS, Erich

Grades: Generalmajor (Brigadier General)—1 Apr 39.
Generalleutnant (Major General)—1 Mar 41.
General der Artillerie (Lieutenant General)—1 Oct 42.

Assignments: CofS, Eighteenth Army—5 Nov 39-10 Dec 40.
CG, 101st Light Infantry Division—10 Dec 40-26 Jun 41.
Officers Reserve Pool—26 Jun 41-15 Mar 42.
CG, 337th Infantry Division—15 Mar-28 Sep 42.
CG, LXVI Corps—28 Sep-Nov 42.

MODEL, Walter

Grades: Generalleutnant (Major General)—1 Apr 40.
General der Panzertruppen (Lieutenant General)—26 Oct 41.
Generaloberst (General)—1 Feb 42.

Assignments: CofS, Sixteenth Army—23 Oct 39-13 Nov 40.
CG, 3d Panzer Division—13 Nov-26 Oct 41.
CG, XLI Corps—26 Oct 41-15 Jan 42.
CG, Ninth Army—16 Jan 42-5 Nov 43.

PAULUS, Friedrich
Grades: Generalleutnant (Major General)—1 Aug 40.
General der Panzertruppen (Lieutenant General)—1 Jan 42.
Generaloberst (General)—30 Nov 42.
Assignments: CofS, Sixth Army—3 Sep 40.
ACofS, Operations, Army High Command—3 Sep 40–16 Jan 42.
CG, Sixth Army—16 Jan 42–1 Feb 43.

RAEDER, Erich
Grade: Grossadmiral (Fleet Admiral)—1939.
Assignment: CinC of the Navy—1935–43.

REICHENAU, Walter von
Grade: Field Marshal—19 Jul 40.
Assignments: CG, Sixth Army—Oct 39–3 Dec 41.
CG, Army Group South—3 Dec 41–17 Jan. 42.

RICHTHOFEN, Wolfgang von
Grade: Generaloberst (General)—Mar 42.
Assignments: CG, VIII Air Corps—End of 39–23 Jun 42.
CG, Fourth Air Force—24 Jun 42–10 Jun 43.

ROMMEL, Erich
Grades: Generalmajor (Brigadier General)—1 Aug 39.
Generalleutnant (Major General)—7 Feb 41.
General der Panzertruppen (Lieutenant General)—1 Jul 41.
Generaloberst (General)—1 Feb 42.
Field Marshal—22 Jun 42.
Assignments: CG, 7th Panzer Division—15 Feb 40–14 Feb 41.
CG, Afrika Corps—14 Feb–1 Sep 41.
CG, Panzer Group Afrika—1 Sep 41–30 Jan 42.
CG, Panzer Army Afrika—30 Jan 42–22 Feb 43.

RUNDSTEDT, Gerd von
Grade: Field Marshal—19 Jul 40.
Assignment: CG, Army Group A—20 Oct 39–15 Mar 41.
CG, Army Group South—1 Apr–3 Dec 41.
CG, Army Group D (West)—8 Mar 42–2 Jul 44.

SODENSTERN, Georg von
Grades: Generalleutnant (Major General)—1 Feb 40.
General der Infanterie (Lieutenant General)—1 Aug 40.
Assignments: CofS, Army Group A—15 Feb 40–15 Mar 41.
CofS, Army Group South—1 Apr 41–15 Jul 42.
CofS, Army Group B—15 Jul 42–14 Feb 43.

STRAUSS, Adolf
Grade: Generaloberst (General)—19 Jul 40.
Assignment: CG, Ninth Army—30 May 40–15 Jan 42.

THOMAS, Georg
Grade: General der Infanterie (Lieutenant General)—1 Aug 40.
Assignment: Chief, Armed Forces Economics Office—1 Sep 39–17 Nov 42.

WAGNER, Eduard
Grades: Colonel—1 Oct 37.
Generalmajor (Brigadier General)—1 Aug 40.
Generalleutnant (Major General)—1 Apr 42.
Assignment: CofS, Supply and Administration Division, Army High Command—26 Aug 39–1 Oct 40.
Chief, Supply and Administration Division—1 Oct–22 Jul 44.

WARLIMONT, Walter

Grades: Colonel—1 Feb 38.
Generalmajor (Brigadier General)—1 Aug 40.
Generalleutnant (Major General)—1 Apr 42.

Assignments: Chief, National Defense Division, Armed Forces High Command—26 Aug 39–31 Dec 41.
Deputy Chief, Armed Forces Operations Staff—1 Jan 42–6 Sep 44.

WEICHS, Maximilian von

Grade: Generaloberst (General)—19 Jul 40.

Assignments: CG, Second Army—23 Oct 39–13 Jul 42.
CG, Army Group B—13 Jul 42–10 Jul 43.

ZEITZLER, Kurt

Grades: Colonel—1 Jan 39.
Generalmajor (Brigadier General)—1 Feb 42.
General der Infanterie (Lieutenant General)—24 Sep 42.

Assignments: CofS, XXII Corps—26 Aug 39–5 Dec 40.
CofS, First Panzer Army—5 Dec 40–24 Apr 42.
CofS, C-in-C West—24 Apr–24 Sep 42.
Chief of the Army General Staff—25 Sep 42–20 Jul 44.

Appendix B Chronology of Events

1940

July

16 Hitler issues Directive No. 16, pertaining to the invasion of England.

19 In a speech before the Reichstag assembly Hitler makes a peace overture to Great Britain.

August

7 Directive *AUFBAU OST* is issued, initiating military buildup in German-occupied Poland.

8 German bombing planes open the air offensive against Britain.

September

13 Italy begins drive into Egypt.

17 Invasion of England is indefinitely postponed.

27 Germany, Italy, and Japan sign Tripartite Pact.

October

7 German troops enter Romania.

28 Italian forces attack Greece from Albania.

November

12 Hitler issues Directive No. 18, pertaining to future operations in the Mediterranean theater.

12–13 Molotov visits Berlin.

December

8 British open a surprise drive against the Italians in North Africa.

18 Hitler signs and issues Directive No. 21, Operation BARBAROSSA, pertaining to the campaign against the Soviet Union.

1941

February

17 Hitler asks Jodl to draw up a plan for the invasion of India.

March

11 Lend-Lease Act passed by U. S. Congress and signed by President Roosevelt.

26 Yugoslav *coup d'état.*

April

3 Rommel opens his offensive in Lybia.

6 German troops invade Yugoslavia.

13 Soviet Union concludes a pact of neutrality with Japan.

17 Yugoslav High Command capitulates.

23 Greek Army surrenders to the Germans and Italians.

May

2 Pro-Axis revolt in Iraq is squashed by British troops.

20 German parachute troops invade Crete.

29 Rommel stopped at the Egyptian border.

June

11 Directive No. 32, "Preparations for the Period after BARBAROSSA," is circulated among the services.

22 Operation BARBAROSSA begins.

July

1–2 Riga occupied by German troops.
13 Great Britain and Russia conclude a mutual-aid treaty.
16 Army Group Center captures Smolensk.
19 Hitler issues Directive No. 33 pertaining to the continuation of the Russian campaign.
23 Supplement to Directive No. 33 orders diversion of Army Group Center armor to the south and north.
30 Directive No. 34 orders the withdrawal of the Army Group Center panzer groups to permit their rehabilitation.

August

12 Hitler issues Supplement to Directive No. 34, envisaging the Moscow offensive after the seizure of Leningrad.
25–29 British and Russian forces occupy Iran.

September

6 Directive No. 35 orders Moscow offensive for the end of September 1940.
8 First German attacks against the outer fortifications of Leningrad.
18–19 Kiev and Poltava seized by the Germans.

October

1 First Russian Protocol, signed at Moscow, provides that Great Britain and the United States would supply materials essential to the Russian war effort for nine months.
7 Start of the muddy season in central European Russia.
8 Army Group Center takes Orel.
12–13 Bryansk and Vyazma fall to the Germans.
16 Odessa is seized by Army Group South forces.
20 Soviets lose Kalinin and Staritsa.
21 Army Group North starts the attack on Tikhvin.
24 Kharkov is seized by Army Group South.
End Soviet Government moves from Moscow to Kuibyshev.

November

2 Army Group South takes Kursk.
7 Hitler decides to delay seizure of Caucasus oil fields to following year.
8 Army Group South forces split Russian defense in Crimea.
11 Russians abandon Tikhvin.
15 Army Group Center launches all-out attack on Moscow proper.
20 Army Group South panzers enter Rostov.
28 Russians counterattack at Rostov from three sides.

December

1 Hitler permits Army Group South to evacuate Rostov.
5 German offensive bogs down and Russians begin to seize initiative.
7 Japanese attack Pearl Harbor.
8 Germans evacuate Tikhvin.
8 Hitler issues Directive No. 39, pertaining to the defense of German-held territory.
11 Germany and Italy declare war on the United States.
16 Germans abandon Kalinin.
19 Brauchitsch resigns as commander in chief of the Army; Hitler assumes his responsibility.

1942

January

10 Hitler revises 1942 plans on the basis of recent setbacks.

15 Hitler issues the first order of a large-scale German withdrawal in World War II.

End Russians break through at Izyum.

April

5 Directive No. 41 defines plan for summer offensive of 1942.

May

12 Russians launch spoiling attack near Kharkov.

17 Germans jump off near Izyum.

19 Russian resistance collapses on Kerch Peninsula.

27 Rommel opens second drive into Egypt.

28 Germans win Battle of Kharkov.

June

7 Start of the second German siege of Sevastopol.

11 Master lend-lease agreement signed between the United States and Soviet Union.

19 Outer defenses of Sevastopol are breached.

July

5 End of fighting on Crimea.

6 Germans take Voronezh.

11 Directive No. 43 issued, dealing with flank attack from Kerch across the strait into the Caucasus.

13 Hitler decides to initiate a frontal attack of the Caucasus.

16 Hitler's headquarters moved to Vinnitsa in the Ukraine.

21 Directive No. 44 issued, pertaining to warfare in northern Finland.

23 Hitler issues Directive No. 45, ordering two simultaneous drives into the Caucasus and toward Stalingrad.

29 Last rail line connecting Stalingrad with the Caucasus is cut.

31 Fourth Panzer Army is diverted from the Caucasus to the Stalingrad offensive.

August

6 Army Group A captures Armavir.

9 Maikop falls into German hands.

18 Hitler issues Directive No. 46, pertaining to antipartisan warfare.

18–19 British stage Dieppe raid.

28 Russians counterattack in the Caucasus.

September

1 Germans cross the Kerch Strait.

6 Army Group A forces capture Novorossiysk.

9 Hitler assumes command of Army Group A upon List's resignation.

24 Zeitzler replaces Halder as Army Chief of Staff.

26 Army Group A captures Nalchik.

October

23 Start of Battle of El Alamein.

31 Hitler returns to East Prussia.

November

8 Allies invade North Africa.

11 Germans assume control over Unoccupied France.

12 Rommel expelled from Egypt.

19 Soviets launch Stalingrad counteroffensive.

Printed in Great Britain
by Amazon

55918231R00130